TEACHER'S BOOK

ELEMENTARY

Liz & John Soars

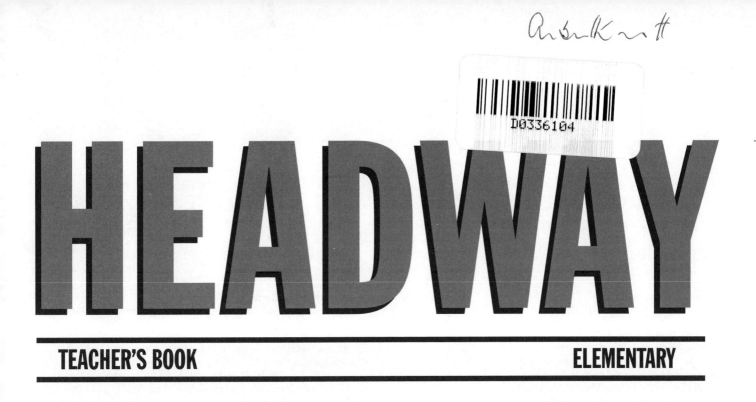

Oxford University Press

Oxford University Press
Walton Street, Oxford OX2 6DP

Oxford New York
Athens Auckland Bangkok Bombay
Calcutta Cape Town Dar es Salaam Delhi
Florence Hong Kong Istanbul Karachi
Kuala Lumpur Madras Madrid Melbourne
Mexico City Nairobi Paris Singapore
Taipei Tokyo Toronto

and associated companies in
Berlin Ibadan

Oxford and Oxford English are trade marks of
Oxford University Press

ISBN 019 433994 7

First published 1993
Third impression 1994

Designed by Holdsworth Associates
Printed in Great Britain by
St Edmundsbury Press Ltd
Bury St Edmunds, Suffolk

Acknowledgements
The *Headway Elementary* Progress Tests written by Tim Falla.

Songs
'What a Wonderful World' by Louis Armstrong used by kind permission of Colin Music Corp., Iron Bridge House, 3 Bridge Approach, London NW1 8BD.
'All the way from America' by Joan Armatrading © 1973 Onward Music Ltd, 1a, Farm Place, London W8 7SX. Used by kind permission of the publishers.

CONTENTS

INTRODUCTION

The *Headway* series

Headway Elementary completes the series of *Headway* course books, which cover all levels from beginners to advanced. The list is as follows:

Headway Elementary
Headway Pre-Intermediate
Headway Intermediate
Headway Upper-Intermediate
Headway Advanced

The first four have pronunciation books that accompany them, and there are videos that go with the first two.

Headway Elementary is designed as a first-year book. It can be used by complete beginners, but given that the *Headway* series was written for adults and young adults aged 14 and above, it is more likely that students will be false beginners when they encounter *Headway Elementary.* That is, they will have a little knowledge of English grammar and they will know a certain amount of lexis. The course has been piloted extensively with both complete beginners and false beginners in the UK and abroad.

The *Headway* series provides thorough coverage of the grammatical and lexical systems of English, combined with extensive practice of the four language skills of speaking, listening, reading, and writing.

The ever-changing world of English language teaching

There have been many stimulating and innovatory developments in language teaching over the past decade. These have produced activities designed to practise language in realistic, communicative activities in the classroom. Teachers have become aware that language exchanges and language exposure should be as real and authentic as possible.

However, we feel that there is a danger in our profession of always rejecting the 'old' in favour of the 'new'. This has led to a certain neglect of many tried and tested approaches, activities, and exercise types which benefited generations of teachers and learners. There is almost an assumption that nobody learned a language successfully before the arrival of the communicative approach. In the *Headway* series, we have always tried to combine the best of the old and the new.

Teaching beginners is different!

Low-level language learners require a very logical, step-by-step approach. Activities and tasks that work perfectly well at an intermediate level and above are not always suitable for learners who have so little language at their disposal.

- **New language** needs to be introduced in a clear, unambiguous presentation. It needs to be practised not only in communicative, meaningful ways, but in drills and exercises where language is used for display purposes only. Students need the support and confidence of merely knowing that they can pronounce and produce the target language.
- **Skills work** (listening, speaking, reading, and writing activities) needs to be manageable and gradual in its development. Listening and reading texts should be selected very carefully and they also probably need to be graded. They may *sound* and *look* authentic, but the language they contain has to be within the abilities of the students, otherwise they become demotivated.

Organization of *Headway Elementary*

The organization of *Headway Elementary* is similar to that of *Headway Pre-Intermediate* and *Headway Intermediate*, that is to say, the Presentation and Practice sections come at the beginning of the unit. These are followed by skills work and vocabulary work. Next there is an Everyday English section and finally a Grammar Summary.

PRESENTATION

There are usually two presentations. The target language is contextualized to illustrate the meaning, and appears in either a reading or listening text (but usually both). Students are given a task which highlights the new language, and then are asked Grammar questions to draw attention to rules of use, form, and pronunciation.
A feature of *Headway Elementary* which is new is the Caution Box, which appears with this symbol.

⚠ We use the Caution Box to warn students of potential hazards! Where possible, we suggest that the information in the box is translated.

You, as teacher, can decide by and large how much use to make of the students' own language. In a multilingual class, it is unlikely that you can exploit L1 terribly much, but in a monolingual class, L1 is there as a tool, and we suggest that you make judicious use of it. You can translate instructions, especially with more complicated activities, and you can explain concepts. Do this as a check of understanding *after* a presentation, rather than as the *medium* of presentation. The Grammar questions could well be asked and answered in L1.

The Grammar Summary at the end of each unit serves to bring together all the target language of the presentation sections. We include lists of preposition collocations, because even at such a low level students find prepositions difficult in English.

Practice

In the Practice section there is a variety of exercise types, involving all four skills. There are pronunciation exercises, pair work and group work, 'mingle' activities, transformation drills and repetition drills. There is a mixture and a balance of both pre-communicative and genuinely communicative activities, and of course, personalization runs throughout.

In nearly every unit there is an exercise called 'Choosing the correct sentence'. This tests the input of the unit, and also revises previous units. It is a recognition exercise, and students often find it reassuring to be able to identify correct and incorrect sentences, despite some teachers' concern that one should never expose students to examples of incorrect English.

SKILLS WORK

A feature of the *Headway* series is the rich variety of texts that engage the learner. The lower the level, the more difficult it is to select interesting yet accessible texts. There is a great deal of satisfaction when beginners / elementary students encounter an extended piece of language and understand it. The converse of this is exposing students to authentic, ungraded pieces too soon, and instead of the satisfaction of meeting a challenge, there is frustration.

All the texts in *Headway Elementary* have an authentic source, from newspapers, magazines, interviews and short stories, but they have all been graded to suit the level. Many of the speaking activities are personalized, where students talk about themselves, each other, and their own environment. The writing syllabus is in the Workbook. There are times in the Students' Book when we suggest that students do some freer writing for homework, and the aim of these exercises is for students to explore what they can do. In the teaching notes we suggest that you don't correct this work too harshly, as this would be demotivating.

● VOCABULARY

There is a strong lexical syllabus in *Headway Elementary*, as in the whole *Headway* series. There are usually two vocabulary exercises per unit in the Student's Book, and a further exercise in the Workbook. Students are encouraged to keep a vocabulary notebook, and to use a bilingual dictionary. Lexical items are systematically recycled.

Several of the vocabulary exercises have a pronunciation element. Students are asked to identify word stress, or match a word with its phonetic spelling.

There are vocabulary lists at the back of the book where students are encouraged to write in a translation of the key items in the unit.

● PRONUNCIATION

Pronunciation work is integrated throughout. There are always examples of the target language on tape for repetition purposes. Salient features of pronunciation are highlighted and practised when necessary.

The phonetic script is introduced in a simple manner in appropriate exercises, and the phonetic chart appears inside the back page for ease of reference.

Systematic pronunciation work also appears in the Pronunciation Book which accompanies *Headway Elementary*.

● EVERYDAY ENGLISH

As well as a grammatical and lexical syllabus, *Headway Elementary* also has a situational syllabus, which appears in the Everyday English section. Students are exposed to the language used in everyday situations such as a café, an airport, a hotel and a railway station, and are given opportunities to practise the language. There are also exercises on survival areas such as the alphabet, numbers, time, and social expressions such as *Excuse me!*, *Sorry*, *Pardon?*, and *Never mind!*.

STOP AND CHECK

There is a Stop and Check revision section after every four units. This can be done in class or at home. We give suggestions on how to exploit this in the teaching notes. At the end of the Stop and Check, students are invited to translate sentences that contain examples of the target language of the previous units. It is very important that students translate the ideas and concepts, and not word by word.

Workbook

The Workbook is an important component of the course. It revises the grammatical input of the Students' Book, and also adds to it. There is at least one extra vocabulary exercise, and the writing syllabus is to be found towards the end of each unit of the Workbook. Many of the exercises are on cassette, for use in class or at home.

Video

A *Headway Elementary* Video, Video Guide, and Activity Book are available as an optional accompaniment to the course. The video is linked to the syllabus and consists of mini-documentaries on topics that reflect those in the Students' Book, and situational language such as in a shop and in a pub.

Teachers are constantly making decisions, both in the preparation and execution of their lessons. We hope that *Headway Elementary* helps you in this process of decision-making and we hope you enjoy using the book.

UNIT 1

am/is/are – Possessive adjectives – Spelling

Introduction to the unit

As you begin *Headway Elementary*, you are probably starting a new course with a new group of students. The title of Unit 1 is 'Hello!', and one important aim is that students get to know each other and you, and you get to know them. Obviously students will have very little English to use, but nevertheless a convivial classroom atmosphere can be established through very basic interchanges. If you are teaching a monolingual group, it would probably be a good idea to use L1 so that everybody can introduce themselves.

Language aims

Grammar

am/is/are

The verb *to be* is introduced in all persons, singular and plural. The focus is on the positive and the question. The negative is dealt with in Unit 2.

Possessive adjectives

My, *your*, *his*, and *her* are introduced in the unit. The other possessive adjectives are given in the Grammar Summary.

Vocabulary

In the Vocabulary section, students look at the organization of a bilingual dictionary entry, and they are asked to examine their own bilingual dictionary. Some everyday objects such as *ticket* and *key* are introduced, and students are encouraged to buy a notebook in which to keep vocabulary records.

Everyday English

The alphabet is introduced and practised by means of both receptive and productive exercises.

Workbook

Nationality adjectives (*German*, *French*) are introduced. The numbers 1–100 and telephone numbers are practised. There are no specific writing development activities in the first two units of the Workbook. The writing syllabus begins in Unit 3.

Notes on the Unit

PRESENTATION (1) (SB page 6)

Note
You could start the lesson by using page 6, but it is perhaps better to introduce the language yourself, and use the coursebook for consolidation.

Say your own name – *I'm John* –, then ask several students *What's your name?* and invite a reply – *I'm Jean*, *I'm Keiko*, etc. Practise the question around the class. When you feel students are ready, they could ask and answer the question across the room with the rest of the class listening (i.e. in *open* pairs). The question and answer could then be practised with the whole class in pairs (i.e. in *closed* pairs). Then you could have a mingle activity, where you ask all the students to stand up and ask everybody the same question. They should try to learn as many names as they can.

If there are not too many students in the class, put their names on the board so everyone can begin to learn the names.

If you think your students won't know and won't understand from context *Where are you from?* and *I'm from ....* then teach these items.

T1a Ask students to read and listen. (Use L1 for instructions if you like.) Play the tape two or three times, repeat as a class first, then practise it in both open and closed pairs.

Point out the contractions in the Caution Box.

Practice (SB page 6)

1 Writing and listening

T1b Ask students to complete the conversation. Play the tape to check. Again, you could practise the dialogue in open and closed pairs.

2 Speaking

This is a mingle activity. If you have followed the suggestion in the **Note**, then you will not want to do it again. Don't let this activity go on too long. If you have a large class, it will be impossible for *all* the students to talk to everyone.

Additional material

Workbook Unit 1

Exercises 1–3 These practise *What's your name? Where are you from?*, *I'm from* ... and *I'm (a)* ... .

PRESENTATION (2) (SB page 7)

Note

This presentation needs to be handled carefully. If you have absolute beginners, then it will seem to you that there is a lot of input in this section. You will have to teach *doctor*, *thirty*, *married*, *two*, *children*, *house*, *south*, *learn*, *job* and a similar amount of vocabulary in the Practice section. This can be done by pictures, drawings on the board, mime, and/or translation.

However, it is more likely that the majority of your class already knows a little English, and the aim of this Presentation and Practice section is to allow students to show you how much English they actually have. In Practice 2, students are asked to write about themselves. For those with only a little English, they can follow the models in the Presentation and Practice 1. For better students, this is an opportunity for them to show off!

The verbs *have*, *live*, and *want* also appear in their Present Simple form. It is *not* the intention that you should embark on a presentation of this tense, however. The verbs appear in their base form, with no inflection. In our experience, students do not wonder whether these verbs are present, past or future. They accept them unquestioningly as referring to all time. We strongly suggest that you do not draw students' attention to Present Simple at this point.

Ask students to read about Manuel. You could read the text aloud, so students are reading and listening at the same time, or they can read in silence.

Make sure students understand *doctor*, *thirty*, *married*, *have*, *two*, *children*, *live*, *house*, *south*, *Spain*, *want*, *learn*, and *job*. This can be done using pictures, and/or dictionaries.

You could ask one or two students to read the text aloud, or it could be practised in closed pairs and the students can help each other with pronunciation.

Practice (SB page 7)

1 Writing and listening

T2 Ask students to complete the text about Mayumi. Make sure students understand *student*, *nineteen*, *not married*, *brother*, *sister*, *flat*, *Japan*, *international*, and *language*. Play the tape to check.

Again, you could practise the text around the class and/or in closed pairs.

2 Writing and speaking

Ask students to write about themselves. After quite a lot of oral class work, some silent, individual work provides variety and balance.

Ask students to read what they have written to the class. Don't worry if there are a lot of pronunciation mistakes. The aim is for students to show what they can do, and to say a little about themselves and their families. You can't do everything at once!

If you have a large class, you won't be able to have all of the students reading out what they have written. Collect it in.

If you have a smaller class, it can be interesting to record the students. When you have recorded everyone, play the recording back and correct a few mistakes.

PRESENTATION (3) (SB page 8)

If you have access to a world map or a globe, it would be useful for this presentation.

1 Read the introduction as a class. Explain *stress* and *stress marks* using the board, e.g. Eng|land. You could use L1 to explain, and you could perhaps take some examples of words with more than one syllable in L1 (if L1 is stress-timed itself, not syllable-timed) to show how there are stressed and unstressed syllables.

   T3 Ask students to read the list of countries as you play the tape. Then they can listen and repeat after the tape the second time. Practise the countries as a class, then in closed pairs.

2 Ask students to look at the photographs and read the words.

⚠ Draw their attention to the Caution Box, which explains the contractions.

3 Ask students in pairs or groups to write where the people are from. Students are *not* expected to know how to say *Hello!* in all the different languages! This is merely a fun way to introduce countries and the third person singular and plural. Some students will know a few, others will know more, and some of the countries can be worked out by a process of elimination.

Answers

1 This is Jean-Paul. He's from France.
2 This is Johann. He's from Germany.
3 This is Fatima. She's from Egypt.
4 This is Paola. She's from Italy.
5 This is Christina. She's from Greece.
6 This is Clara and Bruno. They're from Brazil.
7 This is Ivan. He's from Russia.
8 This is Pablo. He's from Mexico.
9 This is János and Irén. They're from Hungary.

Note
This is a good opportunity to introduce the questions *What's his/her name?* and *Where's he/she from?* Point to some of the pictures, ask the questions yourself, and let the students reply. Then drill the questions and correct any mistakes carefully. Practise the questions and answers in open pairs.

When you have established the right answers, you can point to different photographs and invite students to say *He's from …*, *She's from …*, or *They're from …* .

Practice (SB page 9)

1 Speaking

1 Students work in pairs to ask and answer questions about the people in the photographs.

2 Students ask and answer the same questions in open and/or closed pairs about the people in the class. Obviously this will work better in a multilingual class. In a monolingual class where everyone knows each other, you can give students a new nationality. This practises the vocabulary of the exercise, too.

2 Listening and pronunciation

T4 Play the tape. Ask students to tick the sentence they hear. This is an exercise that tests discrimination, but you can make it productive afterwards by asking students in pairs to practise the pairs of sentences. Pay particular attention to the sounds /ɪ/ and /iː/.

Answers
1 b 2 a 3 b 4 a 5 a 6 a

3 Grammar

Ask students to work in pairs to put *am*, *is*, *are*, *his*, or *her* into the gaps. Afterwards, you can ask them to make the contractions in b, d, f, h.

Answers

a Where *are* you from?
b I *am* from Italy.
c 'What's *his* name?' 'Peter.'
d Christina *is* twenty-nine years old.
e Mike and Rosie *are* from London.
f Clara *is* married.
g 'What's *her* name?' 'Mayumi.'
h He *is* a doctor.
i I have a daughter. *Her* name's Kate.
j János and Irén *are* married. They have a son.

4 Choosing the correct sentence

See page 5 of the Teacher's Book for an explanation of this exercise type.
Ask students to work in pairs or small groups to choose the correct sentence. If/when students make mistakes, decide how much to explain by gauging how they feel. If they are tired, just give them the correct answer. If you feel they would benefit from an explanation, then explore the mistakes.

Answers
1 b 2 a 3 a 4 a 5 b 6 a 7 b 8 a 9 b 10 a

Additional material

Workbook Unit 1
Exercises 4 and 5 Third person *is* and *are*, and short and long forms.
Exercises 6 and 7 Possessive adjectives.
Exercises 8 and 9 Countries and nationalities with stress practice.

● LISTENING AND SPEAKING (SB page 10)

Hello and goodbye

If you feel your students will be familiar with most of the language in this activity, do it as suggested in the Student's Book. If, however, you think a lot will be new, teach the new items, perhaps by means of dialogue builds on the board, then use the Student's Book for consolidation.

1 Ask students to write the conversations in the correct order.

T5 Play the tape to check.

Answers
a A Hello, Mary. How are you?
B Fine, thank you. And you?
A I'm OK, thanks.
b A Hi, Dave! How are you?
B Not bad, thanks. And you?
A Very well. How are the children?
B They're fine.
c A Goodbye, Chris.
B Goodbye, Anne. Have a nice evening.
A Thanks, Chris. See you tomorrow!

2 Students practise the dialogues in closed/open pairs. Then ask them to stand up and make similar conversations with other students.

● VOCABULARY AND PRONUNCIATION (SB page 10)

1 Using a bilingual dictionary

Ask students to look at the dictionary entry. Check that they all have a bilingual dictionary. Ask them to find *apple* in their dictionary. You could have a conversation in L1 to compare the dictionary entries, but don't let this go on too long.

2 What's this in English?

1 Students use their dictionaries to match a word and a picture.

Answers

a a dictionary	g an apple	m an envelope
b a map	h a ticket	n an orange
c a notebook	i a bag	o a postcard
d a suitcase	j a stamp	p a newspaper
e a key	k a magazine	
f a letter	l a camera	

2 **T6** Play the tape. Practise the vocabulary. You could do this in several ways. You could stop the tape after each vocabulary item and drill it. Having done this, you could point to one of the photographs and ask a student to tell you what it is. Students could do the same in closed pairs.

3 Ask students to look at the words. Some might know the rule.

Answers
A goes before a word with a consonant, *an* goes before a vowel.
The letters *a*, *e*, *i*, *o*, and *u* are vowels.

3 A vocabulary notebook

Look at the notebook as a class. Encourage your students to buy a notebook, preferably one they can carry in their pocket or bag. You will need to check from time to time that students are actually filling in the notebook, and you will need to give them an awful lot of encouragement! It requires a lot of effort on the part of students, and you can expect many of them to stop trying.

Additional material

Workbook Unit 1
Exercises 10 and 11 *a/an*

● EVERYDAY ENGLISH (SB page 12)

Spelling

1 The letters of the alphabet are grouped according to vowel sound. Explain to the students about the IPA spelling on the left hand side. The students will have to deal with phonetic script later, so it's a good idea to make them aware of it now. But it is best not to spend much time on this here as students have to learn the letters of the alphabet first.

T7a Students listen to the tape. Practise the letters as a class and in closed pairs. The following letters seem to cause problems for many students: a, j, e, g, i, y, u, w, r

2 **T7b** Listen to the song and let the students sing it if they want to. It certainly helps them to remember the pronunciation of the alphabet!

3 **T7c** Students listen to the words and write them down. Pre-teach *double* for spelling.

Answers

1 name	6 house
2 sister	7 letter
3 flat	8 married
4 student	9 apple
5 doctor	10 job

4 **T7d** Students read and listen to the conversation, then practise the two questions in closed pairs. Students might wonder, either consciously or subconsciously, what *do* means. It would not be a good idea to start explaining how to form questions in the Present Simple. The best idea is to tell them not to worry!

5 Students ask and answer questions about things in the room. Teach *I don't know* idiomatically. Again, it is probably not worth trying to explain how to form negatives in the Present Simple.

GRAMMAR SUMMARY **(SB page 12)**

Read the Grammar Summary as a class. Encourage students to ask any questions.

Don't forget!

Workbook Unit 1
Exercises 12–14 These are exercises on numbers and telephone numbers which students need to know to begin Unit 2. Take some time to go over the numbers in class if the students are unfamiliar with them.

Word List
Look at the Word List on page 123 of the Student's Book as a class. Tell students that the most important words from the unit are here. They could translate the words, or look at them at home, or transfer some of the words to their vocabulary notebook.

Pronunciation Book Unit 1

UNIT 2

Questions and negatives – Possessive *'s* – Prices – *Can I have ...?*

Introduction to the unit

The title of Unit 2 is 'People', and various characters are introduced to practise the grammar. There is the first real fluency activity of *Headway Elementary* in the reading and listening exercise, Paola's letter to David. It is important that even at such a low level students are exposed to language in a natural context. They should not always be engaged in presentation and practice, accuracy-based activities. (Incidentally, the characters Paola and David appear in the video that accompanies *Headway Elementary*.)

Language aims

Grammar

Questions and negatives

The verb *to be* is given further practice in all persons, with an emphasis on questions, negatives, and short answers. The question words *what*, *where*, *who*, *how old*, and *how much* are introduced and/or revised.
Note that in the negative, the contracted forms of *not* are introduced, not the contracted forms of the verb *to be*. We introduce *she isn't*, *they aren't*, *you aren't*, *we aren't*, and not *she's not*, *they're not*, *you're not*, *we're not*. Try to keep to these forms as you speak to the class. However, the contraction **I amn't* isn't possible, and this is pointed out in the Caution Box in Practice 2.
Having been introduced to contracted forms, students are tempted to use them in short answers, for example, *Are you married? *Yes, I'm.* Short answers are a feature of English. Where other languages will answer an inverted question with simply *yes* or *no*, English prefers to add a short answer. Without the short answer, the speaker can sound rather abrupt.

Possessive *'s*

It can come as quite a surprise to students to learn that not only does *s* signify a plural noun, but *'s* is both the contracted form of the verb *to be* and an indicator of possession. This needs to be pointed out very carefully.

Vocabulary

Members of the family (*father*, *aunt*, etc.) are introduced in Presentation (2). Common adjectives and their opposites are introduced in the Vocabulary section.

Everyday English

This section practises the language required in a café. *Can I have ...?* is taught idiomatically. Vocabulary to do with food and drink is introduced, and prices are practised. There are two exercises in the Workbook, Exercises 13 and 14, which practise saying prices. You might feel your students would benefit from doing these two exercises before doing the Everyday English section.

Workbook

The alphabet is revised. In the Vocabulary section, *What's the matter?* plus some adjectives such as *tired*, *thirsty*, *bored* are introduced. The rules governing the spelling of plural nouns are given.

Notes on the Unit

PRESENTATION (1) (SB page 13)

Questions and negatives

Note
This presentation begins with a listening activity that revises and practises numbers. Numbers and phone numbers were introduced in Unit 1 of the Workbook, but you might feel that your students need more classroom work on these areas before they can begin this activity.

Learners of English often experience difficulty in recognizing and producing the difference between the 'teen' numbers (13–19) and the corresponding 'ten' numbers (30, 40, 50, etc.). Point out the different word stress.

● •   • ●
thirty thirteen

1 **T8** Play the tape. Ask students to write down the numbers and phone numbers. Explain that you want them to write the number, not the spelling, i.e. 6, not *six*.

Answers
Numbers
5 20 16 32 50 12

Phone numbers
791 463 859 622
503 971 010 331 46 58 93 94

2 Ask students to read about Mary Hopkins. Check that all the vocabulary is understood.

3 If you think that your students will be familiar with most of the question words in this presentation, you can ask them to do this exercise in pairs. Otherwise, do it as a class.

T9 Play the tape so students can check their answers. Point out that *isn't* is the negative, and that *n't* is the short form of *not*.

Answers
a What's her surname?
b What's her first name?
c Where's she from?
d What's her job?
e What's her address?
f What's her phone number?
g How old is she?
h Is she married?

Before you ask students to practise the questions and answers in pairs, have a reasonable amount of open pair practice. English has a very wide voice range, and this is apparent in questions. Questions with a question word start high and fall.

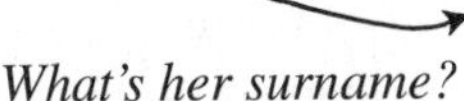

What's her surname?

You will need to encourage your students strongly to start high! Listen to the models on tape and ask students to imitate them. Inverted questions usually rise at the end.

Is she married?

Try to practise the questions as much as possible without boring the class! Have a mixture of open and closed pairs.

4 Encourage students to ask you questions about Mary's brother. Again, insist on good intonation. You can give any information you want, but here is a sample profile.

Mary's brother

Surname	Hopkins
First name	Jack
Country	England
Job	Travel agent
Address	72, Station Road, Manchester
Phone number	061 753 8991
Age	26
Married?	No

Practice (SB page 13)

1 Speaking

1 You will need to photocopy the charts on page 124 of the Teacher's Book. They are repeated so you can cut them up and save paper.

Note
This is the first information gap activity in *Headway Elementary*, and it might even be the first time your students have ever done such an activity. The mechanics of such an exercise can be difficult to grasp. Students may find it strange that Student A has different information from Student B, so explain this activity very carefully, in L1 if you can. Stress that they mustn't show each other the information! Read the instructions as a class. Allocate the pairs, and give the information to Student B. You could do the first two questions yourself as an example. Give students as long as they want to do the exercise.

2

> **Note**
> Students first saw a short answer (*No, she isn't*) in Exercise 3 of Presentation (1). This speaking exercise introduces two more (*Yes, I am* and *No, I'm not*). You could embark on an explanation of what short answers are and how they operate, but this is probably inadvisable. You run the risk of overloading students with too much information. It is perhaps a better idea to let students see them in context and use them in controlled exercises.
> The area of short answers is further complicated by the fact that we do not contract the verb *to be*. We cannot say **Yes, she's.*

Read the instructions as a class. Point out the short answers *Yes, I am* and *No, I'm not*. The students ask you the same questions. Correct mistakes carefully.

3 You will need to photocopy the forms on page 124 of the Teacher's Book. They are repeated so you can cut them up and save paper. This is a mingle activity. Read the instructions as a class. Students stand up and ask and answer questions. Don't let this go on too long. Let students finish, but stop it before they get tired.

4 Ask four or five students to tell the rest of the class about one of the students. They could well have problems with the shift from first and second persons to third person, i.e. *your* to *her*, *are* to *is*, etc.

2 Negatives and short answers

> **Note**
> This is the first time that students have seen all the negative forms of the verb *to be* and short answers, so deal with the information in the Caution Box very carefully. You might want to drill the negative sentences, and practise the short answers in open pairs.

> Read the information in the Caution Box together with the class. Point out especially that we cannot say **I amn't.*

1 Read the instructions and the example. Drill the question and answer in open pairs. Students ask and answer questions about Mary and Martin.

Answers

a	Is she a doctor?	No, she isn't.
	Is she a teacher?	No, she isn't.
	Is she a journalist?	Yes, she is.
b	Is she eighteen?	No, she isn't.
	Is she twenty-one?	No, she isn't.
	Is she twenty-three?	Yes, she is.
c	Is his surname Smith?	No, it isn't.
	Is his surname Jones?	No, it isn't.
	Is his surname Peters?	Yes, it is.
d	Is he American?	No, he isn't.
	Is he English?	No, he isn't.
	Is he Scottish?	Yes, he is.
e	Is he a taxi-driver?	No, he isn't.
	Is he a shop assistant?	No, he isn't.
	Is he a policeman?	Yes, he is.

2 Students ask more Yes/No questions about the other students in the class. Don't let this go on too long unless students are enjoying it. They will already have done a lot of work on a similar area. Notice that first, second, and third persons singular are practised.

3 Grammar

This exercise serves to consolidate the verb *to be* in all persons, and allows students to make some sentences about themselves. Check that students know *at home* and *at work*.

Answers

There can be no set answers for a–f!

g Champagne *isn't* a drink from Portugal.

h Egypt and Morocco *aren't* in Europe. They *are* in Africa.

> **Additional material**
> **Workbook Unit 2**
> **Exercises 1–7** Verb *to be*, questions, negatives, short answers, short forms, and long forms.

PRESENTATION (2) (SB page 14)

Possessive *'s*

> **Note**
> You could begin this presentation with a personalized example. Talk about your own family, e.g. *I have two children, a boy and a girl. The boy's name is Tony and the girl's name is Lucy.*
> Put the last sentence on the board, and draw students attention to the possessive *'s*. Say that this isn't the verb *to be*, but that it shows possession. Use L1 if you can.

T10 Students look at the photograph. They read and listen and put the names next to the right person.

> Read the information in the Caution Box together with the class.

● Grammar question

Students work in pairs to find other examples of *'s* = possession and *'s* = is.

Answers	
possession	*is*
wife's name	She's a dentist.
daughter's name	She's twenty-three
son's name	she's a hairdresser
Alison's boyfriend	He's nineteen and he's a student.

Practice (SB page 15)

1 Speaking

1 Students ask and answer questions about Martin's family.

Answers	
Who's Jennifer?	She's Alison and Andy's mother.
Who's Alison?	She's Martin's/Jennifer's daughter.
	She's Andy's sister.
	She's Joe's girlfriend.
Who's Andy?	He's Martin's/Jennifer's son.
	He's Alison's brother.
Who's Joe?	He's Alison's boyfriend.

2 Students ask you questions about the names of your family, i.e. *What's your mother's name?* not *Who's* ... as in Exercise 1. This is practised in the speaking activity later.

2 Vocabulary

Students use their dictionaries to fill in the gaps.

Answers	
husband	wife
son	*daughter*
father	*mother*
brother	sister
uncle	*aunt*
nephew	niece
grandfather	*grandmother*

Drill some of the words to practise the pronunciation.

3 Speaking

Students write down the names of some of their relatives on a piece of paper. Then they exchange pieces of paper with a partner and ask and answer questions about each other's families.

Additional idea

You could revise the possessive *'s* at the beginning of the next lesson by asking ten or so students for a personal belonging of theirs. Put them all in the middle of the room. Students then have to point at an object and say *That's Maria's book*, etc.

4 Choosing the correct sentence

Students work in pairs or small groups to identify the correct sentence.

Answers
1 b 2 a 3 b 4 a 5 a 6 a 7 b 8 a

Additional material

Workbook Unit 2
Exercises 8 and 9 Possessive *'s*

● VOCABULARY (SB page 15)

Adjectives

1 Students use their dictionaries to match the opposite adjectives.

Answers
1 difficult – easy
2 expensive – cheap
3 old – young
4 hot – cold
5 horrible – lovely
6 new – old
7 small – big
8 right – wrong

Drill the words to practise pronunciation. You could ask students to mark the stress on the words with two syllables or more, as in the Vocabulary section in Unit 1.

Answers		
● • •	• ● •	● •
difficult	expensive	lovely
horrible		

2 The aim of this exercise is to practise the vocabulary and to revise the verb *to be*.

Students write sentences for each picture.

Answers	
a It's big.	i It's easy.
b It's small.	j It's difficult.
c She's old.	k They're old.
d She's young.	l They're new.
e They're expensive.	m They're hot.
f They're cheap.	n They're cold.
g It's horrible.	o It's right.
h It's lovely.	p It's wrong.

T11 Play the tape so students can check their answers. Students could practise saying the sentences in pairs.

● READING AND LISTENING (SB page 16)

Note

This is the first piece of extensive skills work in *Headway Elementary*. Students are encouraged to read and listen to the letter at the same time even though this might be deemed an unnatural activity. Learners of English find reading an easier skill than listening because they can recognize cognates with L1 without the interference of different pronunciation. However, if they read the letter silently at their own speed, they could become distracted by unknown and not terribly important vocabulary.

The aim of this activity is to show students a lot of the language that they have been exposed to in a relatively natural context. If you feel your students would not be able to cope with the activity as it stands, you could pre-teach the following items of vocabulary, or set them as a homework task prior to the lesson.

penfriend	funny	park
class	top	beautiful
with	friendly	centre
other	understand	use (v)
all	interesting	Underground
different	weather	now
nice	sunny	soon

However, if you feel your students don't need so much support, pre-teach the following items, and try to encourage them not to worry about other unknown words.

penfriend	weather
nice	beautiful
friendly	Underground
understand	

Read the introduction as a class.

T 12a Students read and listen to the letter.

Comprehension check

1 Ask students to match a picture with a part of the letter. There are more pictures than paragraphs, so students will use words to refer to the relevant part of the letter.

Answers (anti-clockwise from top left)
Picture 1 – English coffee is horrible.
Picture 2 – The Brown family.
Picture 3 – The parks are beautiful.
Picture 4 – In class with Peter Briscall.
Picture 5 and tube ticket – The Underground is expensive.

Having established gist comprehension, you might want to play the tape and ask students to read again.

2 If you feel your students would be happy to answer the true/false questions in pairs or small groups, ask them to do this. Otherwise, answer the questions as a class. You could ask them to provide the correct information for the false statements.

Answers
a True.
b False. (She's at a school of English.)
c False. (It's a small class – nine students.)
d False. (One student is from Japan, one from Argentina, and one from Thailand.)
e True.
f False. (It's expensive.)
g False. (It's OK.)

3 With this exercise, the focus of attention shifts from fluency to accuracy. Students often have problems with the formation of questions, so it is worth taking the opportunity to provide some practice.

Again, if you feel students would be happy to work in pairs or small groups to answer these questions, let them do so.

Answers
a Where are the (other) students from?
b What's her/the teacher's name?
c How old is Thomas?
d Is the weather good?
e Is the coffee good?

You could drill the questions for pronunciation practice. Careful with intonation!

4 With this listening, the focus of attention again shifts, from accuracy to fluency. Students hear the five conversations, and there will inevitably be words that they don't know. However, there are enough clues for them to work out where Paola is and who she is with. Note that students will not know the word *ticket seller*.

T 12b You could play the tape once and ask students to answer the two questions for each situation. Then ask them to look at the tapescript, and play the tape again. It can be very rewarding for students to explore sound/spelling relationships at this level.

Answers
1 She is with Kurt, a student.
2 She is in the Underground with a ticket seller.
3 She is in class with her teacher and the other students.
4 She is in a café with the assistant and another student, Kurt.
5 She is at home with Catherine and Thomas Brown.

Writing

This is a free writing activity, as explained on page 5 of the Teacher's Book. Set it for homework, and mark it sympathetically and selectively, i.e. only correct those things that students have learnt and can be expected to get right!

● EVERYDAY ENGLISH (SB page 17)

In a café

> **Note**
> This exercise practises, among other things, prices. If you feel your students need some work on this prior to the lesson, see the Workbook Unit 2, Exercises 13 and 14.
>
> Exercise 5 suggests that you should use real English money if you can. This is not only for authenticity and curiosity, but because when one is in a foreign country, it is so much easier to hand over a note rather than try to work out the exact money! The consequence of this is that you end up with a pocketful of coins (not to mention being shortchanged!).

1 Students look at the menu, and check new words in their dictionary.

2 **T13a** Students listen and repeat. Do this chorally, stopping the tape, and individually. See the tapescript for the text.

The question *How much ...?* might be new, so check this if necessary. Make sure students practise the intonation of the *How much ...?* questions, and draw attention to word-joining, e.g. cup of tea, an orange juice.

3 Students ask and answer questions about prices. Do this first in open pairs, then in closed pairs. Correct pronunciation carefully.

4 **T13b** Students listen to the conversations and fill the gaps.

> **Answers**
> a B Can I have a *ham sandwich*, please?
> A One pound *fifty*, please.
> b B A *cup of tea*, please.
> B *How much* is that?
> c A *Can I have* a hamburger and a cup of coffee, please?
> B OK. *Here you are.*
> B *Three pounds* twenty.

5 Students practise the conversations in pairs. You can then make the activity a little freer by roleplaying. Take the role of the person working in the café yourself first. Give out the English money to one of the students, and ask him/her what he/she wants. You can increase the vocabulary load of your language according to the level of your students, asking for example *Do you want any mayonnaise in your sandwich?*, *Diet Coke?*, etc.

Then ask students to take both roles. You could record some conversations for later examination and correction.

GRAMMAR SUMMARY (SB page 18)

Read the Grammar Summary as a class. Encourage students to ask any questions.

> **Don't forget!**
>
> **Workbook Unit 2**
> **Exercise 10** A revision of the alphabet.
> **Exercise 11** This exercise introduces the question *What's the matter?* and several answers to the question.
> **Exercise 12** Spelling of plural nouns.
>
> **Word List**
> Encourage students to study the Word List on page 123 of the Student's Book, and translate the words into L1.
>
> **Pronunciation Book Unit 2**
>
> **Video**
> A video accompanies *Headway Elementary*. There is a section for every two units throughout the course. The first one is called *A Day in London* and features David, who is English, showing his Italian friend, Paola, round London.

UNIT 3

Present Simple (1) – *What time is it?*

Introduction to the unit

Work and jobs are the themes of this unit as they lend themselves to the practice of the grammatical aim, which is the introduction of the third person singular of the Present Simple. The skills work includes a reading text about a man who works in England, but lives in France. This was chosen to complement both the themes and grammar of the unit.

Language aims

Grammar

Present Simple (1)

The Present Simple is the most used tense in the English language. It is therefore important to introduce it early in a beginners'/elementary course. In *Headway Elementary* the introduction is staged over two units. In this unit only the third person singular with its questions and negatives is presented and practised. All the other persons are introduced in Unit 4.

Problems

1 The English language does not have many inflections. Unfortunately this seems to mean that the few that exist cause a disproportionate amount of difficulty for foreign learners. The *s* on the third person singular of the Present Simple is a classic example of this. Therefore we introduce it first in the hope that it will be more memorable and students will be less likely to omit it.

2 The pronunciation of the *s* can be realized in three ways:

comes /kʌmz/
works /wɜ:ks/
teaches /ti:tʃɪz/

So you need to spend some time highlighting the /s/, /z/, /ɪz/ endings and practising them.

3 The use of *does* in the question and negative will seem very strange to your students. This is not only because this will be the first time they meet an auxiliary verb, but also because the absence of the auxiliary *do/does* in the positive makes its sudden appearance in the question and negative seem quite bizarre to many learners.

Note

For the first nine units of *Headway Elementary*, the verb *have* is introduced and practised as a full verb with its *do/does* forms. *Have got* is introduced in Unit 10. This is for several reasons.

1 By introducing the *do/does* forms, the verb *have* operates like any other verb in the Present Simple (with the exception of *has* in the third person singular).

2 When students have just learned the Present Simple and have been introduced to the auxiliary verbs *do/does*, it is very difficult and confusing for them when they come across the verb form *have got*, which operates differently.

3 Although *have got* is common, especially in the spoken language, the full verb *have* with its *do/does* forms covers all the uses in a way that *have got* doesn't. *Have got* expresses possession, but it cannot express a habitual action. So students can learn *How many children have you got?*, but then it is very confusing when they are introduced to *What time do you have lunch?*. We cannot say **What time have you got lunch?*.

4 Finally, *have* with its *do/does* forms is becoming more common in spoken British English. It is of course the standard form in American English.

Vocabulary and pronunciation

A variety of jobs with related activities are introduced. This lends itself to further practice of the Present Simple. Dictionary work is encouraged and there is a certain amount of work on the phonetic spelling of some of the words.

Everyday English

Students are introduced to how to tell the time in English. This is practised in short dialogues.

Workbook

The spelling of the third person singular is illustrated and practised (*watches*, *goes*).
Question words such as *Where?* and *How much?* are practised.
Verbs of daily routine (*get up*, *get dressed*) are introduced, and some verbs and nouns that go together (*cook dinner*, *wear a uniform*).
The writing syllabus of *Headway Elementary* begins in this unit. Object pronouns (*me*, *him*, *them*) are introduced and practised.

Notes on the unit

PRESENTATION (1) (SB page 19)

Present Simple

Note
We suggest that *before* you start this unit you set the following vocabulary homework in preparation for the presentation texts. This will save a lot of classroom time where you would have to teach new words either by mime, dictionary work, or translation (in a monolingual class), and it will give you more time to focus on the grammar.

Homework prior to lesson
Ask students to use their bilingual dictionaries and look up the meaning and write the translation of the following words and *learn* them for the lesson:

Verbs	Nouns	Adjectives
come	countryside	green
go	mountain	free (time)
have	language	
like	shop	
live	summer	
love	village	
play	winter	
speak		
teach		
walk		
work		

Pre-teach *nun* and *ski-instructor*.

1 Ask students to look at the photographs. Ask them *What's her job? (teacher), What's his job? (ski-instructor).*

Then ask them to look quickly at the texts and ask *Where is she from? (Ireland), Where is he from? (Switzerland).*

T14 Now play the tape and ask your students to read and listen to the texts at the same time. If you think your class will experience some difficulty you could deal with the texts one at a time, doing the grammar questions *with* them for the first text and then asking them to repeat the process on their own for the second.

● Grammar questions

Ask your students to work on their own to underline the verbs and then check their answers with a partner before you conduct a full class feedback. You could ask them to call out the verbs for you to write on the blackboard. It would be a good idea to write them in columns according to their pronunciation (see below) to highlight the differences and help your students practise saying them later.

Answers

/z/	/s/	/ɪz/
comes	works	teaches
lives	likes	
loves	speaks	
goes		
plays		
is		
has		

Ask the whole class what the last letter is and point out that this is the ending for the third person singular – *he, she, it* – of the Present Simple tense.

2 Before you ask your students to practise the verbs in pairs, ask them to chorus them with you from the blackboard and draw their attention to the different pronunciations of the endings.

You may also want to point out that *is* and *has* are irregular.

Now ask them to practise in pairs and read one of the texts to each other. Go round and check whilst they are doing this. You could round off the activity by asking one or two students to read a text aloud to the whole class.

Practice (SB page 19)

1 Grammar

Ask your students to write in the answers on their own and then check with a partner before you go through the exercise with them. Make it clear that each gap represents a word.

Answers

a She comes from Ireland. He *comes from* Switzerland.
b He lives in a village, but she *lives in* a town.
c She works in a school. He *works in* a sports shop.
d He *teaches* skiing. She *teaches French* and Spanish.
e She *lives* near the sea, but he *lives* in the mountains.
f He likes his job and she *likes her job*, too.
g He *has two* sons.
h She *goes* walking in her free time. He *plays football* with his sons.*
i He *speaks* four languages. She *speaks* three.

* Note that *play/go* + activity are dealt with in Unit 4.

2 Speaking

The aim of this activity is to give students the chance, not just to produce single sentences, but to speak at some length to describe the characters. It is both useful and satisfying for low level students to use language for 'display' purposes only in this way and not always engage in the more 'natural' question and answer activities.

Ask the whole class to look at the picture of Georges. Use the notes about him to build a profile of him orally with contributions from different students in the class.

Then ask one or two individuals to speak at length about Georges.

Sample answer
Georges is a taxi driver. He comes from France and he lives in Paris. He works in the centre of Paris. He isn't married, but he has a dog. In his free time he goes walking with his dog and he plays football.

Now ask your students to do the same thing in pairs for Keiko and Mark. Go round the class to check and help them. Round off the activity by bringing the whole class together again, and asking one or two students to tell the others about Keiko and Mark.

3 Writing

You could set this exercise for homework, but if there is time it is often motivating to do such personalized activities in class. Ask your students to write a few lines on their own and then read them aloud either to a partner, or to the class as a whole.

Additional material

Workbook Unit 3
Exercises 1, 2 and 4 These provide further practice of the third person positive of the Present Simple. Exercise 2 focuses on the spelling.
Exercise 3 This is a vocabulary activity in preparation for Exercise 4. It should be done with a dictionary. (It is *not* an opportunity to practise other persons of the Present Simple, only to see the verbs in their infinitive forms!) It would be a good idea to set this exercise for homework and then follow it in class with Exercise 4 because the pictures of the daily routine of Pamela's life are particularly suitable for a classroom activity, where the story is built orally *before* students are asked to write it.

PRESENTATION (2) (SB page 20)

Questions and negatives

Note
This will be the first time your students have met an auxiliary verb in English (apart from *do* in *How do you spell your name?* in Unit 2), so be prepared for some students to be surprised at the sudden appearance of *does/doesn't* to form the question and negative. In the Present and Past Simple tenses, where there is no auxiliary in the positive, the introduction of the auxiliary verbs can seem very strange. Many students feel that it would be much more logical to say:

**Lives he in Paris?*
**Where lives she?*
**She lives not in London.*

The short answers *Yes, he does./No, he doesn't.* also cause problems and need highlighting for students.

1 You need to signal that you are going to introduce the question form. You can do this by drawing a large question mark on the board and/or repeating the sentences yourself with exaggerated intonation.

T15a You can teach the questions either yourself or using the tape. Ask your students to listen, then repeat both chorally and individually. Then get them to ask and answer the questions in open pairs across the class.

Note
Encourage good pronunciation at all times. Isolate the weak and strong forms of *does* for repetition, and then ask for repetition in the context of the questions and answers:

the weak /dəz/ in all the questions *What does she do? Does she speak French?*
and the strong form /dʌz/ and /dʌznt/ in the short answers *Yes, she does. No, she doesn't.*

Also take care with the intonation, falling at the end in the *wh-* questions and rising in the inverted questions.

Where does she come from? /weə dəz ʃɪ kʌm frɒm/

Does she speak French?

Read the Caution Box as a class. This will reinforce and summarize the form and meaning of the oral work you have been doing.

2 **T 15b** Ask your students to complete the sentences on their own and then check their answers with a partner. Play the tape and get them to listen and check. Finally ask individuals to read aloud their answers to the class and check the pronunciation.

Answers
a Where *does* Hans *come* from? Switzerland.
b What *does* he *do*? He's a ski-instructor.
c *Does* he *speak* French and German? Yes, he *does*.
d *Does* he *speak* Spanish? No, he *doesn't*.

Practice (SB page 20)

1 Writing and speaking

1 Ask your students to work on their own and write the questions about Georges, Keiko, and Mark on a separate piece of paper.

Answers
a Where does she/he live?
b What does he/she do?
c Where does she/he work?
d Does he/she speak French or Spanish?
e What does she/he do in her/his free time?
f Does he/she play tennis?
g How many children does she/he have?
h Does he/she have a dog?

Check their questions quickly round the class, getting students to read them aloud.

2 Ask your students to close their books. Write the names Georges, Keiko, and Mark on the blackboard, then ask students to work in pairs and take it in turns to ask and answer questions about any of the three characters. Don't make the activity too laborious by insisting they ask *every* question about *every* character, as this would probably take too long, so let your students choose which questions and which characters they use.

Round off the activity by asking for a few questions in open pairs across the class.

3 This is a personalized activity. You may need to suggest a suitable family member, perhaps an aunt, an uncle, or a cousin. Go round and check as they do it. Ask one or two students to tell the whole class about their or their partner's relative to round off the activity.

2 Listening and pronunciation

1 Do this exercise as briskly as possible with the whole class. Illustrate the nature of the activity by going through the sample sentences with them and practising the responses *Yes, that's right* and *No, he/she doesn't.*

T 16a Play the tape or read the sentences yourself and nominate individuals in the class to respond. Encourage other members of the class to correct if a wrong answer is given. It should be quick and fun to do, so *don't* insist on the full correct answer if it slows down the activity. *No, he/she doesn't* is enough.

Answers
He works in the centre of Paris.
Yes, that's right.
In his free time he plays tennis.
No, he doesn't. (He plays football.)
Keiko comes from China.
No, she doesn't. (She comes from Japan.)
She lives in Washington.
No. she doesn't. (She lives in New York.)
She speaks French and German.
No, she doesn't. (She speaks Russian and English.)
She's married to an American. *Yes, that's right.*
Mark comes from England. *Yes, that's right.*
He works in Liverpool.
No, he doesn't. (He works in Moscow.)
He speaks Italian.
No, he doesn't. (He speaks Russian and German.)
In his free time he goes walking.
No, he doesn't. (He plays tennis.)

2 **T 16b** This should follow on immediately from the previous exercise. Play the tape. Ask students to tick the sentence they hear. This is an exercise that tests reception, but you can make it productive afterwards by asking students to practise the pairs of sentences in pairs.

Answers
1 b 2 a 3 a 4 b 5 b 6 a

3 Choosing the correct sentence

See page 5 of the Teacher's Book for an explanation of this exercise type.
Ask students to work in pairs or small groups to choose the correct sentence. Ask them to work quite quickly, then conduct a full class feedback on which are the correct answers. Try to get students to correct each other and explain any mistakes they hear.

Answers
1 a 2 b 3 b 4 a 5 b 6 a 7 a 8 b

Additional Material

Workbook Unit 3
Exercises 5–9 Questions and negatives in Present Simple third person singular.
Exercises 12 and 13 This may also be a good time to do the writing activity because it is the rewriting of a short text about Keiko.

● VOCABULARY AND PRONUNCIATION

(SB page 21)

Jobs

1 Ask students to look at the pictures and tell you any of the jobs they know already. Then get them to work in pairs and match a picture with a job in column A, checking any words that are still unknown in their dictionaries. You could ask them to mark the stress.

Conduct a full class feedback on the correct answers and drill the words both chorally and individually as you go, taking care with the stress (see below). Keep revising as you go by asking *Tell me again! What's a? What's d?* etc.

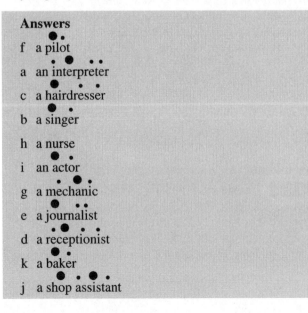

Answers
f a pilot
a an interpreter
c a hairdresser
b a singer
h a nurse
i an actor
g a mechanic
e a journalist
d a receptionist
k a baker
j a shop assistant

2 Ask them to work in pairs or small groups and match a line in column A with a line in column B. They will probably need to continue to use their dictionaries *or* if you have a monolingual class and you think dictionary work will take too much time, you could give quick translations of any words they ask about. Afterwards you could either conduct a full class feedback (try not to make this too laborious with too much correction), or alternatively, you could ask different students to come up to the board and write the answers for the others to comment on and read aloud.

Answers
A pilot flies a plane.
An interpreter translates things.
A hairdresser cuts hair.
A singer works in a night club.
A nurse looks after people in hospital.
An actor makes films.
A mechanic mends cars.
A journalist writes for a newspaper.
A receptionist works in a hotel.
A baker makes bread.
A shop assistant sells things.

3

Note
The idea of this activity is to give a very short introduction to and practice of the phonetic script. It is also an opportunity to start getting your students familiar with the phonetic chart on the back cover of their book.

You need to make clear what exactly phonetic script is, i.e. that it is only the *sounds* of the words that are transcribed and that it is important to know this in English because the spellings and the sounds often do not relate exactly.

We are attempting throughout the book to stage the introduction of the phonemes, therefore in this exercise we have limited the words to those with single vowel sounds only. We have not included those words which contain diphthongs.

Address the whole class and ask them to look at all the phonetic spellings and say if they can recognize any of the words. Ask them to turn to the inside back cover, *not* to study it, but so that they get the idea of what phonetic spelling is.

Now ask them to write the spellings of the words and then check them with a partner and practise saying them together. Let them use the phonetic chart to help them.

Answers

a nurse	d actor
b interpreter	e singer
c receptionist	f mechanic

If you have time you could put a few additional words in phonetic script on the blackboard for them to do after you have asked for feedback on the words in the exercise. For example:

/bred/	(bread)
/hɒspɪtəl/	(hospital)
/pɪ:pl/	(people)
/wɜ:ks/	(works)
/lʊks/	(looks)
/selz/	(sells)
/kɑ:z/	(cars)

4 Make this exercise fun, like a game, and do it as quickly as possible. Ask your students to learn the sentences by heart, then to close their books. You call out the name of a job and tell your students to call out to complete the sentence.

Teacher	**Student(s)**
A journalist ...	*writes for a newspaper!*
An actor ...	*makes films!* etc.

Finally ask them to work in pairs for a few minutes with their books still shut, and ask and answer questions about the jobs. Demonstrate the first example yourself to remind them of the question, e.g.

What does an interpreter do? An interpreter translates things.

Additional material

Workbook Unit 3
Further vocabulary exercises:
Exercise 10 This practises more verbs and nouns that go together, e.g. *cook dinner.*
Exercise 11 This revises a selection of vocabulary from all the units so far. It requires students to sort words into related groups.

● READING AND LISTENING (SB page 22)

Note
This is an important activity because it brings together in a text much of the grammar your students have been studying so far. It should give them great satisfaction to feel that they can already master a piece of continuous prose of this length.

Frank Garret is a real person and the text is based upon a newspaper article about him. However it has been carefully simplified and graded to make it manageable for students of this level.

You could begin the lesson by asking students:
Is your home near school? How far is your home from school?
If you have a strong class you could even teach and practise:
How long does it take to come here? (to school)
Then ask and answer quickly round the class.

Pre-reading task

1 Ask students to look quickly at the pictures on the page and tell you a little about what and who they can see. Now focus their attention on the map and ask the whole class which countries they are and the names of their capital cities. They can write them in their books (if it is their own copy and not a class set!).

Answers
The country at the top is, of course, England and across the Channel is France.
The two *big* dots are the capitals, London and Paris.

2 It would be a good idea to set this little vocabulary exercise for homework *prior* to the lesson to save time now. (Check it in class through translation if you have a monolingual group.) Otherwise do it as *quickly* as possible in class, asking your students to work in pairs with their bilingual dictionaries. Go round and help them as they do it.

Don't forget to tell them to record the words in their vocabulary notebooks (if they are keeping them!).

Reading

Ask students to read the text quite quickly this first time (you could even set a time limit of perhaps three minutes) and answer the three questions. Tell them they will get a chance to read it more carefully later. Ask them to check their answers with a partner and then with the whole class.

Answers
a He lives in France.
b He's a teacher.
c He works in England *and* France.

Comprehension check

Ask students to work in pairs or small groups to do this. They can consult the text whenever necessary to complete the task.

1 Do this and check the answers *before* asking students to move onto the questions in 2.

Answer

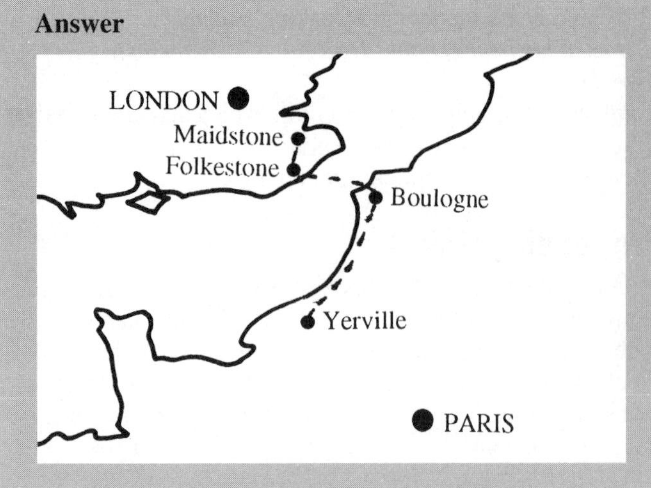

2 Ask students to do question 2 and get feedback before moving to 3. You decide according to the speed and ability of your students whether to settle for quick short answers or whether you want fuller answers (see brackets).

Answers

a No, he isn't. (He's English.)
b Two. (He has two jobs: he teaches French in England and English in France.)
c No, he doesn't. (He drives to Boulogne.)
d In Boulogne. (He leaves his car in Boulogne.)
e In Folkstone. (He catches the train in Folkestone.)
f It's cheap. It costs only £16.
g No, he doesn't. (He (only) works in Manor School on Mondays.)
h Because he loves his home in France, but he also loves his job in England.

3 Make it clear to your students that this text is about Mr Garret's journey *back home* and they only need insert the correct verb.

Answers

Mr Garret *leaves* Manor School at 3.30 in the afternoon and he *catches* the train to Folkstone, where he *catches* the ferry to Boulogne. Then he *drives* from Boulogne back to his village. The journey *takes* six hours. He *arrives* home at 9.30.

Ask one or two members of the class to read aloud their completed texts. Listen carefully to their pronunciation of the verb endings. You could take the opportunity to revise /s/, /z/, /ɪz/ by asking your students to identify which verbs have which endings:

/s/	/z/	/ɪz/
takes	leaves	catches
	drives	
	arrives	

Language work

After all the pairwork it may be a good idea to vary your approach and do this activity with the whole class. Ask individuals to complete the questions orally and establish the correct answers with open question and answer practice across the class. Aim for good pronunciation not only of the sounds but natural falling intonation in all these *wh*-questions. Now ask your students to write in the correct answers and finally practise them again with a partner.

Answers

a What time *does he arrive* at Manor School?
b What time *does he leave*?
c When *does he arrive* home in the evening?
d How much *does* the journey *cost*?
e How long *does* the journey home *take*?
f How many students *does* he *have* in his English class?

Listening and speaking

1 **T17** This is a dictation activity. Tell your students that they are going to hear some conversations from Mr Garret's day and ask them to listen and write in the missing words. Stop the tape after each conversation.

Answers

a A *Good morning*, sir. Can I see your *ticket*?
B Yes, of course. Here you *are*.
A Thank you. Maidstone next *stop*.
B Thank you.

b A *Good morning*, boys and girls.
B *Good morning*, Mr Garret.
A *Can I have* your homework, please?
B It's on your *desk*, Mr Garret.
A Thank you.

c A *Goodbye*, Frank. Have a good *journey*!
B Thank you very *much*.
A See you next *Monday*.
B Yes, *of* course. Goodbye!

d A *Excuse me*. Is this seat *free*?
B Yes, it is.
A Thank you. It's *cold* this evening.
B *It* certainly *is*. And the sea's very *black*!

e A Hello darling! Are you *tired*?
B Yes, I am. And *cold*.
A Sit down and *have* a glass of wine.
B Mmmm! Thank you. I'm *hungry*, too.

Ask students to check their answers with a partner. Then play the tape again and conduct a full class feedback after each dialogue to establish the correct answers.

2 Do this with the whole class. Ask them to look again at the conversations and tell you what time of day and where each one is taking place, and who is talking to Frank Garret.

Answers

a Morning. On the train from Folkestone to Maidstone. A ticket inspector.
b Morning. At school. School children.
c Afternoon. At school. A teacher.
d Evening. On the ferry. A ferry passenger.
e Evening. At home. Frank's wife.

3 Put your students into pairs to practise the conversations. An additional idea is to ask them to choose *one* of the conversations and learn it by heart to act out to the rest of the class. You could also perhaps encourage the more confident students to improvise some further dialogue. (Asking students to get to their feet and act out really seems to help their pronunciation, particularly stress and intonation.)

● EVERYDAY ENGLISH (SB page 24)

What time is it?

1

Note
The first eight clocks on this page are positioned in such a way that those with gaps underneath are next to clocks with *similar* times which students can use to help them write in the correct answers.

The next eight practise the time in five minute intervals around the clock. You probably will *not* need to point out the above to students when you ask them to do the exercise. It should be obvious what to do from the pictures.

Ask students to work in pairs, look carefully at the clocks, and write in the times.

Answers

It's five o'clock.	*It's eight o'clock.*
It's half past five.	*It's half past eleven.*
It's quarter past five.	*It's quarter past two.*
It's quarter to six.	*It's quarter to nine.*
It's five past five.	*It's ten past five.*
It's twenty past five.	It's twenty-five past five.
It's twenty-five to six.	It's twenty to six.
It's ten to six.	*It's five to six.*

T18a Now play the tape for them to check their answers. Then practise saying the times either from the tape or repeating them after you. If possible bring a toy clock with moveable hands to the lesson because at this stage it is the obvious way to get further practice. First *you* can change the times on the clock and then your students can also have turns, coming to the front of the class, moving the hands, and asking *What time is it?*

2 *Exactly*, *nearly*, and *just after* are introduced because they are useful time expressions.

Read through the examples with the class and practise with the toy clock (if you have one!) or by drawing further examples on the board.

3 **T18b** Play the tape and ask your students to repeat the sentences giving very special attention to the stress and intonation. Tell them that they must try to sound *very* polite. Really encourage good imitation from the tape, or by giving the sentences yourself. Practise the dialogue across the class with your own examples first, then ask everyone to draw about three clocks on a piece of paper and practise the conversation again in pairs. Round off the lesson by asking one or two pairs to act out the conversations in front of the class. Tell them to imagine that they are stopping someone in the street to ask the time and that they must be very, very polite.

Note
The *more* you insist on good stress and intonation in such activities the *more* fun it will be!

Additional material

Workbook Unit 3
Exercises 14 and 15 These give more practice of telling the time and writing about daily routines.

GRAMMAR SUMMARY (SB page 24)

Read the Grammar Summary together as a class. Encourage students to ask questions.

Don't forget!

Workbook Unit 3
Exercises 12 and 13 You might want to do the writing activities now, if you haven't done them earlier.

Word List
Remind your students of the Word List at the back of their book. Ask them to look at the list for this unit on page 123. Tell them that they could write in the translations, study them at home and/or write *some* of the words in their vocabulary notebook.

Pronunciation Book Unit 3

UNIT 4

Present Simple (2) – Articles – Social English

Introduction to the unit

The theme of this unit is 'Free time'. This lends itself to much practice, personalized and otherwise, of the main grammatical aim, which is the introduction of *all* other persons (those without the *s*!) of the Present Simple tense. We also include a brief and simple introduction to the use of articles in English. The skills work includes a listening where people from three different countries talk about their favourite season and what they do. This provides the opportunity to bring together and revise all persons of the Present Simple.

Language aims

Grammar

Present Simple (2)

This unit follows on from the introduction of the third person in Unit 3 and introduces all other persons of the Present Simple, *I*, *you*, *we*, *they*, and the question and negative. The verb forms with these are all the same, without the inflection *s*, and tend to cause less difficulty as a result. The third person is constantly revised alongside the other persons so that students can perceive the differences in form.

Articles

We feel that the use of articles is often ignored for too long in language teaching and that *perhaps* something can be gained from trying to provide a little insight into how they operate, even at this low level. However, we have limited the information on their use to bare essentials. Students make so many mistakes with articles, and are constantly being corrected without knowing why, e.g. 'Use *the* in *Close the door.* Use *a* with professions. There's no article in *go home*.' Students will probably continue to make mistakes in article usage for much of their language learning career, but it is hoped that a few basic rules might help to explain some of their mistakes.

Obviously it would be useful for you to be aware of differences between article use in English and your students' language(s), but this will probably only be possible if you are teaching monolingual groups.

Vocabulary

A variety of free time activities (sports and hobbies) are introduced and these are practised in a personalized activity with the verb *to like*.

The use of *play* or *go* with sports is introduced after the reading and listening texts.

Everyday English

Some common and useful social expressions are introduced and practised in short dialogues.

Workbook

Adverbs of frequency, e.g. *always*, *sometimes*, *never* are presented and practised.

In the vocabulary section, opposite verbs, e.g. *love/hate*, *open/close*, *leave/arrive* are revised.

The writing syllabus continues with an introduction to informal letter writing via a letter to a penfriend.

Notes on the unit

PRESENTATION (1) (SB page 25)

Present Simple

Note
We suggest that you set some vocabulary for homework before you start this unit in preparation for the presentation texts. This will save a lot of classroom time and give you more time to focus on the grammar. However, it is also worthwhile to get your students used to the idea of taking some responsibility for the learning of vocabulary. Encourage them to enter the new words in their vocabulary notebooks.

Homework prior to the lesson

1 Ask your students to learn the days of the week in English. You could give them a handout with phonetic script such as this:

Monday /mʌndɪ/	Friday /fraɪdɪ/
Tuesday /tʃu:zdɪ/	Saturday /sætədɪ/
Wednesday /wenzdɪ/	Sunday /sʌndɪ/
Thursday /θɜ:zdɪ/	

2 Give them the following list of new verbs to look up in their bilingual dictionaries.
Ask them to learn them and write down the translations.

bring _____	go out _____
chat _____	listen to _____
cook _____	relax _____
eat _____	stay _____
get up _____	visit _____

1 Use a calendar as a visual aid, and get your students to go through the days of the week. Say the days yourself and ask them to repeat each one both chorally and individually. This will obviously take less time if you have set the above for homework.

Problems
Take particular care with the pronunciation of *Tuesday* /tʃu:zdɪ/ and *Thursday* /θɜ:zdɪ/ which students can easily confuse because they sound quite similar. Also the pronunciation of Wednesday /wenzdɪ/ can be a problem because of the spelling, and the consonant cluster /nzd/ that results from it being pronounced as *two* syllables not three.

Ask *What is the day today?* Also ask *Which days are the weekend?* This will check that your students understand the word *weekend* which is needed in the exercises.

Now chorus through the days of the week with the whole class and then make the individual practice fun by getting one student after another to give consecutive days *very* quickly round the class until they are firmly fixed.

If time, you could then ask one or two students to go through the whole week and perhaps also ask them to spell some of the days, to revise the alphabet.

2 This text reminds students of the third person of the Present Simple before they are introduced to the other persons. Ask them to look at the photograph and read the text. Ask a few questions about the text to revise the third person.

Examples

Teacher	**Student(s)**
Where does she live?	*In London.*
How old is she?	*Thirty-four.*
What does she do?	*She works for the BBC.*
What time does she get up?	*Three o'clock in the morning.*
What time does the programme start?	*Half past six.*
Does she like her work?	*Yes, she does.*
Why does she like it?	*Because she meets interesting people.*

3 Ask students to work in pairs and check through the verbs in the box. This can obviously be done quite quickly if they have done the preparatory homework.

4 **T19a** Play the tape and ask students to read and listen only first of all. Tell them that Ann McGregor is talking about her weekends.

5 Now put your students into pairs and ask them to work together to complete the text with the verbs from the box. You will need to make clear that some of the verbs will need an *s* because they are third person singular. The others can be copied exactly from the box. Play the tape again so that they can check their answers.

Answers
On Fridays, I *come* home from the BBC at about 2.00 in the afternoon and I just *relax*. On Friday evenings I don't *go out*, but sometimes a friend *comes* for dinner. He or she *brings* the wine and I *cook* the meal. I *love* cooking! We *listen* to music or we just *chat*.
On Saturday mornings I *get up* at 9.00 and I *go* shopping. Then in the evenings I sometimes *go* to the theatre or the opera with a friend. I *love* opera! Then we *eat* in my favourite Chinese restaurant.
On Sunday ... Oh, on Sunday mornings I *stay* in bed late, I don't *get up* until 11.00! Sometimes in the afternoon I *visit* my sister. She *lives* in the country and *has* two children. I *like* playing with my niece and nephew, but I *leave* early because I *go* to bed at 8.00 on Sunday evenings!

Ask one or two students to read parts of the text aloud to the rest of the class. If time, ask students to read parts of it to each other in pairs.

Grammar questions

Ask your students to tell you the four verbs that end in *-s*.

> **Answers**
> comes, brings, lives, has.

Ask why they end in *-s*. Your students should be able to attempt to say that it is because of *he* or *she*, or they could explain in L1 if it is a monolingual class.
Ask them to find and tell you the two negatives. Write these on the board. Ask them the negative for the *he* and *she* forms and write these next to the others on the board.

> **Answers**
> I don't go out ... I don't get up ...
> She/he doesn't go out ... She/he doesn't get up ...

Complete the rules by reading this aloud to the class, encourage their suggestions to fill the gaps and establish the correct answers.

> **Answers**
> In the Present Simple positive we add <u>-s</u> to the verb with *he, she,* and *it*, but not with *I, you, we,* and *they*. With *I, you, we,* and *they*, the negative is <u>*don't*</u> + infinitive. With *he, she,* and *it*, the negative is <u>*doesn't*</u> + infinitive.

PRESENTATION (2) (SB page 26)

Questions

1 **T19b** Ask students to read the questions and answers and at the same time either play the tape or model them yourself. Practise them in open pairs across the class so that you can correct any mistakes. Take particular care with the pronunciation:

Sounds
The weak vowel sound /dʊ/ not the strong /du:/ in the question, and the strong vowel sound /du:/ in the short answer.

Do you stay at home? Yes, I do.

/djʊ steɪ ət həʊm/ /jes aɪ du:/

Stress and intonation
The intonation rises at the end of inverted questions and falls at the end of short answers and *wh-* questions.

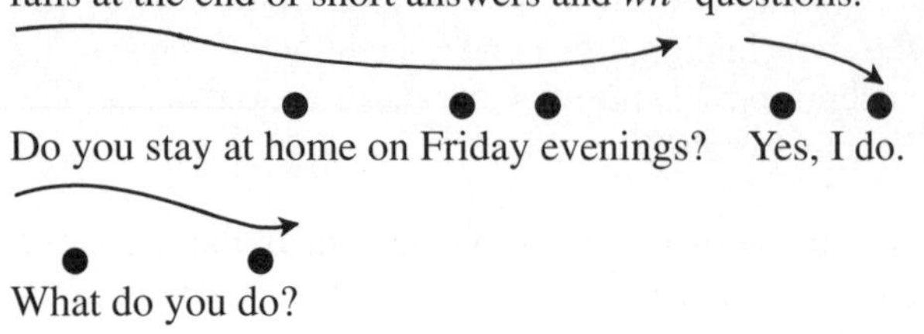

Do you stay at home on Friday evenings? Yes, I do.
What do you do?

2 Ask students to work in pairs and take it in turns to be Ann McGregor. Tell them to read the text again first but then to turn back to this page and try to remember what she does at different times at the weekend. They should be encouraged to ask a mixture of inverted and *wh-* questions, using the examples on the page to help them. Go round and check as they do it.

Grammar question

Read aloud the rule to your students and ask for suggestions to complete the gaps.

> **Answers**
> The auxiliary verb in questions with *I, you, we,* and *they* is <u>*do*</u>. With *he, she,* and *it*, the auxiliary verb is <u>*does*</u>.

Practice (SB page 26)

1 Questions and answers

Ask students to work on their own to do this and then check their answers with a partner. Conduct the feedback by asking students to ask and answer the questions across the class. Don't forget to encourage good pronunciation.

> **Answers**
> What time do you go to bed? At 11 o'clock.
> Where do you go on Saturday evenings? To a disco.
> What do you do in the evenings? I watch TV.
> When do you do your homework? After dinner.
> Who do you visit on Sundays? My grandmother.
> Why do you like your job? Because it's interesting.
> How do you travel to work? By train.

Make this activity as brisk as possible because it is being done in preparation for the next personalized activity.

2 Speaking

1 This activity gives practice of the first and second persons only. Ask your students to work in pairs to ask and answer questions about their routines on weekdays and weekends. You could tell them that they should try to think of about five to six questions each. Go round and check as they do it because they may need help to use a diversity of types of questions (see the examples and Practice 1). Try to discourage them from just repeating *What do you do on Friday evenings?/Sunday mornings?* etc.

> **Note**
> It would be a good idea to do Exercises 9–11 in the Workbook to introduce adverbs of frequency before doing this activity.

2 This activity practises the third person singular alongside the other persons. It also pulls the class together after the pairwork. Ask a few individuals to tell the rest of the class about themselves and their partner. (Unless you have a small class it would probably take too long to give everyone a turn.)

3 Listening and pronunciation

T20 Play the tape. Ask the students to listen carefully and tick the sentence they hear. Play the tape again. Stop after each one and ask students to discuss the answer with a partner before you establish the correct one. This is a receptive exercise but you can make it productive by asking students to read aloud the pairs of sentences.

Answers
1 a 2 b 3 a 4 b 5 a 6 a

4 Speaking and writing

1 The students begin this activity by asking *you* the questions so that you have the opportunity to help and correct them before they continue it with partners.

Ask individuals to ask you the questions, encourage good pronunciation with rising intonation because these are all inverted questions.

Ask all the class to stand up and 'mingle' to do the next part of the activity (if there is enough space to do so!). Tell them to take it in turns with two other students to ask and answer the questions.

2 Then ask them to sit down and quickly fill in the boxes about themselves.

3 This part of the activity is designed to revise the third person singular again alongside the other persons. (It could be set for homework or in fact done orally rather than in writing.)

Ask your students to use the information they have collected and write and compare themselves with either you or another student. Then ask one or two students to read aloud what they have written for the others to comment on.

Sample answer
I smoke, but my teacher doesn't. She drinks a lot of wine. We both like Chinese food and cooking, and we both sometimes play cards. My teacher also plays tennis, but I don't. We both read and listen to music a lot. She also watches TV often, but I don't.

5 Grammar

This exercise revises the verb *to be* alongside other verbs in the Present Simple.
It could be set for homework, but it can be in fact quite fun doing it orally in class. They could then write it afterwards. Do it briskly with the whole class.

Answers
a She speaks German.
b They don't want to learn English.
c We're not/aren't tired and we don't want to go to bed.
d John doesn't like watching football on TV, but he likes playing it.
e I don't work at home because I don't have a word processor.
f Sarah's happy because she has a nice flat.
g I don't smoke, I don't drink, and I go to bed early.
h He smokes, he drinks, and he doesn't go to bed early.

Additional material

Workbook Unit 4
Exercise 1 This practises the first person of the Present Simple with the verbs *like* and *love*. It also introduces *so* and *but*, and two adverbs of frequency *often* and *always*.
Exercises 2–4 These practise all persons of the Present Simple. Exercise 4 focuses on question formation.
Exercise 5 This practises *do* and *does* alongside the forms of the verb *to be*.
Exercises 6–8 These practise questions and negatives in the Present Simple.
Exercises 9–11 These introduce and practise more adverbs of frequency.

PRESENTATION (3) (SB page 27)

Articles

This is an attempt to give a simple introduction to the use of articles in English. This area is often fraught with difficulties because of the differences in article use, or lack of article use in other languages.

1 **T21a** Ask your students to work in pairs to fill the gaps. Then play the tape so that they can listen and check their answers. Note that this article is designed to see how aware students are of article usage. They are not expected to know the rules.

Answers
Mr and Mrs Forrester have (a) *a* son and (b) *a* daughter. (c) *The* son lives at (d) / home and (e) *the* daughter is (f) *a* student at (g) / university. Mr Forrester is (h) *a* journalist. He works for (i) *The* Times. He writes (j) / articles about (k) / restaurants. 'I love (l) / food!' he says.

2

Note
This is the only time we actually suggest that the Grammar Summary is read as part of the presentation. However there is no reason why you should not do this more frequently if you feel your students would benefit from explanation of the grammar *before* they move on to practise it.

Ask your students to turn to page 31 and read the summary of Articles aloud to them, clarifying any points in L1 if possible or necessary. Now ask them to look back at the first text and find examples of the rules. (These are numbered for ease of reference.)

Answers
a and b = 1
c and e = 3
d and g = 6
f and h = 2
i = 4
j, k, and l = 5

3 **T21b** Now ask your students to work on their own to complete the next text using the Grammar Summary on page 31 to help them. Ask them to check their answers with a partner before you play the tape and conduct a full class feedback on the correct answers. Invite them to give you the rule number from the summary as you do this. (The number in brackets next to the answer refers to this number.)

Answers
'Every spring a) *the* (3) children go skiing, so my wife and I go to Paris on b) / (6) holiday. We stay in c) *a* (1) hotel near d) *the* (4) River Seine. We have e) / (6) breakfast in f) *the* (3) hotel, but we have g) / (6) lunch in a restaurant. h) / (5) French food is delicious! We walk a lot, but sometimes we go by i) / (6) taxi. After four days we don't want to go j) / (6) home and go back to k) / (6) work.'

Practice (SB page 28)

1 Listening and speaking

Make this activity as quick and as much fun as possible. Students enjoy being given the opportunity to contradict their teacher and it provides good pronunciation practice particularly of stress and intonation.
You could add to the challenge by asking students to read the texts again and try to *remember* the information. However if you think it is too difficult, allow them to look at the texts as you go through the exercise.
Do the example from the book with them first to illustrate the activity, saying your incorrect statement firmly and with conviction. Ask for contributions to correct it from the class as a whole, but focus on one student to establish the right answer and then repeat the incorrect statement to a few others, encouraging indignant and exaggerated patterns of stress and intonation.

Teacher: *The son lives with friends.*

Students: *No, he doesn't. He lives at home (with his parents).*

Further incorrect statements and answers.
(They have all been chosen because the answer necessitates use or lack of use of articles.)

1 **T:** The daughter is at school.
Ss: No, she isn't. She's at university!
2 **T:** Mr Forrester is a teacher.
Ss: No, he isn't. He's a journalist!
3 **T:** He writes about sport.
Ss: No, he doesn't. He writes about restaurants!
4 **T:** Every spring he goes to Paris to work.
Ss: No, he doesn't. He goes to Paris on holiday!
5 **T:** He and his wife stay in a hotel near the sea.
Ss: No, they don't. They stay in a hotel near the River Seine!
6 **T:** They always walk in Paris.
Ss: No, they don't. They sometimes go by taxi!

2 Grammar

If you can, move straight to this activity as a contrast to the previous one. Ask students to do it on their own and then check their answers with a partner. Conduct a full class feedback to establish the correct answers.

Answers

a Oxford is *a* town in / England, on *the* River Thames.
b *The* Queen lives in *a* very big house in London.
c I have / breakfast in / bed on / Sundays.
d Do you go to / work by / car?
e My sister is *a* student. She comes / home at weekends.
f Do you like / Chinese food?

3 Choosing the correct sentence

This exercise revises all the grammar they have just been doing. It should be done quite quickly to round off this stage of the lesson. Ask students to work in pairs to do it. Go round the class and check as they do it.

Answers

1 a 2 b 3 a 4 a 5 b 6 b 7 a 8 b 9 a

Additional material

Workbook Unit 4
Exercises 12 and 13 These give further practice of articles.

● VOCABULARY (SB page 28)

Free time activities

1 Ask students to work in pairs or small groups. First ask them to look at the pictures and match as many as they can with the activities listed. Ask them to check the others in their bilingual dictionaries. Encourage them to enter any new words in their vocabulary notebooks (if they keep them!).

2 First build a dialogue with one or two members of the class yourself, using the example in the book and highlighting *like +-ing*, and then perhaps telling them some true things about yourself and what you do and don't like doing. (Students are often interested to find out about their teacher!) Encourage them to respond to your likes and dislikes as in the example.

Now ask them to continue in pairs and go round the class to check and help them. Make sure they use the *-ing* form.

Finally, ask a few students in the class to report back on themselves and their partners (thereby practising different persons of the Present Simple). Particularly encourage them to tell you about other activities that they do which are not on the list.

● READING AND LISTENING (SB page 29)

Note

Homework prior to lesson
It would save time in the lesson if you could ask your students to learn the names of seasons and months in English for homework before the lesson. You could provide them with the following list to learn by heart and then test them in class.

Seasons

spring /sprɪŋ/	autumn /ɔ:təm/
summer /sʌmə/	winter /wɪntə/

Months

January /ʤænjərɪ/	July /ʤu:laɪ/
February /febrʊərɪ/	August /ɔ:gʌst/
March /ma:tʃ/	September /septembə/
April /eɪprɪl/	October /ɒktəʊbə/
May /meɪ/	November /nəʊvembə/
June /ʤu:n/	December /dɪsembə/

1 Use a calendar as a visual aid, and check that your class know the seasons and months by first illustrating them yourself and then saying them in chorus and individually round the class. Make it fast and fun if you can.

Ask which months the different seasons are. If you have time and you feel it is necessary, check further by asking:

What's before/after September? etc.
When's your birthday?

(Make sure that they give only the month in their answers *not* the actual date.)

2 **T22a** Ask your students to look at the pictures and see if they can identify which season the pictures represent. Then ask them to read the text and listen to the tape at the same time. Ask them to find the seasons which are mentioned and the speaker's favourite season (to check whether they were right about the photographs).

It may be wise to pause after *each* text to ask for feedback. You can also ask for the *nationality* of the speaker. (Careful with the stress in naming the nationalities.)

Answers

Al Wheeler is Canadian. His favourite season is autumn.

Manuela da Silva is Portuguese. Her favourite season is summer.

Toshi Suzuki is Japanese. His favourite season is spring.

Comprehension check

1 Ask students to do this in groups of three if possible. Ask each one in the group to read again about *one* person only, each taking a different person. Then as they go through the questions they can share the information with the others about their person to answer the questions. Thus more speaking will be generated than in just answering the questions. Ask someone in the group to write down their answers. Give them 5–10 minutes to do the exercise and then bring the whole class together to conduct the feedback. Encourage them to give short answers where applicable but then to expand on these if possible (see suggestions in brackets in the answer key).

Answers

a No, they don't. (Toshi doesn't. Al plays baseball and ice-hockey and goes ice-skating and fishing. Manuela goes windsurfing.)

b Al goes ice-skating and plays ice-hockey. Manuela meets friends in bars and chats.

c Yes, they do. (Manuela likes going to Brazilian bars. Toshi likes relaxing in a bar near his office.)

d Near a lake.

e In spring.

f They drive to the beach, sunbathe, and go windsurfing.

g No, we don't. We only know Toshi's job. (He works for Pentax cameras.)

h Because he likes the colours of the trees.

i Toshi watches his friend Shigeru. Shigeru likes singing Karaoke in the bars.
Toshi doesn't sing because he is shy.

j Red, gold, orange, yellow, brown, grey.
(Ask your students to point to things of these colours in the room to check their understanding.)

2 Ask your students to remain in their groups to find the five mistakes in the summary.

Ask them to correct the mistakes and get one or two students to read aloud the corrected version to the rest of the class.

Answers

Al comes from Canada. In winter he plays ice-hockey and goes (1) *ice-skating*. He has a holiday home near (2) *a lake*. Manuela comes from (3) *Portugal*. She likes sunbathing and windsurfing in summer. Toshi comes from Japan. He (4) *doesn't have* a lot of free time. He likes taking photographs, but he (5) *doesn't like* singing pop songs in bars.

3 **T22b** This should be quite a short activity. Play the tape and stop it after each conversation. Ask *Who is it?*, *Where are they?*, *How do you know?*

Answers

Conversation 1: Manuela. (She is with some Portuguese friends and an English friend called Jane.) They are in a Brazilian bar. We know this because they talk about the music and have drinks.

Conversation 2: Toshi. (He is with a British colleague, Ann Jones from London.) They are in Tokyo in an office (the headquarters of Pentax). We know this because Toshi says *Welcome to Tokyo.*

Conversation 3: Al. (He is with a Scottish friend called Mick.) They are at Al's holiday home, near the lake. We know this because they talk about going fishing.

If time, and you feel it worthwhile, you could round off the activity by playing the tape again and suggesting that your students read the tapescripts on page 115 at the same time.

4 This is an attempt to generate some personalized discussion and give further freer practice of the Present Simple. Don't worry if at this level it turns out to be quite a short activity. Just a little free speaking is still worthwhile.

It can be helpful to ask students to discuss the topic together in small groups first to collect their ideas before you conduct feedback with the whole class.

It would also be a nice idea to encourage them to ask *you* questions about *your* favourite season.

Vocabulary

This is an additional vocabulary activity to revise sports and sort out the use of *play* or *go,* as this can often cause confusion and students have already met examples of each. During the feedback you could ask them if they can see a rule. It would be enough for them to realize that it is *go* + *-ing* and *play* + the others (all of which use balls).

Answers

play + football, golf, ice-hockey, volleyball, baseball, tennis (games).

go + swimmimg, fishing, walking, ice-skating, windsurfing, sailing, dancing, skiing (activities).

● EVERYDAY ENGLISH **(SB page 30)**

Social English

The aim of these dialogues is to introduce and practise some of the more frequent little expressions that 'lubricate' all day-to-day conversational exchanges.

1 **T23** Ask students to work in pairs and complete *all* the dialogues. Then play the tape for them to listen and check their answers.

Answers
See the tapescript on page 116 of the Student's Book.

2 Ask them to practise the conversations in pairs. You could play the tape again *before* they do this so that they can copy the stress and intonation. Ask each pair to learn one of the dialogues by heart and then act it out for the rest of the class. Acting out can improve their pronunciation considerably.

GRAMMAR SUMMARY **(SB page 31)**

Read the Grammar Summary together in class, and/or ask your students to read it at home. Encourage them to ask you questions about it.

Don't forget!

Workbook Unit 4
Exercise 14 This is an exercise to revise prepositions covered so far.
Exercise 15 This vocabulary exercise practises verbs with opposite meaning, e.g. *love/hate.*
Exercise 16 The writing activity is an informal letter to a friend.

Word List
Remind your students of the Word List at the back of their book. Ask them to look at the list for this unit on page 123. Tell them that they could write in the translations, learn them at home, and/or write some of the words in their vocabulary notebooks.

Pronunciation Book Unit 4

Video
There are two video sections that can supplement Units 3 and 4 of the Student's book.
Report (Section 2) *The Train Driver.* This is a short documentary about a man who is a teacher, but drives a steam train in his free time.
Situation (Section 3) *The Party.* This is a short situation where David takes Paola to a party to meet some friends.

EXTRA IDEAS UNITS 1–4

On pages 125/6 of the Teacher's Book there are two additional activities, a reading text and a song. If you have time and feel that your students would benefit from them, you can photocopy them and use them in class. The reading exercise revises Units 1–4 and could also be done for homework.
An activity to exploit the reading is provided and the answers are below.
You will find the song after the tapescript for Unit 4 on the Class Cassette. You could exploit the song by blanking out some of the words and asking students to listen and fill in the gaps. Alternatively, as the verbs are in the Present Simple, you could blank out some of the verbs the students will know, and put them jumbled up on the board for the students to choose from and fill in. Then they can listen and check their answers. However, don't make the task too complicated or it will detract from the enjoyment and challenge of listening to the song itself.

Answers to the reading
Complete the questions or answers in the interview with Roberta Tomlinson.

a A What's your name?
  B Roberta Tomlinson.
b A How do you spell it?
  B T – O – M – L – I – N – S – O – N.
c A Where are you from?
  B Glasgow, in Scotland.
d A How old are you?
  B I'm forty-three.
e A Are you married?
  B Yes, I am.
f A What's your husband's name?
  B Andrew.
g A What does your husband do?
  B He's a teacher. (He teaches blind children.)
h A Do you have any children?
  B Yes, I do. I have two sons and a daughter.
i A Do you have any brothers or sisters?
  B Yes. I have two brothers.
j A Do you enjoy your work?
  B Yes, I do.
k A Why do you enjoy your job?
  B Because I meet a lot of people.
l A Where do you live?
  B We/I live in Glasgow.
m A Do you have a garden?
  B Yes, I/we do.
n A What do you like doing in your free time?
  B Having friends for dinner, going to the theatre, and listening to music.

STOP AND CHECK UNITS 1–4

There is a Stop and Check revision section after each quarter of the Student's Book.The idea is that your students pause to check their progress so far. Each test is out of 100. There is a Stop and Check Answer Key on page 140 of the Teacher's Book. You could set it in class as an informal progress test or you could use the following procedure.

1 Give your students the Stop and Check to do for homework, preferably when they have more time, such as at the weekend.
2 In the next lesson ask them to go over their answers in small groups, trying to agree on the right answer. Allow enough time for this. It can be very productive for students to try and persuade their peers of the right answer. Many previous lessons are recalled.
3 Go over it with the whole class, reminding students of the language items covered.

After all the group discussion everyone *should* have a reasonably high score!

UNIT 5

There is/are – Prepositions – *any/some* – Directions (1)

Introduction to the unit

The theme of this unit is 'Places'. Students describe a living room, a kitchen, and where they live themselves. There is a reading text about Buckingham Palace, which is quite challenging in its length and vocabulary load, but hopefully students will be interested in the sometimes ridiculous extravagance of life in a royal household.

Language aims

Grammar

There is/are

Problems
Students often confuse *It's a ...* with *There's a ...* The difference is that *It's a ...* defines something and gives it a name. *There's a ...* expresses what exists. This is quite a subtle area, and we don't suggest that you explore it with students, unless absolutely necessary, and preferably in L1, using translation as a support.

Learners confuse *there* and *their.* For such a short structural item, there are a lot of pronunciation problems. Many nationalities have difficulty with the sound /ð/. In *There's*, the *r* is often silent. In *There are* and the question when the following word begins with a vowel, the *r* is pronounced as a linking sound. Again, students need to be encouraged to start questions 'high' and fall, ending with a rise in inverted questions. It is worth working on these pronunciation areas, but not to the point of exhaustion!

Prepositions

Simple prepositions of place, such as *near* and *in front of,* are introduced and practised.

any/some

In this unit, *any* and *some* are presented only with countable nouns. In Unit 9, they are presented with both countable and uncountable nouns.
In Presentation (1), *any* is seen in the question only. In Presentation (2), *some* appears with countable nouns in the positive, and *any* in negatives.

Problems
Some also presents problems of pronunciation with its weak form /səm/.

Some as a concept has a tangible meaning, i.e. a certain, unspecified number of (something). The same cannot be said of *any*. It is a determiner used often (though by no means exclusively) in questions and negatives. We suggest you do not go into the deeper areas of *any* expressing fundamentally negative ideas, or *any* expressing *It doesn't matter what*, as in *Take any book you want*. This is probably unnecessary, and difficult for the level.

Vocabulary

There is quite a high vocabulary load in this unit, with the descriptions of the rooms and the lexis in the text about Buckingham Palace. For this reason, the Vocabulary section aims to recycle words to do with people, places, food and drink, rather than introduce yet more new words.
It is worth checking from time to time how students are progressing with their vocabulary notebooks. Are they still adding to them? Have they started a new one? Do they try to revise regularly? Have they thought of new ways of organizing their notebooks?

Everyday English

This is the first activity on directions. This topic is picked up again in Unit 10, where prepositions of movement are introduced.

Workbook

This, *that*, *these*, and *those* are introduced and practised. You might decide to do this in class, as they are such high-frequency items. In the vocabulary section, rooms and objects are introduced, such as *soap* and *bathroom*, via a vocabulary network. There is also an exercise on verb and noun collocations.
In the writing section there is the first exercise on linking words, *and*, *so*, *but*, and *because*. Students are invited to write a description of their house or flat.
Numbers 100–1,000 are presented and practised, and some letters of the alphabet are revised.

Notes on the Unit

PRESENTATION (1) (SB page 34)

There is/are – *any* – Prepositions

Note
We suggest that you set some vocabulary for homework before you start this unit to maximize classroom time.

Homework prior to the lesson
Look up the following words in your dictionary, and put them in your vocabulary notebook.

chair	armchair	table	sofa	picture
lamp	mirror	stereo	fire	plant
window	living room	bathroom	kitchen	bedroom

1 Ask students to name the rooms in a house or flat. Make sure you include *living room*, *kitchen*, *bedroom*, *bathroom*. You might want to add others, perhaps *toilet* (as it is an important word!), but avoid going into words such as *balcony*, unless students really want to know.

Ask students to think of one or two things we do in the rooms. Do this either as a class, or with students working in pairs. Don't let this go on too long, and avoid over-correcting.

2 Students look at the photograph of the living room and find the objects. If they have looked up the words for homework, this shouldn't take too long.

Model the words yourself, and drill them around the class. Correct pronunciation carefully.

3 Read the rubric and the example sentences as a class. In a monolingual class, you might want to ask for a translation of *There's* and *There are*. You could ask 'Why *is* and why *are*?' to establish singular and plural.

Again, model the sentences yourself and do some individual drilling. Students can then work in pairs to produce more sentences. Note that with plural nouns they need to state the exact number. You do not want them to try to produce *some* at this stage.

Get the feedback to the pairwork and correct mistakes carefully.

Answers

There's a sofa.	There are two plants.
There's a television.	There are two lamps.
There's an armchair.	There are four pictures.
There's a chair.	
There's a stereo.	
There's a telephone.	
There's a table.	
There's a mirror.	
There's a fire.	

4 **T24** Students listen to the questions and answers. Practise them in open pairs. Take care with all aspects of pronunciation (sounds, intonation, stress).

Students work in pairs to ask and answer questions. Notice that the words in columns 1–3 are singular, and the words in columns 4 and 5 are plural.

Go round the class monitoring the pairs. You can expect a lot of mistakes, as students are having to deal with a lot of different problems, so give help as necessary.

After a while ask one or two pairs to repeat their questions and answers in open pairs.

Answers

Is there a table?	Yes, there is.
Is there a fire?	Yes, there is.
Is there a mirror?	Yes, there is.
Is there a dog?	Yes, there is.
Is there a stereo?	Yes, there is.
Is there an armchair?	Yes, there is.
Is there a desk?	No, there isn't.
Is there a camera?	No, there isn't.
Is there a newspaper?	No, there isn't.
Are there any lamps?	Yes, there are.
Are there any flowers?	No, there aren't.
Are there any photos?	Yes, there are.
Are there any pictures?	Yes, there are.
Are there any plants?	Yes, there are.
Are there any books?	Yes, there are.

5 This exercise practises prepositions. If you think they will be new to your class, you will need to present them first. Do this very simply, perhaps using the classroom, an object such as a book or chair, or the students themselves (*Juan is next to Maria*). Note that *next to* is two-dimensional, whereas *near* is three-dimensional.

Ask students to work in pairs to put a preposition into each gap. Ask for feedback.

Answers
a The telephone is *on* the table.
b The table is *next to* the sofa.
c The chair is *near* the stereo.
d The lamp is *behind* the chair.
e The dog is *in front of* the fire.

You can expect some students to argue that the chair is in front of the stereo, not near it. Deal with this as you please! Point out that *in front of*, like *next to*, is two-dimensional. You can do this by using gestures.
You could practise the prepositions further by using your actual classroom, if you haven't already used this situation to present the items.

Practice (SB page 35)

1 Grammar

Students work in pairs or small groups to complete the sentences.

Answers
a There *are* two books *on* the sofa.
b The sofa is *in front of* the window.
c There *is* a lamp *next to* the television.
d The telephone is *near* one of the lamps.
e '*Are* there *any* pictures on the wall?' 'Yes, *there are*.'
f There *isn't a* desk.
g There's a plant *behind* the sofa in front of the window.
h Is *there a* fire?
i '*Are* there *any* people in the living room?' 'No, *there aren't*.'
(Note that students often think the word *people* is singular, not plural.)

2 Speaking and listening

1 You will need to photocopy the pictures on page 127 of the Teacher's Book, enough copies for half of the class to see picture A and half picture B. Read the instructions as a class. This is another information gap activity, so use L1 if you want to clarify what students have to do. Naturally, the most important thing is that they don't see their partner's picture!

Look at the example sentences, pointing out the question *How many ...?*, and ask students to work in pairs to find the ten differences. Point out that we say *on the sofa*, but *in the armchair.* Allow enough time for this activity. When students have finished, get some feedback.

Answers
Here are the differences.

Picture A
There are two people on the sofa, a man and a woman.
There is one chair (not an armchair) in the room.
There is a cat in front of the fire.
There are four pictures on the walls.
There are two magazines on the big table.
There isn't a clock.
There is a plant next to the fire.
There isn't a lamp.
There is a photo on the TV.
There are two children on the floor in front of the TV.

Picture B
There is a man on the sofa, and there is a woman in the armchair.
There are two chairs (not armchairs) in the room.
There is a cat on the sofa.
There are three pictures on the walls.
There are two books on the big table.
There is a clock on the wall.
There isn't a plant.
There is a lamp behind the sofa.
There isn't a photo.
There aren't any children.

2 **T25** Read the instructions as a class. Students listen and shout 'Stop!' when they hear a mistake. You could do some work on contrastive stress as students correct the mistakes.

Example
There aren't three people. There are four people.

Answers
These are the mistakes.

Picture A
There isn't a mirror.
(There aren't three people. There are four people.)
There isn't a lamp.
There isn't a clock.
There isn't a glass of beer. There are two cups.
The television is on.

Picture B
The woman isn't on the sofa. She's in the armchair.
The cat isn't in front of the fire. It's on the sofa.
There aren't four pictures. There are three.
There aren't any plants.
There isn't a telephone.

Additional material
Workbook Unit 5
Exercises 1–4 *There is/are*, *any*, and prepositions.

PRESENTATION (2) (SB page 35)

some and *any*

Note
We suggest you set the following vocabulary items for homework prior to this lesson.

modern	clean	cupboard	washing machine
fridge	cooker	dishwasher	radio
plate	sink (n)		

Take care with the pronunciation of *cupboard* /kʌbəd/. Students often confuse *cook* and *cooker*, thinking quite logically that *cooker* should be a person not a thing.

1 Ask students to look at the photograph and say what they can see. Do not expect or encourage the use of *some*. Correct mistakes of pronunciation.

Answers
A fridge, a cooker, a table, cupboards, and a radio near the cooker. A washing machine.
Books and glasses, apples, and oranges.
Pictures on the wall.
Cups and plates next to the sink.
Flowers.

2 **T26** Students listen to the description of the kitchen and fill in the gaps. Let them check in pairs, then play the tape again. Ask for feedback. Notice that students are not expected to produce *some* until they have seen and heard it three times already.

Answers
It's a modern kitchen. Nice and clean with a lot of cupboards. *There*'s a washing machine, a fridge, and a cooker, but there isn't a dishwasher. There are some lovely *pictures* on the walls but there aren't any photographs. There's a radio *near* the cooker. There are some flowers, but there aren't *any* plants. On the table there are some apples and oranges. Ah! And there are *some* cups and plates next to the sink.

● Grammar questions

Look at the Grammar questions as a class. Allow students time to think before you come in with the answer.

Answers
We say *There isn't a ...* with singular nouns. We say *There aren't any ...* with plural nouns.
Two books gives us the exact number. *Some flowers* doesn't give us the exact number.

Read the information in the Caution Box together with the class.

Practice (SB page 36)

1 Speaking

1 Students have not yet been asked to say any sentences containing *some*, so now is the time! Ask students to look at the picture of the kitchen. Model some sentences yourself, containing both singular nouns and noun phrases with *some*. Make sure *some* is weak /səm/. Drill the sentences around the class, correcting mistakes carefully.

Examples

There's a washing machine.	There are some pictures.
There's a radio.	There are some flowers.

You could ask your students to close their books and in pairs try to remember what is in the kitchen.

2 This topic for discussion might not interest your students in the slightest! However, with some classes, especially multilingual classes, an interesting discussion might result. Kitchens over the world are very different, mainly because of climate, but also because of people's eating habits and life-styles. In some parts of the world it is very unusual to have a washing machine in the kitchen. The washing machine is kept in the bathroom, or in a special room on its own, or on a balcony. You could ask questions like *Where's the fridge? How big is it? Where do you keep food?* Don't correct grammar mistakes unless incomprehensible. The emphasis here is on fluency.

2 Grammar

1 Students work in pairs or small groups to fill the gaps.

Answers
a In our classroom there are *some* books on the floor.
b There aren't *any* flowers.
c Are there *any* German students in your class?
d There aren't *any* Chinese students.
e We have *some* dictionaries in the cupboard.
f There are *some* pens on the table.

2 If students are getting fed up of talking about rooms, do this activity quickly.

3 Listening and speaking

1 **T27** Students listen to a man describing what is in his briefcase, and tick the things they hear.

Answers

a newspaper ✔	some pens ✔	a bus ticket ✘
a dictionary ✔	a notebook ✔	an address book ✘
a sandwich ✘	a letter ✔	some stamps ✘
some keys ✔	some photos ✔	

2 Ask one or two students to say what is in their bag. This can be very interesting! However try not to be over-curious! Some students may consider it too personal.

4 Choosing the correct sentence

Students work in pairs to choose the correct sentence.

Answers
1 a 2 a 3 b 4 a 5 a 6 a 7 b 8 b 9 a

Additional material

Workbook Unit 5
Exercises 5 and 6 *some/any* and short answers

● READING (SB page 36)

Pre-reading task

1 Students look at the photographs and try to answer the questions. Don't tell them the answers now. Let them check their answers in the text.

Answers
They are in London. One is 10, Downing Street, where the British Prime Minister lives. The other is Buckingham Palace, where the Royal Family lives.

Extra ideas

1 You might want to have a short discussion about the British Royal Family, what they do, and any recent news stories about them. You could do this before you read, or after you read (when you could also ask them what they think of the Queen's lifestyle).
2 You could tell the class that they are going to read an article about Buckingham Palace and the Queen's day. Ask if there are any questions that they would like answered.

Example
How many rooms are there?
Is the garden big?
Is there a swimming pool?
What time does the Queen get up?
What does she have for breakfast?

If you do this, get the feedback to the answers before Comprehension Check question 1.

2 Check the meaning of the words. Put on the board the abbreviations in brackets with their full form if necessary. If you have a monolingual class, it would be quicker to translate the items yourself, or ask for translations. It is easy to overdo dictionary work in class, and some students find it a waste of valuable classroom time. Careful with *grow up*, *like*, *own*, and *course*, as students might have difficulty finding the word, or could find the wrong definition.

Reading

Students read the text. You might decide to read the text aloud whilst students read (although some people would argue that this is mixing two skills, reading and listening). There are several advantages to you reading aloud.

1 Your pronunciation, sentence stress, and intonation will aid comprehension.
2 You can check any words students might be unsure of.
3 Students will not be able to stop at unknown words and lose the thread of the text.

Having read it aloud, you could ask students to read the text silently and answer the Comprehension Check questions.

Comprehension check

Students work in pairs or small groups to answer the questions.

Answers
1 a True.
  b False. It is famous because it is where the Royal Family lives.
  c False. Seven people look after her.
  d False. They have their own bedroom.
  e False. They meet at Buckingham Palace.
2 a Because it is a family house and a place where important people go to meet the Queen.
  b Because there are a lot of different places in it, for example, a police station, a swimming pool, post offices.
  c Yes. Three hundred.
  d Eight or nine.
  e *The Times.*
  f Scottish music.
  g For different drinks – water, red wine, white wine, port, and liqueur.
  h She speaks to the person on her left for the first two courses, and the person on her right for the rest of the meal.
  i Everybody finishes!

Language work

1 Students work in pairs to ask and answer questions about Buckingham Palace. Conduct the feedback in open pairs.

Answers

Is there a swimming pool?	Yes, there is.
Is there a supermarket?	No, there isn't.
Is there a school?	No, there isn't.
Is there a bar?	Yes, there is.
Is there a sports club?	Yes, there are two.
Is there a cinema?	Yes, there is.
Is there a disco?	Yes, there is.
Is there a hospital?	Yes, there is.

2 Students work in pairs or small groups to write the questions. Again, you could get the feedback in open pairs. Careful with the pronunciation of the questions. Make sure the voice starts high.

Answers
a Where does the Prime Minister live?
b How many rooms are there in Buckingham palace?
c How many clocks are there?
d What does the Queen have for breakfast?
e Where do her dogs sleep?
f When does the Queen meet the Prime Minister?

● VOCABULARY AND PRONUNCIATION

(SB page 38)

Places, people, food and drink

1 Students work in small groups to put words in the right columns, and mark the stress. Notice the pronunciation of liqueur in English /lɪkjʊə/.

Places	People	Food and drink
world	Prime Minister	breakfast
palace	family	coffee
centre	children	toast
house	presidents	eggs
town	kings	gin and tonic
police station	politicians	whisky
post office	queen	dinner
hospital	men	wine
bar	piper	water
sports club		port
disco		liqueur
cinema		
swimming pool		
room		
bedroom		

2 Students could add more words in class or for homework.

● LISTENING AND SPEAKING (SB page 38)

Note
The listening texts contain quite a lot of words that may be new, or that students might not remember. We intend that this listening exercise is for gist understanding only, so students should be encouraged, if possible, not to worry about unknown words.

You *could* ask them to look at the tapescripts while they listen, or you could do this after they have heard the texts once or twice and then study the vocabulary. However, try if possible not to do this – but only you know your class!

Even for gist comprehension, you will need to check the following words first.

south farmhouse animal plane
floor (of a block of flats) alone

You could ask students to look at the tapescript for homework.

1 **T28** Students listen to the five people talking about where they live and fill in the chart.

Answers

	Anne-Marie	Harry	Dave and Maggie	Thanos
House or flat?	House (farmhouse)	House	House	Flat
Old or new?	Old	New	Old	New
Where?	The South of France (Provence)	Texas	Dublin	Athens
Number of bedrooms?	Three	Fourteen or fifteen	Two	Two
Garden?	Yes	Yes	Yes	No
Live(s) with?	2 dogs and 8 cats	His wife and 4 children	Their son, Thomas	Lives alone

2 Have a discussion about where students live. You might decide to do this as a class or in groups.

Writing

3 Students write about where they live for homework. Before you set this, do the writing Exercises 13 and 14 in the Workbook, which will prepare them for the task.

● EVERYDAY ENGLISH (SB page 39)

Directions (1)

1 Ask students to look at the street map. Make sure they understand the words on the map.

Problems
Students often confuse a library and a bookshop. Also, there might not be the direct equivalent of a newsagent's in your students' countries. A newsagent sells newspapers, magazines, cigarettes, sweets, and little items such as birthday cards and soft drinks.
As a class, ask where you can buy the items.

Answers
bread at a baker's or supermarket
a CD (compact disc) at a music shop
cigarettes at a newsagent's or supermarket
a book at a bookshop
a plane ticket at a travel agent's

2 **T29** Students listen to the conversations and complete them. You might want to play them all through first before students begin to write, or you might want to pause the tape recorder after each conversation to allow students time to write. Play the tape again to check answers.

Answers
a A Excuse me! Is *there* a chemist's *near* here?
B Yes. It's over *there*.
A Thanks.
b A *Excuse* me! Is there a *sports* club near here?
B Yes. *It's in* Queen Street. Take the second *street on the* right.
A Thanks.
c A Excuse me! Is there a *newsagent's* near here?
B Yes. There's *one* in Church Street *next to* the bank, and there's one in Park Lane opposite the *swimming pool*.
A Is that one *far*?
B No. Just two minutes, that's all.
d A Is there a cinema near here?
B *Take* the first left, and it's *on the* left, *opposite* the flower shop.
A Thanks a lot.

Check that the class understand *Excuse me!*, *over there*, *second*, *far*, and *opposite*.

3 Students work in pairs to practise the conversations, then make more conversations using the map. You could ask some of the pairs to act out their dialogues for the rest of the class.

4 Students talk about their own situation. You could do this as a group activity or as a class.

GRAMMAR SUMMARY (SB page 00)

Read the Grammar Summary as a class. Encourage students to ask any questions.

Don't forget!

Workbook Unit 5
Exercises 7 and 8 Vocabulary of rooms and objects found in them, and verbs and nouns that go together.
Exercises 9–12 These exercises introduce and practise *this/that/these/those*.
Exercises 15 The numbers 100–1000
Exercise 16–18 A revision of the alphabet

Word List
Encourage students to study the Word List on page 124 of the Student's Book, and translate the words into L1.

Pronunciation Book Unit 5

UNIT 6

can/could – was/were – At the airport

Introduction to the unit

Skills and ability are the themes of this unit. These are particularly suitable topics to introduce and practice *can/can't* (ability). However, the unit has two main aims in that we also introduce some past tenses for the first time: the past of *can* (ability) – *could* and the Past Simple of the verb *to be – was*, and *were*. The skills work includes a jigsaw reading about two teenage geniuses and provides a further context for and practice of the grammar.

Language aims

Grammar

can/can't

Students have already met the form *can* in the Everyday English section of Unit 2, but it is used only as a polite request *Can I have ...?* In Unit 2 it is introduced idiomatically because it is a useful expression, and the grammar is not explored.
Here, in Unit 6, the use is extended to ability, and all aspects of the form (statements, questions, negatives) are fully explored and practised.

Problems

1 Sometimes after all the practising of the Present Simple, students want to use *do/don't* and *does/doesn't* to form the question and negative.
**Do you can swim?*
**I don't can swim.*

2 A major problem with *can* and *can't* is the pronunciation. Often students find the different realizations of the vowel sounds (/ə/ or /æ/ in *can* and /ɑ:/ in *can't*) confusing and, because the final *t* in *can't* tends to get lost, they can't recognize whether the sentence is positive or negative and they have difficulty producing the correct sounds themselves.

I can swim.	/aɪ kən swɪm/
Can you swim?	/kən ju swɪm/
Yes, I can.	/jes aɪ kæn/
I can't come.	/aɪ kɑ:ŋk kʌm/

For these reasons we highlight the pronunciation in the unit and include exercises both for recognition and production.

was/were and *could*

These three are the first introduction to a past tense. We have chosen to present them in a simple and straightforward manner by having students complete a table about the present and past.

Problem

Again pronunciation is a problem. The vowel sounds in *was* and *were* have both weak and strong realizations: *was* /ə/ and /ɒ/; and *were* /ə/ and /ɜ:/.

He was at home.	/hɪ wəz ət həʊm/
Was he at home?	/wəz hɪ ət həʊm/
Yes, he was./No, he wasn't.	/jes hɪ wɒz/ /nəʊ hɪ wɒznt/
Were they at home?	/wə ðeɪ ət həʊm/
Yes, they were./No, they weren't.	/jes ðeɪ wɜ:/ /nəʊ ðeɪ wɜ:nt/

The pronunciation is highlighted and practised in the unit.

Vocabulary and pronunciation

We focus on words that sound the same but have a different spelling and meaning, i.e. homophones, for example *see* and *sea*. This provides the opportunity to give more practice of phonetic script.
There are many homophones in English (because of the non-phonetic spelling), and students confuse the two meanings, especially when hearing them (as opposed to seeing them when reading).

Everyday English

Useful vocabulary and expressions related to air travel are introduced and practised. (There is a documentary on Heathrow Airport in the *Headway Elementary* Video.)

Workbook

The question *How much ...?* is practised with *is* and *was*.
Students are introduced to how to say years (1915 – *nineteen fifteen*).
More words that commonly go together are practised (*ask a question, get up early*).
The writing syllabus continues with work on simple formal letters.

Notes on the unit

PRESENTATION (1) (SB page 40)

can/can't

1 This is quite a simple presentation. The aim of the pictures is to illustrate the meaning of *can* and *can't*. The sentences are on tape to provide models of the different realizations of the vowel sounds and to raise students' awareness of these from the start.

First ask students to look at the pictures and read the sentences. (Most of the vocabulary should be familiar or obvious from the picture, but check that there are no isolated difficulties.)

T 30a Play the tape and ask them to match the sentences with the pictures. They could write the appropriate letter on the picture. Ask them to discuss their answers with a partner before conducting a full class feedback on the correct answers.

Answers
1 'Can you speak Japanese?' 'No, I can't.'
2 I can't hear you. The line's bad.
3 'Can you use a word processor?' 'Yes, I can.'
4 I can't spell your name.
5 Cats can see in the dark.
6 She can type fifty words a minute.

2 Now is the time to start focusing on the pronunciation. Play the tape again and this time get your students to read and listen very carefully to the pronunciation of *can* and *can't*. First ask generally *Can you hear differences?* If necessary repeat the sentences yourself, exaggerating the vowel sounds in *can* and *can't* and isolating them /ə/, /æ/, /ɑ:/, so that your students can fully appreciate the differences. (The sentences are produced below in phonetic script.)

1 /kən jʊ spi:k dʒæpəni:z/
/nəʊ aɪ kɑ:nt/
2 /aɪ kɑ:nt hiə jʊ ðə laɪnz bæd/
3 /kən jʊ ju:z ə wɜ:d prəʊsesə/
/jes aɪ kæn/
4 /aɪ kɑ:nt spel jɒ neɪm/
5 /kæts kən si: ɪn ðə dɑ:k/
6 /ʃɪ kən taɪp fɪftɪ wɜ:dz ə mɪnɪt/

Read aloud the questions with the whole class and ask individuals to give the answers and others to repeat them to establish the differences.

Answers
The pronunciation of *can* in the positive and in questions is /kən/.
The pronunciation of *can* in short answers is /kæn/.
The pronunciation of *can't* is /kɑ:nt/.

Read through the Caution Box with the whole class.

Ask students to work in pairs and take it in turns to give the correct sentence(s) for each of the pictures.

3 **T 30b** This is a dictation to check that your students can recognize what they hear. Ask them to listen and write in the answers. Pause the tape after each sentence. Then ask them to check their answers with a partner. Play the tape again as you conduct a full class feedback. (They could read the tapescript on page 116 of their books as you do this.)

Answers
a I *can type*, but I *can't spell*.
b He *can sing* and he *can dance*.
c '*Can* you *cook*?' 'Yes, I *can*.'
d They *can ski*, but they *can't swim*.
e We *can read* and we *can write*.
f '*Can* she *drive*?' 'No, she *can't*.'

Although this is a recognition exercise, you can make it productive by asking your students to read some of the sentences aloud to each other.

Practice (SB page 41)

1 Listening and speaking

1 **T 31** This again is a recognition exercise that goes to production. This time the tape is much more natural sounding, not being a series of sentences for dictation, but a girl talking about her abilities.

Play the tape and ask your students to put a ✔ or a ✘ next to each activity.

Answers

(✔) She *can* ...	(✘) She *can't* ...
type	draw
use a word processor	drive
play tennis	ski
swim	speak Italian or Spanish
cook	play the piano
speak French and German	

Put them into pairs to compare their answers. Then conduct a full class feedback to establish the correct answers. Let them listen again if necessary.

2 The exercise now becomes personalized and productive. In pairs they take it in turn to ask and answer questions about each other using the words in 1.

Note

1 Make sure that they use appropriate rising intonation with the inverted questions, and falling intonation with the short answers.

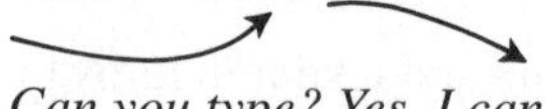

Can you type? Yes, I can.

2 Make sure that they pronounce the *t* on the end of the negatives. The two consonants *nt* together are difficult for many nationalities.

Go round and monitor and help as they do this. Then round off the activity by asking one or two members of the class to tell the others about their partner's abilities. This will reinforce the fact that *can* is the same in all persons, e.g. *Maria can type but she can't use a word processor ...*

2 Speaking

This can be quite a contentious activity because students tend to disagree about what exactly computers can do, and/or the degree to which they can do it. There is currently a growing belief that the initial very high expectations of computer ability in terms of real human-like behaviour have not been met. Put your students into small groups to do this. (We are hoping that discussion and disagreement will generate some freer speaking in English, in which case the activity can last some while. However be grateful at any efforts at expressing their opinions and don't worry if the activity is quite short.)

In the sample answers we have included an extra column (*They can ... but ...*), which is for your information only. You can choose how/if you deal with the extra information.

Sample answers

They can ...

count   play chess   forecast the weather

check spellings

They can ... but ...

translate (but word for word, not overall meaning)

speak English (only in limited fashion with unnatural intonation)

hear (they can recognise some speech, but limited)

make music (but not like Mozart!)

have conversations (but limited with many misunderstandings of context.)

They can't ...

do crosswords   see   smell   write books

think (because they work completely in numbers)

Conduct a feedback session with the whole class. This could be quite lively. Finally, you could ask them what people can do that computers can't do, *or* you could list some things that you think computers can't do and encourage the class to react: *drink*, *eat*, *sleep*, *fall in love*, etc.

Additional material

Workbook Unit 6

Exercises 1–3 These practise *can* and *can't*.

PRESENTATION (2) (SB page 41)

was/were – could

This is a very direct presentation of the past of the verbs *to be* and *can*. It revises the present of the verbs and then moves straight to the past tense equivalents.

1 Let the students work in pairs to write in the answers. Before you do this, teach them the word *yesterday*, by doing the first example with them. When they have finished, go through the exercise with them, modelling the questions and answers for them to repeat, and highlighting the weak vowel sounds of *was* and *were* (/wəz/ and /wə/) in statements and questions, and the strong vowel sounds (/wɒz/, /wɒznt/, /wɜː/, /wɜːnt/) in short answers and negatives.

Problem

The negatives

The groups of consonants in the negatives *wasn't* /wɒznt/, *weren't* /wɜːnt/ and *couldn't* /kʊdnt/ may be difficult for some students and may need extra choral and individual repetition.

Also, as you go through, keep backtracking by asking individual students to answer the earlier questions again.

Finally get your students to ask and answer the questions in open pairs across the class. Use the opportunity to check and correct them carefully. It may prove too laborious to follow this with practice in closed pairs, but if you feel they need it, do it.

● Grammar questions

Put your students into pairs to do this and then quickly check through with the whole class.

Answers

	Positive	**Negative**
I	was	wasn't
you	were	weren't
he/she/it	was	wasn't
we	were	weren't
they	were	weren't
	could	couldn't (all persons)

⚠ Look at the Caution Box on page 42 together to reinforce the rules of pronunciation.

2 **T 32** This is a repetition exercise with some more questions and answers. There are pauses on the tape for students to repeat. (You could omit it if you feel it is not necessary for your students and move on to the freer speaking in the next exercise.)

3 Put students into pairs to take turns in asking and answering the questions. Go round the class to help them. Encourage them to ask about times other than those listed in the book. Round the activity off by asking one or two students to tell the others about their partner.

Practice (SB page 42)

1 Listening and pronunciation

1 **T 33** Set the scene of the conversation by asking your students to look at the picture and telling them that two friends are talking about a party. Check that they realize that they can only use *was*, *were*, *wasn't*, and *couldn't* to fill the gaps.

Ask them to work in pairs to do the exercise. Play the tape for them to listen and check their answers. If necessary play it again and ask them to focus on the pronunciation, not only of *was* and *were*, but of the stress and intonation of the questions and answers.

Ask one or two pairs of students to take the parts of Sue and Bill and read aloud the conversation across the class. Encourage lively and natural pronunciation.

Answers

Sue: *Were* you at Eve's party last Saturday?
Bill: Yes, I *was*.
Sue: *Was* it good?
Bill: Well, it *was* OK.
Sue: *Were* there many people?
Bill: Yes, there *were*.
Sue: *Was* Tom there?
Bill: No, he *wasn't*. And where *were* you?
Sue: Oh, I *couldn't* go because I *was* at Adam's party! It *was* brilliant!

2 Now ask the class to practise it again in closed pairs. Go round and help and check them as they do this. (Don't let this go on too long otherwise it will become boring!)

Move to the other situations. You could just get them to continue in their closed pairs, but it is much more interesting if you put some skeletal dialogue prompts on the blackboard and ask pairs of students to come to the front of the class and act out the other situations, e.g.

... last Sunday?
... good?
... many people?
... (Tom) there?
... brilliant!

Note
Much better than using the situations in the book would be if your students had real parties or other events they had been to recently and they could use these to make similar conversations.

2 Speaking

1 This activity brings together *could*, *couldn't*, and *was* and it also introduces *until*. It is an oral drill, hopefully made a bit more interesting by the inclusion of some famous characters.

First ask students to look at the pictures and see if they can recognize the people. Do the exercise as a class as a contrast to the pairwork in the previous activity, and so it can be done quite quickly. Ask one student to construct the sentence and then ask others to repeat. (It really is true that Einstein couldn't speak until he was eight!)

Answers

a Mozart *could* play the piano *when he was* three. I *couldn't* play the piano *until I was* ten.
b Picasso *could* draw *when he was* one. I *couldn't* draw *until I was* six.
c Nureyev *could* dance *when he was* three. I *couldn't* dance *until I was* seven.
d I *could* speak *when I was* two. Einstein *couldn't* speak *until he was* eight!

Ask your students to memorize some of the sentences and then close their books and tell you or a partner the sentences again.

You could also personalize the activity. The students could compare in small groups or pairs at what age they could walk, talk, swim, speak a foreign language, etc., *or* they could think of some famous talented people that they know and make similar sentences about them. At the end of either activity get feedback from the whole class.

Note

Workbook Unit 6

Exercise 8 This shows students how to say years in English. Therefore it might be a good idea to set it for homework, or do it in class *before* doing the next activity which requires students to say years.

2 This exercise aims to introduce *to be born.*

Note

I was born is taught here as an expression, *not* as an example of the passive. Don't be tempted to go into the grammar. Some students translate from their own language and want to say **I am born.*

Put students into pairs to do the first part of the exercise. Get feedback from the whole class.

Answers

Mozart was born in Salzburg.
Picasso was born in Malaga.
Nureyev was born in Siberia.
Einstein was born in Ulm.

Introduce the questions *Where were you born? When were you born?* Get the class to repeat them in chorus and individually. Make sure the students can hear the difference between *where* and *were.* It is much more fun if you make the following question and answer session a 'mingle' activity, i.e. ask students to get up and walk round the class asking as many people as possible *when* and *where* they were born. Tell them that you are going to see how much they can remember when they sit down. After a few minutes ask them to sit down and tell you what information they can remember, e.g. *Maria was born in Barcelona in 1969. Peter was born in Frankfurt, but I can't remember when!*

3 Choosing the correct sentence

See page 5 of the Teacher's Book for an explanation of this exercise type. This exercise practises the grammar of the unit.

Ask students to work in pairs or small groups to choose the correct sentence. Ask them to work quite quickly, then conduct a full class feedback on which are the correct answers. Try to get students to correct each other and explain any mistakes they hear.

Answers

1 b 2 b 3 a 4 b 5 a 6 b

Additional material

Workbook Unit 6

Exercises 4–6 These practise *was* and *were.* Exercise 5 is also very suitable for oral work and could well be used in class either to supplement or replace one of the activities in the Student's Book. Exercise 6 brings together past and present tense forms covered so far.

Exercise 7 This practises *could* and *couldn't* with *was, were,* and *can.*

● READING AND SPEAKING (SB page 43)

Note

This activity is a jigsaw reading. This means that it should result in not only reading practice, but also some freer speaking.

The class divides into two groups and each group reads a different but similar text about a teenage genius and answers the questions. After this, students from the different groups get together to exchange information about the boy in their text. This means that they should get some speaking practice whilst their main attention is on the completion of the reading task.

These texts are based on real newspaper articles but have been simplified and rewritten to include examples of the grammar taught in this and previous units.

Pre-reading task

Ask everyone in the class to write three things that teenagers like doing. (This revises *like + -ing* from Unit 4). For example: *They like riding motor bikes/listening to pop music/dancing.* Get feedback on their ideas. Then set the scene for the reading texts by saying that they are going to read about two teenagers who like doing different things from usual teenagers.

Reading

Note

You need to be very clear when giving instructions for any jigsaw activity. If necessary and possible, give them in L1.

Ask everyone to look at the photographs of the two boys. Encourage some general comments.
Divide the class into two groups. Tell Group A to read about Ivan Mirsky and Group B to read about Jaya Rajah. Most of the vocabulary in the texts should be known, but allow dictionaries to be used to check. However make it clear that they should *first* read through as quickly as possible to get a general understanding, and only then look up any words.

When they have read the texts they could either go through the questions on their own and then check with others from the same group, or work with a partner from the same group to answer the questions. Each group has the same questions to answer.

Comprehension check

The main idea of these questions is to check understanding, therefore short answers are perfectly acceptable. However, when you have a full class feedback you might want to encourage further language production such as you can see in the brackets in the answers below.

Answers

Group A – Ivan Mirsky

a He's thirteen.
b No, he doesn't.
c (He was born) in Russia.
d (He lives) in America.
e (He lives) with his father.
f His father doesn't have a job.
g He could ride a bike at/when he was eighteen months; he could read before he was two; he could play cards at three; and play the piano at four.
h He practises chess problems/plays chess.
i No, he can't. (Ivan translates for him.)
j No, he doesn't. (Other teenagers are boring.)
k He only plays chess. (He doesn't like playing sports or watching TV.)

Group B – Jaya Rajah

a He's fourteen.
b No, he doesn't. (He studies medicine at New York University.)
c (He was born) in Madras in India.
d (He lives) in New York.
e (He lives) with his mother, father and brother.
f His father is a doctor.
g He could count before he could say 'Mummy' or 'Daddy'; he could answer questions on calculus when he was five; he could do algebra when he was eight.
h He studies at home.
i Yes, he can.
j No, he doesn't. (Other children are boring.)
k He sometimes watches TV.

Speaking

1 Tell each student to find a partner from the other group and go through the questions and answers together, telling each other about the boy in their article.

2 Tell them to read the other text as soon as they have discussed the answers. At this point conduct a full class feedback and get answers about both boys, encouraging your students to elaborate the answers a little and compare the boys as you go. Finally (if time) you could get one or two individuals to speak at length and give a summary about their boy using the questions in the Comprehension Check as prompts, e.g. *Ivan is sixteen but he doesn't go to school. He was born in Russia but now he lives in America with his father. His father doesn't work. He just practises chess with Ivan.*, etc.

3 Lead from 2 to this more general discussion. You could ask your students to discuss the *What do you think?* questions in small groups.

Possible problem

If students become involved in discussion activities, they often start to talk in L1 in their frustration at not being able to get their point across. Don't worry too much if this happens, at least it shows that they are interested! Gently encourage them to try and express something in English as this is such good practice, and don't correct them too much. If they get their point across, that's enough. The aim of this activity is fluency not accuracy.

Roleplay

You might find that you have no time for the roleplay or that it might be too difficult for your students as it stands, therefore we suggest an alternative approach.
Photocopy the interview on page 128 of the Teacher's Book and ask your students to complete the gaps either in class or for homework. They can choose which boy is being interviewed.

They could act out the interview in class.

●VOCABULARY AND PRONUNCIATION

(SB page 44)

Words that sound the same

This activity introduces your students to words that have different spellings and meanings but *sound* the same, i.e. homophones. Of course, it is not important that your students learn the linguistic term *homophone*, but it is important that they are aware of such words, as there are so many in English and they can be particularly confusing when listening. The use of phonetic script in the activity serves not only to continue the process of getting to know it, but also to highlight the fact that there is often no relation between sounds and spellings in English.

1 This is to illustrate what is meant by *words that sound the same.* Ask your students to read aloud the sentences to themselves and then ask for suggestions about the words underlined. They should easily notice that the words sound the same but are spelt differently and have different meanings.

/aɪ/ = *eye* and *I*
/nəʊ/ = *no* and *know*

2 Ask students to work in pairs to do this. Most of the words are taken from previous units and should be familiar, but allow them to check new words either with you or in their dictionaries. Whilst they are doing the exercise write the words in box A on the board in a column.

Bring the class together to go through the exercise and invite students, in turn, up to the board to write the words that sound the same next to each other.

Answers

A	B
hear	here
see	sea
write	right
eye	I
there	their
for	four
know	no
by	buy
knows	nose
wear	where
son	sun
hour	our
meat	meet
cheque	check
too	two

3 This exercise puts some of the words which have the same sound but different spelling in context and should be good fun to do. Again ask students to work in pairs to do it. Then check through with the whole class, asking individuals to read the sentences aloud and spell the correct word.

Answers

a I can *hear* you but I can't *see* you.
b *There* are three bedrooms in *our* house.
c John *knows where* Jill lives.
d My *son* lives near the *sea*.
e Don't *wear* that hat when you *meet* the Queen.
f They *know* Anna *too*.
g You were *right*. Sally and Peter don't eat *meat*.
h *Their* daughter could *write* when she was three.
i I want to *buy two* new pens.
j *Check* that your answers are *right*.

4 You could begin this by asking the class to chant through the phonetic transcriptions all together to check their progress in reading them.

Ask students to work on their own to do the exercise and then check their answers with a partner before you go through it.

Answers

a	/nəʊz/	knows	nose
b	/sʌn/	son	sun
c	/mi:t/	meat	meet
d	/tʃek/	cheque	check
e	/tu:/	too	two
f	/raɪt/	write	right
g	/hɪə/	hear	here
h	/weə/	wear	where

Additional material

Workbook Unit 6
Exercise 9 This is a vocabulary exercise that practises words that go together, e.g. *climb a mountain, get up early.*

●EVERYDAY ENGLISH (SB page 45)

At the airport

1 **T34a** Get students to look at the picture and ask which airports *they* know. Play the tape and tell them to listen carefully to complete the chart. Then go through it with the whole class.

Answers

Flight Number	Destination	Gate number	Remark
BA 516	Geneva	14	Last call
SK 832	Frankfurt	7	Last call
AF 472	Amsterdam		Delayed 30 mins
LH 309	Miami	32	Now boarding
VS 876	New York	20	Now boarding

2 Ask students what they can see in the picture and then get them to do this activity in pairs or small groups. Go through it quickly as a class.

Answers

2 passport control
5 baggage reclaim
1 the check-in desk
4 the plane
6 the arrival hall
3 the departure lounge

3 **T34b** Play the conversations and pause after each one for students to discuss in their groups or pairs where they are taking place.

Tray will be a new word for your students so be prepared to illustrate or translate it quickly as you go. Delay full class feedback until the after the last conversation has been played. Then you can go through the answers and ask *How do you know?* for each conversation.

Answers

passport control	b
baggage reclaim	e
the check-in desk	c
the plane	d
the arrival hall	f
the departure lounge	a

4 Do this as a class in order to help students with the vocabulary.

a Two passengers.
b Passport officer and a passenger.
c Check-in assistant and passenger.
d Air steward and passenger.
e Two passengers.
f An English couple and a foreign visitor (Marie-Thérèse from Switzerland).

5 **T 34c** This should be done quite quickly with the whole class offering suggestions after each line, and you choosing who should try to provide the answer. The others can then comment on it.

Sample Answers

a Was it Gate 4 or 14? *I think it was 4.*
b Can I see your passport, please? *Yes, of course. Here you are.*
c Smoking or non-smoking? *Non-smoking, please.*
d Can I have your tray, please, madam? *Yes. Here you are.*
e Excuse me. I think that's my suitcase. *I'm sorry. My suitcase is red, too.*
f Welcome to England! Was your flight good? *Yes, thank you very much.*

You could play it through for a final time and this time give very little time indeed for them to come up with a suitable reply.

6 This might be quite difficult for some students. However it can be fun, especially in small groups and if these groups act out their situations to the rest of the class. You could make up some rolecards and situations for your students if you feel that they couldn't manage on their own.

GRAMMAR SUMMARY (SB page 46)

Read the Grammar Summary together in class, and/or ask your students to read it and *learn* the grammar at home. Encourage them to ask you questions about it.

Don't forget

Workbook Unit 6
Exercise 10 Prepositions
Exercise 11 The writing activity is a simple formal letter applying for a job.

Word List
Remind your students of the Word List at the back of their book. Ask them to look at the list for this unit on page 124. Tell them that they could write in the translations, learn them at home and/or write some of the words in their vocabulary notebooks.

Pronunciation Book Unit 6

Video
There are two video sections that can supplement Units 5 and 6 of the Student's Book.
Report (Section 4) *Heathrow*. This is a mini-documentary about Heathrow Airport, past and present. It is particularly suitable for use either before or after the Everyday English Unit 6, *At the airport.*
Situation (Section 5) *At the bank.* This is a short situation where Paola exchanges traveller's cheques at a bank.

UNIT 7

Past Simple (1) – Special occasions

Introduction to the unit

The distant past (the early part of the 20th century) and more recent past (the 1980s) are the themes of this unit. Within these contexts both regular and irregular forms of the Past Simple are presented. The formation of the question and negative is introduced, but the latter is only minimally practised because it is one of the main grammatical aims of Unit 8. The skills work includes a reading text which is a short biography of Charles Dickens. This obviously provides further practice of the Past Simple. It's worth noting that the theme of famous British writers is taken up in the Headway Elementary Video, where there is a short documentary about William Shakespeare.

Language aims

Grammar

Past Simple (1)

The learning of the Past Simple is facilitated by students' knowledge of the Present Simple, in that both tenses use a form of *do* as an auxiliary in the question and negative. It is not such a big leap to learn that the same auxiliary is used in its past tense form, *did*, to make the Past Simple tense, especially as this form remains constant in all persons. Many of the exercises in this unit provide opportunities to contrast the Present and Past Simple tenses.

Problems

1. The different realizations of the pronunciation of *-ed* at the end of regular verbs is a problem. Students always want to pronounce the *-ed* in its entirety – /ed/ – and not the /t/, /d/, /ɪd/ endings, for example:

   cleaned */kli:ned/ instead of /kli:nd/
   worked */wɜ:ked/ instead of /wɜ:kt/
   visited */vɪzɪted/ instead of /vɪzɪtɪd/

   There is an exercise to practise these, but basically we are wary of too much time being spent on this at this stage, when there is so much else for students to grapple with.
2. Although students should be helped by their knowledge of the Present Simple (see above), the use of *did* still causes problems and students forget to use it, for example:

   * Where you went last night?
   * When she start school?
   * She no liked her job.
3. There are a large number of irregular verbs to learn. From now on students should be encouraged to consult the irregular verb list on page 127 and learn the irregular verbs as and when needed. You could start setting some to learn for homework and giving short tests on them at the beginning of some lessons!

Vocabulary and pronunciation

Words with silent letters are focused upon, for example *debt*, *know*, *listen*. Again the point being emphasized is that English spelling is not phonetic. The phonetic script is further practised with short and long vowel sounds.

Everyday English

Common expressions for special occasions, such as *Happy birthday* and *Merry Christmas* are introduced and practised. This provides the opportunity for some very interesting discussion on cross-cultural traditions, especially if you have a multilingual class. What occasions different nationalities celebrate, and how they celebrate them, is fascinating!

Workbook

More irregular verbs are introduced.
In the vocabulary section there is an exercise on recognizing parts of speech.
The writing syllabus continues with a piece of narrative writing about *My last holiday.*

Notes on the unit

PRESENTATION (1) (SB page 47)

Regular verbs

Note

You could ask your students to bring to class any old photographs they have of their grandparents when young, and/or you could bring in some of your own family to set the scene. You can introduce the idea of the past via these.

It is always interesting looking at old photographs, so take care that the scene-setting doesn't go on too long and take up too much lesson time!

1 Set this for homework prior to the lesson. Get your students to look up these words and enter them in their vocabulary notebooks. (Point out that it is *retire from work*, not the old-fashioned *retire to bed*, that is needed.)

2 Ask about your students' grandparents: *Do they like talking about the past? Do their grandmothers look like Ellen in the picture?*

Ask them to read about Ellen Peel in Text A. (This text is about Ellen's life now and revises the Present Simple before moving to the introduction of the Past Simple.)

Ask a few questions about Ellen now.

How old is she?	*Over ninety.*
Where does she live?	*In a village.*
How many cats does she have?	*Five.*
Is she married?	*No, she isn't.*
What does she often think about?	*Her past.*

3 **T35a** Establish the answer to this last question clearly and tell your students that they are going to listen to and read about Ellen's past. Play the tape and then immediately go through the grammar questions as a class.

● Grammar questions

Read aloud the questions and establish the answers clearly.

Answers

- Text A is about the present. Text B is about the past.
- Ellen *was* twelve years old.
  The last two letters of the other verbs are *-ed*.
- To form the Past Simple of regular verbs add *-d* or *-ed* to the infinitive.

4 **T35b** Text C is an exercise which gives more information about Ellen's past and requires students to write regular Past Simple forms in the gaps. You could ask them to try and fill the gaps with the verbs in the box *before* they listen, then to listen and check their answers with a partner. Or, if you think that it would be too difficult for them, let them listen to the text first, then fill in the answers afterwards.

Answers

She *worked* from 5.30 in the morning to 9.00 at night. She *cleaned* all the rooms in the house before breakfast. She *earned* £25 a year.
In 1921 she *moved* to another family. She *liked* her new job because she *looked* after the children. There were five children, four sons and one daughter. She *loved* them, especially the baby, Robert. She *stayed* with that family for twenty years.
Ellen never married. She just looked after other people's children until she *retired* when she was seventy years old.

Go through the answers as a class, getting students to take turns at reading aloud part of the text. Correct their pronunciation of the past tense verbs in preparation for the exercise on pronunciation in Practice 2.2.

Practice (SB page 48)

1 Grammar

Put students into pairs to do this exercise. (The pronunciation of the verb endings is given in brackets in the answer key.)
The next exercise, 2, has the answers on tape for the students to listen and check, so wait until then to establish the correct answers with the whole class.

Answers

	A	B
a	I was only twelve years old	when my mother *died* (/d/) and I *started* (/ɪd/)work.
b	I was always tired in my first job	because I *worked* (/t/) very long hours.
c	I started work at 5.30 in the morning	and I *finished* (/t/) at 9.00 in the evening.
d	Now I live in a village,	but in 1920 I *lived* (/d/) in London.
e	Now I look after my five cats.	In the 1920s I *looked* (/t/) after five children.
f	I loved all the children,	but I *loved* (/d/) Robert especially.
g	Robert's over seventy now and I still see him.	He *visited* (/ɪd/) me just last month.

2 Listening and pronunciation

1 **T36a** Play the tape and tell students to listen to Ellen speaking and check their answers.

Ask them to repeat the sentences and start focusing on the pronunciation, particularly of the endings of the verbs in the Past Simple. (See brackets in B in the answer key.)

2 **T 36b** Isolate the sounds /t/, /d/, /ɪd/ for your students and get them to listen and repeat them. Play the tape and ask them to put the verbs in the correct column according to the ending. Get them to check their answers with a partner and then conduct a full class feedback, asking students to practise saying the verbs as you go.

Answers

/t/	/d/	/ɪd/
worked	lived	started
finished	died	visited
looked	loved	
liked	cleaned	
	stayed	
	moved	

PRESENTATION (2) (SB page 48)

Questions and negatives

Note
This presentation of questions and negatives stays with the old-time theme, but moves from Ellen to more famous figures from British history, Queen Victoria and her husband Prince Albert. All the verbs used are still regular (apart from *have*, but the irregular past form *had* is avoided at this stage and only the negative is included) and there is only scant introduction to the negative: *She didn't have any brothers or sisters*. The negative is dealt with much more fully in the next unit, Unit 8.

1 Ask your students to look at the picture. Do they know the people? Ask them to read through the whole text to find out who they are. Tell them not to worry about the gaps. Now ask them to work in pairs and look at the questions.

You could at this point direct them to the Caution Box so that they can see how the Past Simple is formed in comparison with the Present Simple.

Go back to the text and read it aloud pausing at the first gap and encouraging the students to ask the right question.

Note
The first question revises *was born* and is not a *did* question. Also, it asks *Where was she born?* not *When?*

The idea is that your students ask you the correct question for the gap and you tell them the answer which they write in.

Answers

Student(s)	Teacher
Where was she born?	*In London.*
When did she die?	*In 1901.*
When did her father die?	*When she was eight months old.*
When did she marry Prince Albert?	*In 1840.*
Where did they live?	*In Buckingham Palace.*
How many children did they have?	*Nine. Five girls and four boys.*

2 **T 37** Play the questions from the tape one by one (or say them yourself) and get students to repeat them both chorally and individually. Ask other students to provide the answers. These are all *wh-* questions so encourage natural falling intonation on each one.

When did she die? In 1901.

If you haven't already read through the Caution Box with your class, read it now.

● Grammar question

Read the rule aloud or write it on the blackboard and ask your class to tell you what should go in the gaps.

Answer
To form questions in the Past Simple, we use the auxiliary verb did and the infinitive (without to).

Practice (SB page 49)

The practice activities bring together *was/were* and *did*, so that students become aware of the difference between the past of the verb *to be* and full verbs.

1 Speaking

Photocopy the Student A, Student B cards on page 129 of this book.

Note
This is an information gap activity, so you need to give very clear instructions as to how to do it, if possible in L1. Each student looks at his or her text. The texts are the same but *different* information is blanked out. Student A must ask Student B questions to complete her/his text and vice versa. Again stress that they must not *show* their texts!

Put your students into pairs and tell them that they are going to get other texts with some more information about Queen Victoria and Prince Albert. Give out the A and B versions of the text to each pair.

Demonstrate how to do the activity using the example in the Student's Book. You ask the questions and get a couple of students to give you the answers.
Go round and help and check the pairs as they do the activity.
When they have completed it, ask a Student A with a different Student B to go through the questions and answers again in open pairs *across* the class so everyone can hear the right answers.

Answers
Student A's questions to B
Where did they marry? (London.)
When did they visit the French king? (In 1843.)
How old was Albert when he died? (42.)
Why did she love Scotland? (She went there on holiday.)
How old was she when she died? (81.)

Student B's questions to A
What nationality was Albert? (German.)
Who did they visit? (The French king, Louis Philippe.)
When did Prince Albert die? (1861.)
Where did she live? (Windsor and Scotland.)
When did she die? (1901.)

Round off the activity by asking a student to read aloud the completed text to the class.

Complete text
Prince Albert was German and they married in London in 1840. Soon after they married, they visited the French king, Louis Philippe. They visited him in 1843. Unfortunately, Prince Albert died in 1861 when he was only 42. Queen Victoria was terribly unhappy and she never lived in London again. She lived in Windsor and Scotland. She loved Scotland because she often went there on holiday with her family.
She died in 1901. She was 81.

2 Grammar and speaking

1 Get your students to do this on their own. They should be able to do it quite quickly.

Ask them to write in the correct answers and then ask for feedback from the whole class, asking individuals to read out their answers.

Answers
a Where *were* you born? Where *was* your mother born?
b When *did* you start school?
c How many schools *did* you go to?
d What *was* your favourite subject?
e Where *did* you live when you *were* a child?
f *Did* you live in a house or a flat?

2 This is a 'mingle' activity (done only if you have room in your classroom!), i.e. ask students to get up and walk round the class asking two or three other students (probably *two*, given the time factor) the questions, and answering about themselves in return. Or, if you don't mind a lot of movement, ask students to ask each question to a *different* student. Tell them that you are going to see how much they can remember when they sit down.

3 After a few minutes ask them to sit down and tell you what information they can remember.

Note
Be careful with the answer to *c* because this involves the irregular past *went*. You could simply give them the word and use this as an opportunity to introduce the idea of irregular verbs, which are the main aim of the next presentation.

Sample answer
Peter was born in Frankfurt and his mother was born in Stuttgart. He started school in 1974. He went (careful!) to three schools. His favourite subject was History. He lived in a flat in Frankfurt when he was a child.

You could ask students to write the answers to the questions about themselves in a short paragraph. They could do this for homework.

Additional material

Workbook Unit 7
Exercises 1 and 2 These practise regular verbs, questions, and answers in the Past Simple.

PRESENTATION (3) (SB page 49)

Irregular verbs

Now the theme moves to the more recent past. Life in the 1980s provides the context for the introduction of irregular verbs.

1 You need to draw your students' attention to the irregular verb list on page 127. It is important that they learn to consult it.

Ask your students to work with a partner and turn to the list. Ask them to use their dictionaries to look up new words and check the list to find out which three are regular and what the irregular forms of the others are.

Note
All these verbs appear at some point later in this unit, so your students need to learn them. You might therefore want to set this exercise for homework prior to the lesson and then go through it in class.

Answers

have	*had*	work	*worked* (reg.)
leave	*left*	get	*got*
become	*became*	change	*changed* (reg.)
lose	*lost*	buy	*bought*
come	*came*	go	*went*
hate	*hated* (reg.)	give	*gave*
write	*wrote*	win	*won*
find	*found*	sell	*sold*

Ask your students to read out the correct answers.

2 **T 38** Play the tape (or model them yourself) and ask students to listen and repeat the verbs.

3 Write *1980* in large numbers on the board and, if you think your students need dates practice, ask the whole of your class to *chant* the years from 1980 to this year.

Ask your students how old they were in 1980 and what they can remember, not only about their own lives, but also the world, especially sport and politics. You could put them into groups to do this, if you have time and if you feel that your students would respond well. One or two ideas will do, just in order to set the scene for tapescript 39 and Kevin's reminiscences.

4 **T 39** Let students read the text first and check it for any unknown vocabulary (*unemployed*, *computer software*, and *video recorder* will probably be new). Play the tape. Tell your students to listen to Kevin and ask *What can he remember?*

Let them look at the text at the same time if they want to, but tell them *not* to write anything yet. The text in the book is only a summary. There is more information given by Kevin on the tape, but students are required only to sift out certain points to practise certain verbs.

After listening, ask them to work in pairs and fill the gaps with verbs in the Past Simple. They are all from the list in Exercise 1.

Now play the tape again so that they can check that they have used the correct verbs in the correct form.

Answers
About him
a He *left* school in 1982. He was unemployed, but then he *got* a job in an office. He *sold* computer software.
b His parents *bought* a video recorder in 1985 and his brother *got* a video computer game for his birthday in 1986.
c Kevin *lost* his job in 1990.

Sport
d The USSR *didn't go* to the Olympics in 1984, but both the United States and the USSR *went* to Seoul in 1988.
e Argentina *won* the World Cup in 1986.

Politics
f Reagan *became* the US president in 1981, Gorbachev *gave* the world *glasnost* and *perestroika*, and the Berlin Wall *came* down in 1989.

5 Ask students to work in pairs to write the questions. Read through the example with them and then go round and check as they do exercises. Ask individuals to read aloud the answers in a full class feedback session.

Answers
a What did he sell?
b When did his parents buy a video recorder?
c What did his brother get for his birthday in 1986?
d When did he lose his job?
e When did Argentina win the World Cup?
f When did the Berlin Wall come down?

Practice

1 Speaking

1 Read this aloud to your students and then get them to take turns to make the expressions round the class.

2 Demonstrate how to do this activity with a student then put them into pairs to do it. You could suggest that they take notes about each other. Go round and help and check them. Bring the class together and ask a few students to report back on their partner, thereby getting practice of irregular pasts. Note that students will need the irregular verbs *saw* and *took*.

2 Choosing the correct sentence

Ask students to do this on their own and then check with a partner before you go through the exercise as a class.

Answers
1 a 2 a 3 b 4 b 5 b 6 a 7 b 8 b

Additional material

Workbook Unit 7
Exercises 3–5 These practise irregular verbs in the Past Simple.
Exercise 6 This practises question formation.
Exercise 7 This contrasts Present Simple and Past Simple.
Exercise 8 This is the writing activity: describing a holiday. It provides more practice of the Past Simple.

● READING (SB page 50)

Note
Students may find this quite a challenging reading exercise, but their delight in coping with a text about a famous British writer at such an early stage can provide great motivation and satisfaction.

Pre-reading task

You could reverse the order of these three exercises and do 3, the vocabulary exercise, first.

1/2 These questions are by way of setting the scene. When you ask the questions, write notes on the blackboard of any information your students can give you. They may know the name Charles Dickens, but it is unlikely that they will know much about him. They will learn more about him as they read the text. It is also unlikely that your students will know much about Victorian England, but here are some brief notes for you. (The pictures on page 51 may help them get ideas.)

Victorian England
Victorian England was named, naturally enough, after Queen Victoria. This was the time that saw the British Empire at its largest. The boast was that the sun never set on the British Empire, as it had colonies such as Canada, India, and Australia all over the world. Britain became very rich as a result of having trading links with these colonies. However, domestically, this was also a time of great poverty for many of the people, with no work and poor living conditions. There was a huge gap between the rich and the poor.

3 Students check the new words in their dictionaries, and put one of the words into each gap.

Answers
- a All the students like Anna. She's a very *popular* girl.
- b My mother writes books, but she isn't a famous *novelist*.
- c Alan started work in a bank last week. He's a *clerk*.
- d He has ten clothes shops. He's a rich, *successful* businessman.
- e I don't like borrowing money. I hate being in *debt*.
- f I live near a very big *factory* that makes cars.
- g I went round the world for a year. It was a wonderful *experience*.
- h She often goes *abroad* in her job, sometimes to Hong Kong, sometimes to Canada.

Reading

Ask students to look at the pictures around the text. What can they see? Students read the text about the life of Charles Dickens.

Comprehension check

1 Ask students to answer the true/false questions in pairs. If they seem to have problems doing this, they could then check in groups of four.

Answers
- a True.
- b False. Many of his characters were poor and hungry people.
- c True.
- d False. He went to school.
- e False. The rest of his family went to prison, but Charles went to work in a factory.
- f True.
- g False. He became a journalist when he was sixteen.
- h False. He married and had ten children.

2 Students answer the questions in pairs or small groups.

Answers
- a Fifty-eight.
- b Seven (a total of eight children).
- c Yes. His teachers thought he was very clever.
- d Because his father went to prison, and Charles went to work in a factory.
- e All the family, but not Charles.
- f He washed bottles.
- g He worked for a newspaper.
- h No, he didn't have a happy family life.
- i He never stopped/didn't stop writing until he died.

Writing

Students could write about their past for homework. Don't correct this too harshly, and give credit for good ideas as well as good English. You could allow classroom time for them to read and check each other's work. Also it would be nice to ask one or two students to read theirs aloud to the rest of the class.

● VOCABULARY AND PRONUNCIATION
(SB page 52)

Silent letters

> **Note**
> The aim of this exercise is to show students yet again that English spelling is not phonetic via an exercise on silent letters. It is useful to have a convention when writing words on the board to show students a silent letter. This might be by writing the silent letter in a different coloured pen, or by crossing out the silent letter, e.g. de~~b~~t
>
> You could encourage your students to do the same in their vocabulary notebooks.
>
> The silent *r* in mid-position is practised, and one silent *r* in the end position (daughte*r*). We do not advise you to explain the rule about silent *r* in end position unless the following word begins with a vowel sound, e.g. daughter‿and son. This would probably overload students at this level.
>
> Also, pronunciation work here and on the cassette recording is based on RP. If you are a native-speaker teacher with a different accent, you may like to point this out and explain a little about the many and varying accents of spoken English!

1 Read the instructions as a class. Practise the words from the text about Charles Dickens.

Students work in pairs to cross out the silent letters.

T 40a Students listen and check.

Answers

a wa~~l~~k	e autum~~n~~	i hi~~gh~~
b lis~~t~~en	f fa~~r~~m	j ha~~l~~f
c ~~k~~now	g wo~~r~~k	k fore~~ig~~n
d ~~w~~riter	h sho~~r~~t	l dau~~gh~~te~~r~~

2 Students look at the phonetics and write in the words.

Answers

a work	d autumn
b farm	e writer
c listen	f daughter

3 **T 40b** Students work in pairs to write the other words with silent letters.

Answers

a talk	f white
b born	g knife
c bought	h wrong
d world	i cupboard
e answer	j Christmas

EVERYDAY ENGLISH **(SB page 52)**

Special occasions

This exercise can provide a lot of fascinating information if you have students from different countries, or if some of your students know foreign countries.

1 Students use their dictionaries to decide which are special days. They match the special days to a picture and/or object.

Answers
The special days are birthday (girl with cake), wedding day (wedding couple, horseshoe and confetti), Christmas Day (Christmas tree), New Year's Eve (couple kissing at midnight), Easter Day (Easter egg), Mother's Day (Mother's Day card), and Valentine's Day (card with heart).

Ask your class if they have the same customs for the same days. Here are some notes on what the days mean to British people (though not all British people, naturally).

> **British customs**
>
> **Birthday**
> There is often a birthday cake, with candles to be blown out and everyone sings *Happy birthday.* People send birthday cards, and there is perhaps a birthday party with their friends.
>
> **Wedding day**
> People get married in a church for a religious ceremony or a registry office for a civil ceremony. Rice or confetti is thrown at the bride and groom to wish them luck, and the bride often carries a horseshoe, again to symbolize good luck. (We have no idea why the horseshoe is a symbol of good luck!) There is a party afterwards called a reception, and the bride and groom may go on a holiday called a honeymoon.
>
> **Christmas Day**
> This is the main day for celebrating Christmas in Britain, when presents are exchanged. There is a large dinner, traditionally with turkey and Christmas pudding, which is made from dried fruit. We decorate the house, and have a Christmas tree. For children, Santa Claus (or Father Christmas) visits during the early hours of Christmas morning and leaves presents by the children's beds or under the tree.
>
> **New Year's Eve**
> In Scotland this is a more important celebration than in the rest of Britain. People go to parties and wait for midnight to come, when they wish each other 'Happy New Year'. In London many thousands of people celebrate New Year in Trafalgar Square where they can hear Big Ben (the clock on the Houses of Parliament) strike midnight.

Easter Day
There is no fixed tradition of ways to celebrate Easter. Children receive chocolate Easter eggs and usually eat too many of them!

Mother's Day
This is on a Sunday towards the end of March. Children send cards and a present such as some flowers or chocolates.

Valentine's Day
People send Valentine cards to the person they love. They are usually sent with no name on!
People also put messages in newspapers to their loved one. These can often be quite funny!

2 Students work in pairs to complete the conversations with the days.

T41a Students listen and check their answers, then practise the conversations.

Answers

a A Ugh! Work again! I hate *Mondays*.
B Me too. Did you have a nice weekend?
A Yes. It was wonderful.

b Happy *birthday* to you.
Happy *birthday* to you.
Happy *birthday,* dear Katie.
Happy *birthday* to you.

c A How many *Easter* eggs did you get?
B Six. What about you?
A Five. I had them all on *Easter* morning before lunch.
B Did you?
A And then I was sick!
B Ugh!

d A Congratulations!
B Oh, thank you very much.
A When's the happy day?
B Pardon?
A Your *wedding* day. When is it?
B Oh! We're not sure yet. Some time in June, probably.

e A Hello! Merry *Christmas*, everyone!
B Merry *Christmas*! Come in, come in. It's so cold outside.

f A Wonderful! It's *Friday*!
B Yes. Have a nice weekend!
A Same to you.

3 **T41b** Students listen to the lines and give an answer. They can choose what they say.

Sample answers

a A Did you have a nice weekend?
B *Yes, very nice, thank you. What about you?*

b A Happy birthday!
B *Thank you.*

c A Merry Christmas!
B *Merry Christmas to you, too!*

d A Have a nice weekend!
B *Thanks. And you.*

e A Congratulations!
B *Thank you very much.*

GRAMMAR SUMMARY (SB page 53)

Read the Grammar Summary as a class. Encourage students to ask any questions.

Don't forget!

Workbook Unit 7
Exercise 9 Vocabulary of parts of speech, such as *adjective*, *noun*.
Exercise 10 Prepositions

Word List
Remind your students of the Word List at the back of their book. Ask them to look at the list for this unit on page 124. Tell them that they could write in the translations, learn them at home and/or write some of the words in their vocabulary notebooks.

Pronunciation Book Unit 7

Video
There are two video sections that can supplement Units 7 (and 8) of the Student's Book.
Report (Section 6) *Shakespeare*. This is a short documentary about the life of Shakespeare, which is particularly suitable for use after the reading about Charles Dickens.
Situation (Section 7) *The pub*. David takes Paola to an English pub.

UNIT 8

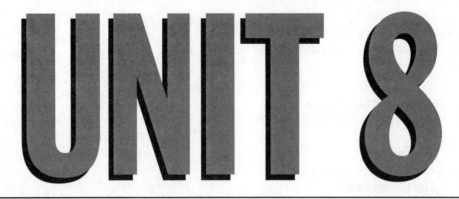

Past Simple (2) – Time expressions – Ordinals and dates

Introduction to the unit

This is the second unit on the Past Simple tense, and it provides further practice and reinforcement of the input in Unit 7, focusing particularly on the negative. The title of this unit is 'Did you know that?'. There are various texts along the lines of how things began, so the topics lend themselves to practice of the Past Simple. There is a picture story which can be exploited to practise both speaking and writing. The main listening exercise is a jigsaw activity, where students listen to two people talking about how they met their husband/wife. This is one of the first extensive listening exercises where students do not have the support of the written word.

Language aims

Grammar

Past Simple (2)

See the introduction to the Past Simple and problems associated with it on page 50 of the Teacher's Book. There is considerable practice of the positive in this unit, but there is also much emphasis on question forms and negatives. These present few problems of concept, but there can inevitably be mistakes of form.

Common mistakes

*When you went home?
*When did you went home?
*Where did go Peter?
*I no went out last night.

ago

Ago is an adverb which is used when the point of reference is the present. It means 'before now', and is used only with past tenses, not present tenses or present perfect tenses. *Ago* always comes after an expression of time.
Different languages realize this concept in various ways.

two years ago – *il y a deux ans* (French)
– *vor zwei Jahren* (German)
– *hace dos años* (Spanish)
– *due anni fa* (Italian)

Common mistakes

*I went there ago two weeks.
*I went there before two weeks.
*My cat died for two years.

Time expressions

The second presentation focuses on preposition and noun collocations, such as *on Monday* and *in winter*. These prepositions cause a lot of confusion and simply have to be learnt – there are no rules!

Vocabulary

There is quite a lot of vocabulary input throughout the unit. The first part of the vocabulary section is an 'odd one out' exercise which revises vocabulary from the unit as well as preparing students for the listening exercise *How we met*. There is also further work on word stress and phonetic script.

Everyday English

This section introduces and practises ordinals and dates.

Problems

The main problem that students face with ordinals is pronunciation. The sound /θ/ always causes difficulty, and there are a lot of consonant clusters, for example, *sixth* /sɪksθ/, *twelfth* /twelfθ/. In rapid speech, sounds are often dropped, for example /twelθ/ instead of /twelfθ/ and /fɪθ/ instead of /fɪfθ/.

Saying dates also causes problems of form. We can begin with the month (*April the third*) or the date (*the third of April*), but in both cases we need to add *the*, which is never written, and in the latter case we need to add *of*, which is also never written.

Note that in American English, *3/8/93* means the eighth of March 1993, whereas in British English it means the third of August 1993.

Workbook

In the vocabulary section, the words for various machines and inventions are introduced. Compounds such as *somebody*, *anybody*, *somewhere*, *anywhere* are introduced and practised.
In the writing section there is further work on linking words, and students are invited to write about their best friend.

Notes on the unit

PRESENTATION (1) **(SB page 54)**

Negatives and *ago*

Note

You will need to pre-teach the word *century*, and you might want to pre-teach *ago*. You could ask questions such as the following and feed in *ago*:

When was your last English lesson? (On Tuesday.)
How many days ago was that? (Two days ago.)
When did you last have a holiday? (In June.)
How many months ago was that? (Five months ago.)
When did you last go to the cinema? (Last Friday.)
How many days ago was that? (Five days ago.)

You could then highlight and explain *ago* (see Language aims on page 58). Translation might help.

1 Ask students what century it is now. They might know the words *nineteenth* and *twentieth* or they might not. Avoid teaching ordinals at this point, as this would distract from the main aim, and they are introduced in the Everyday English section at the end of this unit.

Ask students the other three questions.

2 Students look at the photographs and put a verb under each photograph.

Answers

One hundred years ago, did people …
1 drive cars?
2 ride bikes?
3 watch TV?
4 take photographs?
5 travel by train?
6 travel by plane?
7 make telephone calls?
8 use typewriters?
9 listen to records?
10 wear jeans?
11 write with ball-point pens?
12 eat hamburgers?

3 Model the example question yourself, and get lots of repetition practice. Then practise the question and the three sample answers in open pairs. Do the same for six of the photographs and ask students to ask and answer questions about the remaining six in closed pairs.

4 Students give you their opinions about what people did and didn't do one hundred years ago.

5 Tell students the correct dates. You can expect some disagreement from students, as there is no universal agreement on when or where some of these activities first took place. Also, there is a big difference between, say, the invention of the car and when they were generally available.

Answers

The first cars were in 1893. A Benz went at 18 miles an hour.
The first bikes were in Paris in 1865.
The first television was in 1926.
The first camera was in 1826.
The first train was in 1829.
The first plane was in 1907. The first flight across the Channel was in 1909.
The first phone was in 1876.
The first typewriter was in 1867.
The first record player was in 1878.
The first jeans were in 1850, made by Levi Strauss.
The first ball-point pens were in 1938.
The first hamburgers were in 1885.

● Grammar question

Look at the Grammar question as a class.

Answer

To form the negative in the Past Simple, we use the auxiliary verb <u>*did*</u> + <u>*not*</u> and the <u>*infinitive*</u> (without *to*).

Practice (SB page 55)

1 Reading and listening

1 Ask students to look at the three photos and say what they can see. Students read the three texts, checking new words in their dictionaries. The following words will probably be new:

chef /ʃef/ sailors recipe /resɪpɪ/ transmitted produced

Ask students to try to find three mistakes in each text. This is quite difficult, and made even more so as students are concentrating on understanding the text itself. You could read aloud the first text about the hamburger down to *first hamburgers in 1985* and ask students if they can find a mistake. They should realize from the Presentation on page 54 that the date is wrong. Then let students read the texts in silence. They discuss in pairs to try and decide what facts could be mistakes. They aren't expected to have the answers, of course, apart from the dates given in the Presentation.

2 **T 42** Students listen, correct the mistakes, and see whether they identified any correctly. You could either play the tape all the way through, or stop it after each text. Ask students to make a negative and a positive sentence, and drill them around the room. Be careful with contrastive stress:

He didn't make the first hamburgers in nineteen eighty-five.

He made them in eighteen ninety-five.

Answers
He didn't make the first hamburgers in 1985. He made them in 1895.
Teachers didn't like them. Students liked them.
His son doesn't still sell them. His grandson sells them.
The first television picture wasn't in 1825. It was in 1925.
The first thing on television wasn't a cat. It was a boy.
He didn't send pictures to Paris in 1928. He sent them to New York.
He didn't make the first ball-point pen in 1838. He made it in 1938.
The American Army didn't buy them. The British Army bought them.
The shop didn't sell ten on one day. It sold ten thousand.

You could ask different students to read aloud the texts with the correct information, and correct any pronunciation mistakes.

2 Listening and pronunciation

Note
You will need to photocopy the lists of incredible information on page 130 of the Teacher's Book. They are repeated to help you save paper.

1 **T 43** Students read and listen to the conversations. Make sure they understand *spaghetti*, *really*, *incredible*, *true*, *afraid*, and *believe*. Draw their attention to the wide voice range of the second speaker as he/she expresses incredulity. Practise the conversations in open pairs, and really encourage students to sound surprised!

2 Check students understand the following vocabulary:
painting *alive* *actress* *millionaire*
spell (past tense *spelled*) *snow* *marijuana*
wall *voice*

Take care also with the pronunciation of the following words:
van Gogh (in British English) /væn gɒf/
spelled /speld/
Sahara Desert /səhɑ:rə dezət/
Louis /lu:ɪ/
marijuana /mærɪjʊɑ:nə/

Also, point out how we say kings and queens in English. (Students might not understand Roman numerals.)
King Louis the fourteenth
King Henry the eighth
King Francis the first

Give out the lists of incredible information. Do the first couple as an example. Remember that students will have difficulty in selecting the correct short answer (*wasn't*, *didn't*), so you might want to go through them as a class first. On the other hand, you might decide that as a teacher you can't do everything at once! If students produce a good, wide voice range, and enjoy doing the exercise, maybe that's enough! (This is primarily a pronunciation exercise.)

Sample answers

Did you know that Vincent van Gogh sold only two of his paintings while he was alive?
Really (etc.)? He didn't! I don't believe it (etc.)!

Did you know that the actress Shirley Temple was a millionaire before she was ten?
She wasn't!

Did you know that Shakespeare spelled his name in eleven different ways?
He didn't!

Did you know that in 1979 it snowed in the Sahara Desert?
It didn't!

Did you know that King Louis XIV of France had a bath only three times in his life?
He didn't!

Did you know the American President George Washington grew marijuana in his garden?
He didn't!

Did you know that it took 1,700 years to build the Great Wall of China?
It didn't!

Did you know King Henry VIII of England had six wives?
He didn't!

Did you know that Walt Disney used his own voice for the character of Mickey Mouse?
He didn't!

Did you know that Shakespeare and the Spanish novelist Cervantes both died on the same day, 23 April 1616?
They didn't!

Did you know that King Francis I of France bought the painting *The Mona Lisa* to put in his bathroom?
He didn't!

Did you know when Shakespeare was alive, there were no actresses, only male actors?
There weren't!

Additional material

Workbook Unit 8
Exercises 1–4 Past Simple, regular and irregular
Exercise 5 Past time expressions
Exercise 6 *ago*

PRESENTATION (2) (SB page 56)

Time expressions

Ask students to identify the correct preposition for the time expressions. Some they will know, some will be new. If mistake follows mistake, you can expect some frustration, and possibly amusement, from students. Give them these rules to help:

on + day/date
in + year/season
at + time

This leaves only *at weekends* and *in the evening* to learn.

Answers

in the twentieth century	*on* Christmas Day
in 1924	*on* Saturday
in winter	*on* Sunday evening
in September	*in* the evening
on 10 October	*at* seven o'clock
at weekends	

Practice (SB page 56)

1 Grammar and speaking

Students ask and answer questions with *when*, and answer the questions in the two different ways. Do this first as a class in open pairs. Make sure that the questions are well formed, and that the voice starts high. Only the students know the answers, but again, make sure there are no mistakes of grammar or pronunciation.

2 Listening and speaking

1 Students check the past tense forms of the irregular verbs. They can look at the list of irregular verbs in Appendix 1 on page 127. Check students understand the verb *break into*, meaning to go into someone's house or car without permission, usually to steal something. It's probably not a good idea, however, to explain multi-word verbs at this stage!

Answers
break (into) – broke (into)
steal – stole
eat – ate /et/
drink – drank
feel – felt
fall – fell
wake (up) – woke (up)

2 **T 44** Students look at the pictures and listen to the tape. They then complete the sentences with verbs from the box orally in pairs.

If you think your students will need more help, you can put the following words and phrases on the board haphazardly, including the verbs too (in brackets), if you think it's necessary. These will help weaker students to complete the sentences.

(drank) both bottles	(woke up)	four policemen
asleep the fridge	in Paris	morning
(saw) two bottles of	around his	(stole) two pictures
(broke into)	(went into the)	(ate) all the cheese
(and saw some)	sleepy	a rest

To get feedback, you can elicit a sentence at a time, model and drill it, and every now and again ask a student to retell the story from the beginning.

Alternative approach
You can do this exercise as is suggested in the Student's Book, or you can simply use the pictures for a straightforward narrative build. The aim of a narrative build is for students to speak at length, not simply one sentence at a time. Ask students to look at Picture 1, and ask questions. *Who is he? (A burglar) Which country is he in? (France).* Write on the board *On 1 June, 1992, a French burglar … a house … .*

Elicit the first sentence *On 1 June, 1992, a French burglar broke into a house in Paris.*

Drill this sentence around the class to standardize the line. It is very important that all students say the same thing.

Do the same for the next sentence. Write on the board *He … living room and … .*

Elicit the sentence *He went into the living room and stole two pictures.* Drill this sentence too, then ask one or two students to tell the story from the beginning.

Continue like this for the whole story. Students groan when they are asked to retell the story from the beginning, but generally they get a lot of satisfaction from speaking at length in such a simple, non-threatening activity.

You could then play the tape, and ask students to write the story for homework.

3 Students work in pairs to complete the questions about the story.

Answers
a How many pictures *did he steal*?
b What *did he* see *in the fridge*?
c How *many* bottles *of champagne did he drink*?
d Why *did he go* upstairs?
e When *did he wake up*?
f How many *policemen were there around his bed*?

Practise the questions and answers in open pairs.

4 Students write the story in pairs in class or for homework (except they can cheat by copying out the tapescript!).

● VOCABULARY (SB page 57)

Odd one out

The aim of this activity is to revise some words that have come up in the unit, and to pre-teach some words that will come up in the listening exercise *How we met* on page 58.

1 Read the instructions and the example as a class. Translate *odd one out* if you can. It means *the one that is different*.

Students work in pairs to find the words that are different, using their dictionaries.

Answers
Students might decide that they have alternative answers, which is fine if they can justify them!

a *Photograph* is different. All the others are machines.
b *Recipe* /resɪpɪ/ is different. You can eat all the others.
c *Laughed* is different. All the other verbs are irregular. (This is difficult.)
d *Be retired* is different. All the others are about love and relationships.
e *Warm* is different. All the others are colours.
f *War* is different. All the others are people.
g *Voice* is different. All the others are parts of the body.
h *Clock* is different. All the others are periods of time.
i *Hungry* is different. It is physical. All the others are emotions. (Be very careful with this one. Students confuse the pronunciation of *angry* /æŋgrɪ/ and *hungry* /hʌŋgrɪ/, but far more of a problem is the meaning in *nervous*. It is a 'false friend'. A similar word exists in many languages, but with a different meaning, usually 'angry' or 'irritated'. In English, *nervous* expresses how we might feel before an exam, or before going to the dentist, that is, a feeling of fear *before* something happens.)
j *Television* is different. The others are machines for housework.

2 Students work in pairs to put the words in the right column according to their stress.

Note that students often pronounce *married* with three syllables instead of two */mærɪed/. The same is the case with *engaged*, and students find the consonant cluster at the end difficult /ɪngeɪʤd/.

Answers

●••	•●	•●•	●•
photograph	engaged	computer	married
recipe	machine		camera
century			
dishwasher			

Ask students to practise the words as a class, and in closed pairs.

3 Students practise the words in phonetics. Do this first as a class. *Biscuit*, *laughed*, *angry*, and *hungry* often cause problems.

Answers

a bread	c laughed	e hair	g angry
b biscuit	d war	f married	h hungry

4 Students work in pairs to put one of the words from Exercise 1 (not necessarily the odd ones out) into each gap.

Answers

a My American cousin was a *soldier/pilot* in the Vietnam war.
b My daughter doesn't like parties because she's very *shy*.
c He took a lovely *photograph* of the baby.
d They *laughed* when I told them the joke.
e Can I have that *recipe* for chocolate cake? It was wonderful.
f I *spoke* to our neighbour, Mrs Jones, today. She said she was fine.
g She's a very good singer. She has a beautiful *voice*.
h 'How did you feel before the exam?'
'Very *nervous* .'
j I broke my father's camera yesterday. He was very *angry*.

● LISTENING AND SPEAKING (SB page 58)

How we met

Note

This is one of the first extensive listening exercises in *Headway Elementary* where students are not encouraged to read and listen at the same time. They have to listen to the tape only. Students often find listening to tapes very difficult for the obvious reason that they have no visual support. They cannot see the speakers, or their lips.

However, there are several pre-listening tasks, and students are guided to comprehension via the questions. This is a jigsaw activity (you need two tape recorders and preferably two rooms), so they only hear one of the people speaking. It is therefore quite short. At the end of the activity you could play both of the people talking if students are interested in hearing the other person, too.

Pre-listening task

1 Students work in pairs to put the sentences in order. Ask for some feedback. You will probably get lots of different ideas!

Note that *they got married* means the same as *they were married*. The former is more common. You will probably have to explain that *to go out with someone* means to be with someone as boyfriend or girlfriend in a relationship.

Sample answers

1 Jane and Roger met at a party.
2 He liked her before she liked him.
3 They went out together for a long time.
4 They fell in love.
5 They wrote love letters.
6 They got married.
7 They have two children.

2 Discuss these questions as a class. The discussion could go on for a long time.

3 Students look at the photos of the couples and answer the questions. You will probably have to introduce the word *disc jockey*.

Answers

Oliver and Wendy look about thirty. He's a disc jockey. Trevor and Astrid look about forty. They work in a baker's shop.

4 Students check the new verbs in their dictionary, and find the past tense.

Answers

hear	*heard*	smile	*smiled*	forget	*forgot*
think	*thought*	ring	*rang*	speak	*spoke*
wait	*waited*	tell	*told*	laugh	*laughed*

Listening

T45 Divide students into two groups. Group A listens to Wendy Mint, group B listens to Trevor Richards.
You could ask students to listen first and say if the sentences in Pre-listening task Exercise 1 are true or false.

Answers

Wendy Mint
They got married. True.
They fell in love. True.
They met at a party. False.
He liked her before she liked him. False.
They have two children. False.
They went out together for a long time. False.
They wrote love letters. We don't know.

Trevor Richards
They got married. True.
They fell in love. True.
They met at a party. False.
He liked her before she liked him. True.
They have two children. False.
They went out together for a long time. False.
They wrote love letters. True.

Comprehension check

Students answer the questions about their couple.

Answers

Wendy and Oliver Mint

a They met five years ago.
b She was in the bath and she heard his voice on the radio. She phoned the radio station and spoke to him. He invited her to an Italian restaurant, and they met there the next evening.
c He's a disc jockey.
d Yes, he was when she first spoke to him, but they first *met* in a restaurant.
e She liked his voice.
f They probably are, but we don't exactly know.
g Wendy says that she is usually quite shy.
h Wendy talks about a restaurant because that is where they met for the first time.
i One month later.
j We don't know, but probably not.
k Yes, a baby boy.

Astrid and Trevor Richards

a In the summer of 1976.
b Astrid came into Trevor's baker's shop to buy some sandwiches.
c He's a baker.
d Yes, he was.
e He liked the way she smiled, the way she laughed, and he liked her blue eyes.
f No, she is Swedish.
g He says that he is usually shy.
h Trevor talks about a cake, because when she came back into his shop, he wrote *I love you* on it, and gave it to her.
i In 1978.
j Yes, they do.
k Yes, they have three children.

Speaking

1 Students find a partner from the other group. They tell each other about their person using the Comprehension Check answers as prompts. Ask for some feedback.

2 Tell your students that you are going to ask one or two students to roleplay being Oliver or Astrid. Let students alone or in pairs think about one of the characters first to prepare. If you can, ask the boys/men to imagine they are Oliver, and similarly the girls/women to imagine they are Astrid. Then one or two can tell the class their story from their character's point of view. The rest of the class can ask them questions for more details and the student roleplaying must answer in character.

Additional material

Workbook Unit 8
Exercise 7 This is a gap-fill and comprehension exercise on the same theme of *How we met*.

● EVERYDAY ENGLISH (SB page 59)

1 Ordinals

1 Students work in pairs to put the correct ordinal next to the numbers.

Answers

1st	first	13th	thirteenth
2nd	second	16th	sixteenth
3rd	third	17th	seventeenth
4th	fourth	20th	twentieth
5th	fifth	21st	twenty-first
6th	sixth	30th	thirtieth
10th	tenth	31st	thirty-first
12th	twelfth		

T 46a Students listen and practise saying the ordinals. Stop the tape after each one and drill them around the class, correcting carefully.

2 Students ask and answer questions about the months of the year. You don't need to let this one go on for very long.

2 Dates

Read the Caution Box as a class.

1 Students practise saying the dates. Do this as a class. Correct mistakes very carefully.

Students often have a lot of difficulties saying dates, for the reasons explained on page 58/9 of the Teacher's Book.

T 46b Students listen and check.

2 **T 46c** Students listen and write down the dates they hear. Let them check in pairs before you give the answers.

Answers
a 4 January
b 7 May, 1922
c 30 August, 1965
d 13 October
e 2 June
f 23 April, 1564
23 April, 1616

3 Students work in pairs to answer the questions about dates.

Answers
(We can only give some of the answers.)
c 25 December.
d 14 February.
e It is always on a Sunday towards the end of March.
f July 4.

GRAMMAR SUMMARY (SB page 59)

Read the Grammar Summary as a class. Encourage students to ask any questions.

Don't forget!

Workbook Unit 8
Exercise 8 A vocabulary exercise on different inventions
Exercise 9 This exercise introduces words such as *somewhere*, *somebody*, *something*.
Exercises 10 and 11 There is a further exercise on linking words, *because*, *when*, and *until*. Students are invited to write about their best friend.

Word List
Remind your students of the Word List at the back of their book. Ask them to look at the list for this unit on page 125. Tell them that they could write in the translations, learn them at home and/or write some of the words in their vocabulary notebooks.

Pronunciation Book Unit 8

Video
There are two video sections that can supplement Units 7 and 8 of the Student's Book.
Report (Section 6) is about Shakespeare (if you haven't already played it whilst doing Unit 7). It is a mini-documentary about his life and his plays.
Situation (Section 7) is set in a pub. Students practise the names of drinks, and buying drinks in an English pub.

EXTRA IDEAS UNITS 5–8

On page 131/2 of the Teacher's Book there are two additional activities: a reading text and a song. If you have time and feel that your students would benefit from them, you can photocopy them and use them in class. The reading exercise revises Units 5–8 and could also be done for homework. Activities to exploit the reading are provided, and the answers are below.

You will find the song after Unit 8 on the Class Cassette. You could exploit the song by blanking out some of the words and asking students to listen and fill in the gaps. Alternatively, as the song includes the Past Simple, you could blank out those verbs that they already know and put the verbs jumbled up on the board in the infinitive. Then students can fill in the blanks with the correct verb in its Past Simple form, before listening to the song to check their answers.

Answers to the reading

3 a He can remember the day of any date in any year, and the teams and the scores of every football match in every World Cup.
  b He remembered the order of thirty-five packs of playing cards.
  c No, he wasn't. He couldn't remember his lessons.
  d They said he was stupid.
  e Four years ago. He saw a programme on TV which showed people how to improve their memory.
  f Because he can remember every card.
  g Seven.
  h Three. The other four clubs knew him and didn't want him to play.
  i (No set answer)

4 a What day was April 21, 1876?
  b When did he become world champion?
  c How much can he earn a day on European TV programmes?
  d What does his wife do?
  e How much did he win?
  f What does he like doing in his free time?

5 a He remembered the order of 35 packs of cards.
  b Dominic is 34 years old.
  c He won £1,000 a night (as a professional gambler).
  d He went to 7 clubs (with the interviewers).
  e He had £1,250 in his pocket.
  f Children can learn to improve their memory from the age of five.

STOP AND CHECK UNITS 5–8

There is a Stop and Check revision section after each quarter of the Student's Book. The idea is that your students pause to check their progress so far. Each test is out of 100. There is a Stop and Check Answer Key on page 141 of the Teacher's Book.
You could set it in class as an informal progress test or you could use the following procedure.

1 Give your students the Stop and Check to do for homework, preferably when they have more time, such as at the weekend.

2 In the next lesson ask them to go over their answers in small groups, trying to agree on the right answer. Allow enough time for this. It can be very productive for students to try and persuade their peers of the right answer. Many previous lessons are recalled.

3 Go over it with the whole class, reminding students of the language items covered.

After all the group discussion everyone *should* have a reasonably high score!

UNIT 9

like and *would like* – *some/any* – In a hotel

Introduction to the unit

Unit 9 marks the beginning of the second part of the book. The theme of this unit is 'Food and drink', which lends itself to the presentation and practice of the target items. The verb *like* is contrasted with *would like*, and the determiners *some* and *any* are re-examined with both countable and uncountable nouns (in Unit 5 they were introduced with countable nouns only). There is a reading text about meals in Britain, and an invitation to discuss eating habits in different countries.

Language aims

Grammar

like and *would like*

Would like is introduced for the first time, and this is the first time that students have seen the modal verb *would*. It is easy for students to confuse these two forms. Here are some common mistakes.

*Do you like a coffee?
*I like a cup of tea, please.
Are you hungry? *You like a sandwich?

It is relatively easy for students to perceive the difference between a general expression of liking and a specific request, but you can expect many mistakes for a long time as students confuse the two forms, especially the two auxiliary verbs *do* and *would*.

some/any

Some and *any* were first introduced in Unit 5, but only with countable nouns. This unit sees their introduction with uncountable nouns as well.
The often-repeated rule that *some* is used in positive sentences and *any* in questions and negatives is not entirely true, but it's still useful at this level. However in this unit the use of *some* in requests and offers is also introduced. It is quite a subtle concept for students to grasp that *some* can be used in questions when there is no doubt about the existence of the thing requested or offered. The use of L1 might help to clarify this.
As in Unit 5, we do not suggest that you explore the use of *any* to mean *it doesn't matter which*, as in *Take any book you want*.

Vocabulary

There is quite a heavy vocabulary load in this unit, largely to do with food and drink. For this reason the Vocabulary section revises vocabulary (by means of a word search), and doesn't add any new words.
Words to do with food and drink are introduced in Presentation (1). Shops and things to buy are presented in Practice 1 on page 65, and there is more lexis to do with food in the reading text on page 66.

Everyday English

The requests *Could you ...?* and *Could I ...?* are introduced and practised in a hotel situation.

Workbook

There are exercises on *How much ...?* and *How many ...?*
In the Vocabulary section, there is an exercise on adjective + noun collocations (*medium steak*), and a menu to introduce further vocabulary to do with food.
In the writing section, formal and informal letters are compared and contrasted, and students are invited to write a letter to a hotel.

Notes on the Unit

PRESENTATION (1) (SB page 62)

like and *would like* – *some*

Note
It would save classroom time if you set the vocabulary in the picture on page 62 for homework prior to the lesson. Encourage your students to enter the words in their vocabulary notebooks. All the words are illustrated in the picture.

1 The aim of Exercises 1 and 2 in this Presentation are to revise *like*, but more especially to reinforce the idea of *like* to express an 'all time' preference, in preparation for the presentation of *would like* in Exercise 3, which expresses a preference/request at a specific time.

Students look at the lists of food and drink, and say what they like and don't like. This is probably best done as a class discussion. You might want to feed in *I quite like ...* for those items where students feel neutral about something. Correct mistakes of pronunciation carefully.

2 **T 47** Students listen to the children and tick (or write down) the things they both like. (Students often like listening to children's voices for some reason!) Make sure students understand *cereal* before they listen.

Answers
They both like milk, bread, ice-cream, chocolate, fruit, and hamburgers. (One likes bananas with milk and sugar, the other thinks bananas are OK.)

After students have listened, ask if they can remember what the children said to express that they liked something or didn't like it! The answers are the exclamations *Yummy!* and *Yuk!*. Ask what children say in other languages.

Ask the class if they can remember any of the other things the children said. You could also ask them to look at the tapescripts and practise some of the lines.

● Grammar questions

Look at the Grammar questions as a class. Don't hurry this part. Allow students time to think. If one student knows and wants to give the answer before the others have had time to think, ask him or her to wait a little.

Answers
- There is no *-s* on rice because we cannot count rice. There is an *-s* on apples because we can count them.
- We cannot count the things in list A, but we can count the things in list B. (You might want to feed in the terms countable and uncountable nouns.)

3 **T 48** Students look at the pictures and listen to the conversations.

● Grammar question

Look at the Grammar question as a class. The two questions *Which sentences are about all time?* and *Which sentences are about now?* are intended to guide students to the answer. For some students, this presentation will have been the first time they have encountered the modal auxiliary verb *would*, in which case they will probably not be able to answer the Grammar question. Be prepared to explain! Use L1 if you can.

Answer
I like hamburgers and *Do you like apple juice?* are about all time. *I'd like a hamburger, please* and *Would you like some apple juice?* are about now.

If you have a strong class, you could explore the difference between *hamburgers* (plural and no article because it's a general statement about a countable noun) and *a hamburger* (singular and *a* because it is a specific request), and *apple juice* (singular because it's uncountable, and no article because it's a general statement) and *some apple juice* (*some* because *apple juice* is uncountable).

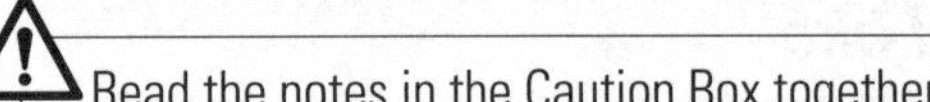
Read the notes in the Caution Box together.

4 Students practise the dialogues in Exercise 3 and make similar dialogues. You could record their dialogues and play them back for intensive correction. Pay attention to all aspects of pronunciation – sounds, stress, and intonation.

Practice (SB page 63)

1 Grammar

Students work in pairs or small groups to choose the correct sentence. Read the instructions and the example as a class.

Answers
a Do you like your teacher?
b Would you like a drink?
c Yes. I'd like a packet of cigarettes, please.
d Well, I like swimming very much.
e Yes. I'd like a steak, please.

2 Listening

T 49a Students listen to what A says and choose the correct answer for B. Let students listen and discuss their answers in pairs, then play the tape again.

Answers
1 b 2 b 3 a 4 b 5 b 6 a

T 49b Students listen and check their answers.

3 Vocabulary

The aim of this exercise is not so much the introduction of new lexis, but practice of *a* and *some* through vocabulary.

1 Students work in pairs to write *a* or *some* before the nouns. If they have broadly understood the presentation up to this point, they shouldn't have too many problems with this exercise. Conversely, if they have difficulty, they haven't grasped the concept of countable versus uncountable nouns!

Answers
a a book
b some air
c some rice
d a mushroom
e some music
f some rain
g some ice
h a kiss
i some bacon
j some money
k a five-pound note
l some fruit

2 Students work in pairs to write *a*, *an*, or *some*. The aim of this exercise is to show that some nouns (here *cake* and *ice-cream*) can be both countable and uncountable.

Answers
a a flower
b some flowers
c a grape
d some grapes
e a cake
f some cake
g an ice-cream
h some ice-cream

Additional material

Workbook Unit 9
Exercises 1–3 *like*
Exercises 6 and 7 *would like*

PRESENTATION (2) **(SB page 64)**

some/any

The aim of this presentation is to show *some* and *any* with both countable and uncountable nouns.

1 Read the instructions and look carefully at the examples. Note that we use the forms of *have* as a full verb, not *have got*, so be careful not to slip into using *have got*. Students look at the picture. Make sure they understand *bacon*, *yoghurt*, *potatoes*, *sausages*, *mushrooms*, *tomatoes*. Students make positive and negative sentences. Do this as a class, giving clear models yourself, and asking students to repeat. Correct mistakes carefully, and pay attention to the weak *some* /səm/.

2 Before students work in pairs to ask and answer questions, practise the question, and point out the use of *any* in the question. You might consider this exercise a little more challenging for students if you ask them to close their books, so they have to remember the picture. Either one student at a time can close his/her book, or you can put all the food as prompts on the board so that both students keep their books closed.

3 **T 50** Students listen to the conversation in the shop, and tick what the man buys. The conversation is supposed to be funny, so if students laugh they are probably understanding it!

Answers
orange juice ✔
potatoes ✔
milk
pizza
coffee ✔
apples
bread
cheese

He doesn't buy …
… milk because the shop keeper sold the last bottle a few minutes ago.
… pizza because the shop keeper doesn't have pizza on Thursdays.
… apples because the shop keeper doesn't sell them.
… bread because there isn't any.
… cheese because the shop keeper doesn't sell it.

The conversation is meant for gist understanding only, but if you want to look more closely at the language you could play the tape again, and ask students to look at the tapescript.

Practice (SB page 65)

1 Speaking

Ask students to look at the price lists. Either ask them to check any new words in their dictionary, or go through them as a class. Give the students some pronunciation practice of the words and the prices. Highlight the pronunciation of *soap* /səʊp/, which students often confuse with *soup*, and the stress on the second syllable of *shampoo*.

Roleplay
Students work in pairs and take it in turns to be a shop assistant and a customer using the price lists. You could ask some of the pairs to act out their dialogues.

2 Questions and answers

1 Students work in pairs to complete the questions using *much* or *many*. The word *petrol* might be new.

Answers
a How *many* people are there in the room?
b How *much* money do you have in your pocket?
c How *many* cigarettes do you smoke a day?
d How *much* petrol is there in the car?
e How *many* potatoes do you want?
f How *many* eggs do you want?
g How *much* beer is there in the fridge?

2 Students choose an answer for each question in Exercise 1. The words *dozen* and *can* might be new.

Answers
a Twenty. Nine men and eleven women.
b Three pounds fifty p.
c A packet of twenty.
d It's full.
e A kilo.
f Half a dozen.
g There are six cans.

3 Correcting the mistakes

Students work in pairs to find the mistakes.

Answers
a I don't like ice-cream.
b Can I have some bread, please?
c I'm hungry. I'd like a sandwich.
d Would you like a cup of coffee?
e I'm thirsty. Can I have a drink?
f I'd like some fruit, please.
g How much money do you have?

Additional material

Workbook Unit 9
Exercises 4 and 5 Countable and uncountable nouns
Exercise 8 *some* and *any*
Exercise 9 *How much/many ...?*

● READING AND LISTENING (SB page 66)

Meals in Britain

Note
You might want to set some vocabulary for homework prior to this lesson.

instant coffee	disgusting	roll (bread)
snack	main (meal)	meat
beef	lamb	pork
vegetable	gravy	juice

Pre-reading task

1 Have a discussion with the whole class and talk about the three questions. This could go on for a long time!

2 Read the instructions. If you think your students will be happy thinking of some questions to ask, they can work in pairs. If you think they won't have many ideas, you might like to do this as a class, giving prompts yourself, and writing the questions on the board:

Examples
Do they often go to restaurants?
Where do they have lunch?
What do they have for lunch?

Reading

Look at the pictures on page 66 of the Student's Book. Ask students to tell you what they can see.

Students read the text and match a photograph with each paragraph. Let students read silently. They can check their answers in pairs. Then ask for some feedback. If there is some disagreement, ask students to justify their decisions, but don't give the answers yet.

Answers
Paragraph 1 – Breakfast, bottom right
Paragraph 2 – sandwich bar, bottom left
Paragraph 3 – afternoon tea, top right
Paragraph 4 – evening meal, centre right
Paragraph 5 – Sunday lunch, centre left
Paragraph 6 – Chinese food, Indian and Italian takeaways, top left.

You could read the text aloud to the class, and ask them to read at the same time. Ask check questions to make sure the vocabulary is understood.

Comprehension check

1 Ask for answers to the questions you wrote on the board in the Pre-reading task.

2 Students work in pairs to answer the true/false questions. Ask for feedback.

Answers
- a False. Many people have a small breakfast.
- b True.
- c True.
- d False. They drink it with cold milk.
- e False. They hate it.
- f False. Some people have sandwiches.
- g True.
- h False. They eat their evening meal between 6.00 and 8.00.
- i True.
- j True.

Listening

T 51 Students listen to the six short conversations, and match each conversation with one of the pictures. What is the relationship between the people?
This exercise is for gist comprehension, so the idea is not that students should understand every word.

Answers
- a Two friends./Afternoon tea.
- b Shopkeeper and customer./Sandwich bar.
- c A mother and her son and daughter./Breakfast.
- d A waiter in an Indian restaurant and a customer./ Takeaway food.
- e A mother, father, their daughter, and son./Evening meal.
- f The same family with the grandmother./Sunday lunch.

If students seem interested, you could play the tape again with students reading the tapescript.

Speaking and writing

Exercises 1 and 2 could provide some interesting discussion, especially in a multilingual class, or if you have some students who have travelled to other countries.
Exercise 3 can be done for homework. When you correct this, don't correct too harshly. The idea is to give students an opportunity for some freer writing, and they will inevitably make a lot of mistakes.

● VOCABULARY (SB page 67)

Food

Students work in pairs to find the words in the word search. All the items have appeared before, mainly in this unit.

Answers

L	C	Y	P	N	C	R	I	S	P	S	M
A	V	Z	O	B	P	B	A	N	A	N	A
M	U	S	T	E	A	K	N	B	T	R	R
B	Z	Q	A	M	O	Y	R	Y	J	A	M
K	G	F	T	G	H	O	D	F	G	H	A
B	A	C	O	N	F	G	R	A	P	E	L
H	J	K	F	I	S	H	T	Y	U	I	A
H	O	N	E	Y	B	U	B	R	E	A	D
R	A	S	D	F	G	R	Z	K	L	P	E
I	B	V	E	G	E	T	A	B	L	E	I
C	Z	X	C	V	B	N	M	L	P	G	J
E	W	E	C	E	R	E	A	L	B	G	U

Students could make a word search of their own using words connected with drinks. This could be done for homework.

Additional material

Workbook Unit 9

Exercises 10 and 11 More language connected with food and restaurants.

EVERYDAY ENGLISH (SB page 67)

In a hotel

Note

This exercise introduces *Could I ...?* and *Could you ...?* for the first time. If you think your students will not be familiar with it, present it yourself, perhaps using the classroom to illustrate meaning:

Jean, could you open the window, please? Maria, could you clean the board, please? Emma, could I borrow your dictionary, please? etc. Then elicit *could* from the students.

Point out that although *could* looks like the past tense, the concept is in fact present. If you think your students would benefit and understand, you could tell them that *Can I ...?* and *Could I ...?* mean the same, but *could* is usually more polite.

However, if you think your class is strong enough, you could use the hotel dialogue as a vehicle for presentation.

You could begin this exercise by asking students if they stay in a hotel when they go on holiday or business, and whether they like hotels or not.
You need to pre-teach or check some vocabulary items before you begin this exercise or you can elicit some vocabulary to do with hotels, if students are false beginners and/or well-travelled:

single/double room	stay (in a hotel)
shower	credit card
sign *(v)*	signature
register	luggage

1 Students read the conversation in a hotel in pairs and put the lines in the right order.

Read the information in the Caution Box as a class.

T 52 Students listen and check their answers.

Answers

1 Good evening. Can I help you?
2 Yes, please. Could I have a room for the night?
3 Certainly. A single room or a double?
4 Single, please.
5 Would you like a room with a shower or a bath?
6 A shower. How much is the room?
7 £72 for the room and breakfast. Would you like an evening meal?
8 No, thanks. Just breakfast. Can I pay by credit card?
9 Yes, of course. We take Visa and Access. Could you sign the register, please?
10 Yes, sure. Do you want my address, too?
11 No. Just a signature. Do you have any luggage?
12 Just this one bag.
13 Here's your key. Your room number is 311. I hope you enjoy your stay.
14 Thanks.

2 Students look at the tapescript and practise the conversation in pairs. Go round, monitor, and correct pronunciation mistakes.

3 Students look at the requests and complete them, using *Could I ...?* or *Could you ...?*

Answers

In the restaurant
Could I have the menu, please?
Could you give me the bill?
Could I have some coffee, please?

In the bedroom
Could I have breakfast in my room, please?
Could you clean my shirts, please?
Could you wake me up at 7.00 tomorrow morning?

At the reception desk
Could I/Could you change some traveller's cheques?
Could you recommend a good restaurant?

4 Students work in pairs to make up and practise some conversations in a hotel using the language from the unit. These could be acted out for the rest of the class.

GRAMMAR SUMMARY

Read the Grammar Summary together in class, and/or ask your students to read it and study the grammar at home. Encourage them to ask you questions about it.

Don't forget!

Workbook Unit 9
Exercise 12 Formal and informal letters. Students are invited to write a letter to a hotel.

Word List
Remind your students of the Word List at the back of their book. Ask them to look at the list for this unit on page 125. Tell them that they could write in the translations, learn them at home, and/or write some of the words in their vocabulary notebooks.

Pronunciation Book Unit 9

UNIT 10

Comparatives and superlatives – *have got* – Directions (2)

Introduction to the unit

This unit is unusual in that it has three presentation sections, each one revising the grammar of the one before.
The theme of the unit is describing places: towns, the countryside, and houses. These are useful contexts to practise comparatives and superlatives. We have deferred the introduction of *have got* until this unit (see **Note** in Unit 3, page 18) and introduce it in a direct comparison with *have* (for possession), which students are already familiar with.
The skills section includes a jigsaw reading about two capital cities in Eastern Europe, Prague and Budapest, and provides further opportunity to practise the grammatical aims of the unit.

Language aims

Grammar

Comparative and superlative adjectives

The following aspects of comparatives and superlatives are introduced:

- the use of *-er/-est* with short adjectives, such as *cheap, cheaper, cheapest.*
- the use of *-ier/-iest* with adjectives that end in *-y*, such as *noisy, noisier, noisiest.*
- the use of *more/most* with longer adjectives, such as *more expensive, most expensive*.
- irregular adjectives such as *good, better, best.*

The presentation of these is staged. In the first presentation pairs of opposite adjectives are revised/introduced and this leads to the introduction of comparative forms. These forms are then revised in the second presentation when *have got* is introduced. Finally superlatives are introduced in the third presentation and at the same time comparatives and *have got* are revised.
Students usually experience little difficulty with the concept of comparatives and superlatives but experience more difficulty in producing and pronouncing the forms because of all the different parts involved. One common problem is that utterances sound very laboured and unnatural because equal stress is given to each word and syllable. For this reason we include pronunciation drills to practise natural sounding connected speech.

Common mistakes
*She's more tall than me.
*He's the most tall student in the class.
*She's taller that me.
*He's tallest student in the class.

have got

The verb *have* for possession was introduced in Unit 3. We purposely have delayed the introduction of *have got* for possession until now because of the complications of production it causes if introduced alongside the Present Simple of *have*, particularly in the question and negative. (See the **Note** in the Language Aims of Unit 3, page 18).
In this unit there are many exercises that contrast *have* and *have got.*

Vocabulary and pronunciation

Pairs of opposite adjectives are introduced as part of the presentation.
In the vocabulary section town and country words are introduced. These are partly in preparation for the reading texts.
The silent *r* in words such as *farm* and *theatre* is highlighted in the pronunciation section and there is further practice in recognizing phonetic script.

Everyday English

There is further practice of getting and giving directions, and prepositions of movement such as *along* and *down* are introduced.

Workbook

Indefinite pronouns such as *everybody*, *nobody*, *everything* are practised.

In the vocabulary section compound nouns to do with towns are introduced such as *traffic lights*, *town centre*, *department store*.

The writing syllabus includes work on relative pronouns. Then students study a model text about London before being guided to write a short piece about their own capital city.

Notes on the unit

PRESENTATION (1) (SB page 69)

Comparative adjectives

1 You could set this (and perhaps the next) exercise for homework if you need to save class time. If you do, begin the lesson by going through it and practising the pronunciation of each word. Otherwise put your students into pairs to do the exercise and then check through it as a class.

Be prepared for students to want to pronounce *interesting* with four syllables, */ɪntɜ:restɪŋ/ and make sure they say it more naturally, /ɪntrəstɪŋ/, with three syllables.

Note
In these pairs of words the opposite of *old* is *modern* (it could also be *new*) not *young*, because in the context of the presentation the adjectives are being used to talk about buildings not people.

Answers

fast	/fɑ:st/	slow	/sləʊ/
small	/smɔ:l/	big	/bɪg/
clean	/kli:n/	dirty	/dɜ:tɪ/
safe	/seɪf/	dangerous	/deɪndʒərəs/
quiet	/kwaɪət/	noisy	/nɔɪzɪ/
old	/əʊld/	modern	/mɒdən/
healthy	/helθɪ/	unhealthy	/ʌnhelθɪ/
friendly	/frendlɪ/	unfriendly	/ʌnfrendlɪ/
interesting	/ɪntrəstɪŋ/	boring	/bɔ:rɪŋ/
expensive	/ɪkspensɪf/	cheap	/tʃi:p/
good	/gʊd/	bad	/bæd/

2 Ask the whole class for feedback on this. You could put the headings *CITY* and *COUNTRY* on the blackboard and write in your students' suggestions as to which adjectives belong where, or you could ask individual students to come up to the board to write in the suggestions themselves. Be prepared for some debate and discussion as there are obviously no prescribed right answers. A lot is to do with personal opinion and experience. Welcome any freer speaking that results.

3 Here you hit the main aim of this section, the grammar! So make it clear to your class that this is an important moment and that this is the structure in English that compares things. If necessary and possible use translation to do this.

Ask them to look at the chart and to work in pairs to make sentences from it. (You may need to point out the use of *more* with longer adjectives, and that *better* is the irregular comparative of *good*, but don't go into the rules too heavily at this stage. They are dealt with more fully later on.)

At this stage don't worry too much about pronunciation as long as they understand the meaning of the structure, just let them try to produce sentences that express their opinions. Get some feedback from the whole class.

4 **T 53** Now is the moment to concentrate on the pronunciation. Play the tape and ask your students to compare their ideas about town and country life with those on the tape.

Ask your students to look at the two examples in the book and say them in chorus either using yourself or the tape as a model. Focus particularly on the /ə/ sound at the end of the comparative and in the pronunciation of *than* /ðən/. Isolate the two words and drill them together as connected speech:

cheaper than	/tʃi:pəðən/
noisier than	/nɔɪzɪəðən/

Drill the other sentences from the tape or by saying them yourself. If necessary, break up the sentences to drill them, particularly the comparative forms + *than.* Try to get a natural 'flow' in the repetition of the sentences as on the tape.

● Grammar question

This is to reinforce and make clear to your students the rules governing the formation of comparative adjectives. Read the grammar question aloud to the class and ask them to try to formulate any rules they can. They may have got a clear idea from doing Exercise 3 or they may need a bit of prompting and guiding, but try not to just give them the rules. You could write the rules up on the blackboard as you go along.

Answers
-er is used with short adjectives such as *cheap, cheaper*.
-ier with adjectives that end in *y* such as *noisy, noisier.*
more is used with longer adjectives such as *more expensive.*
some adjectives are irregular, such as *good, better.*

Practice (SB page 70)

1 Using dictionaries

Some dictionary work is integrated into this exercise to point out to students how dictionaries usually show irregular forms.

1 Ask your students to get out their dictionaries and look up the adjectives *big* and *good.* Tell them to work with a partner or in groups of three and check the information given in each dictionary. Does it give the same information as the example in the student's book?

Big is included here because it illustrates the doubling of the consonant in short adjectives with short vowel sounds. You don't need to describe this to them in such full terms, but do check that they have noticed the doubling of the consonant.

2 Ask them to continue working together with their dictionaries. Ask them to turn back to page 69 and write down the comparative forms of all the pairs of opposite adjectives. Some have already been given in part 3 of the presentation on page 69.

Answers

faster	slower
smaller	bigger
cleaner	dirtier
safer	more dangerous
quieter	noisier
older	more modern
healthier	unhealthier (this is the comparative usually given by dictionaries, but *more unhealthy* is also often used.)
friendlier	unfriendlier (this is the comparative usually given by dictionaries, but *more unfriendly* is also often used.)
more interesting	more boring
more expensive	cheaper
better	worse

Go round and check as they do it. Then go through the exercise with the whole class. Highlight the two irregulars *better* and *worse,* particularly *bad–worse,* because this is the first time students have met this irregular form and they need it for subsequent activities.

3 After all the writing and pairwork this is better done quickly as an oral activity with the whole class. Ask individuals to give their opinion about town and country life using the new comparative adjectives they have written down in part 2 of this exercise.

2 Grammar and listening

This exercise is also good for stress and intonation practice. Put the conversations in a context and tell your students that two people are discussing different cities that they know.

Note
In this exercise we bring in the use of *much* to emphasize comparatives. The students are only asked to recognize it at first, and not produce it until later.

Do the example with your students to illustrate the activity. Then ask them to work in pairs to complete the conversations. Point out that the students have to fill in the opposite adjectives in B's comments to those A uses.

T 54 Play the tape for them to check their answers but also tell them to listen to the pronunciation, particularly the stress and intonation.

Answers

a A The country is *quieter than* the city.
B Yes, that's true. The city is much *noisier.*

b A New York is *safer than* London.
B No, it isn't. New York is much *more dangerous.*

c A The streets of New York are *cleaner than* the streets of Paris.
B No, they aren't. They're much *dirtier.*

d A Paris is *bigger than* Madrid.
B No, it isn't. It's much *smaller.*

e A Madrid is *more expensive than* Rome.
B No, it isn't. Madrid is much *cheaper.*

f A The buildings in Rome are *more modern than* the buildings in New York.
B No, they aren't. They're much *older.*

g A The Underground in London is *better than* the Metro in Paris.
B No, it isn't! The Underground is much *worse.*

To practise the conversations first get individual students to address each other across the class in open pairs. Encourage the Bs to sound really indignant when they disagree with A. Give them exaggerated models yourself or play the tape again to make clear that you want them to produce good stress and intonation and connected speech:

Examples

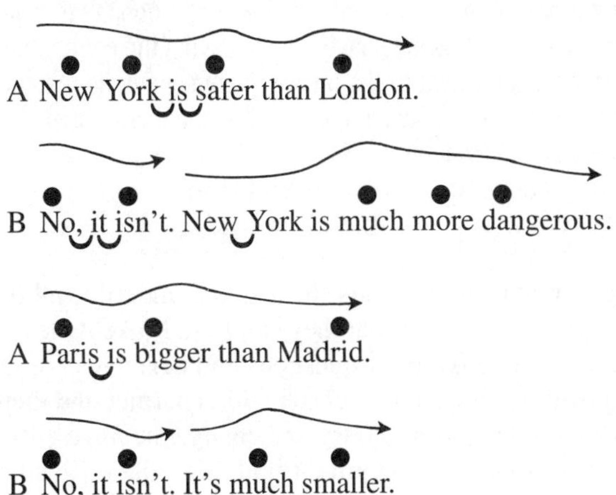
A New York is safer than London.
B No, it isn't. New York is much more dangerous.
A Paris is bigger than Madrid.
B No, it isn't. It's much smaller.

You could personalize the activity at this stage by asking students in a monolingual class to compare towns in their country, or asking students in a multilingual class to compare other cities that they know.

Additional material

Workbook Unit 10
Exercises 1–3 These are homework activities to consolidate the work on the comparatives.

PRESENTATION (2) (SB page 70)

have got

In this presentation comparatives are revised and *have got* is introduced in the context of a telephone conversation where someone has moved from the city to the country.
Read the introduction about Amy and Fran aloud to the class to set the scene. You could ask your students *Why do you think Amy left London?*

1 **T 55** Ask them to listen to and read the telephone conversation. For the moment don't focus on the examples of *have got* in the text. Tell them that many of the adjectives are missing from the conversation but ask them *not* to fill the gaps yet.

When the tape is finished ask them to work in pairs and see if they can write in the missing adjectives. Make it clear that some of them are comparatives and some are not.

Play the tape again for them to check their answers.

Answer
See the tapescript on page 119 of the Student's Book.

⚠ Now draw your students' attention to *have got*. Read through the Caution Box with them. You will need to highlight the fact that the *have* in *have got* contracts but that it doesn't in *have* for possession. They may have trouble saying the contracted forms, especially next to the following consonant, so practise saying the two examples in the box. You could drill them chorally and individually.

I'*ve* got a house /aɪv gɒt ə haʊs/
He'*s* got a car /hɪz gɒt ə kɑ:/

2 Ask your students to study the text and underline all the examples of *have got* that they can find. Make it clear that they are looking for questions and negatives not just the positive. Ask them to check with a partner and then work with that partner to try and change the *have got* sentences to *have*. They might find this quite difficult so go round and help and check as they do it.

Answers

I'*ve got* a better job here.	I *have* a better job here.
I'*ve got* a house here.	I *have* a house here.
How many bedrooms *has it got*?	How many bedrooms *does it have*?
It'*s got* a garden.	It *has* a garden.
But you *haven't got* any friends!	But you *don't have* any friends.
I'*ve got* a lot of friends here.	I *have* a lot of friends here.
Seaton *has got* shops.	Seaton *has* shops.

Also ask your students to find two examples of *have/have got* in the past.
You *had* a good job in London.
And you *had* a beautiful flat in London.

3 Ask students to work in pairs and take the parts in the dialogue to practise *have got*. You can then ask them to go through the dialogue again and encourage them not to follow the dialogue exactly, but to replace the adjectives with others that are suitable. If they have the confidence, encourage them to improvize completely without their books.

Practice (SB page 71)

1 Grammar

This is a very straightforward transformation exercise designed to focus students' attention solely on the difference in form between *have* and *have got* for possession. It is worth bearing in mind that focusing on the form of *have got* at this stage should help students when they meet the Present Perfect Simple in Unit 14.
We suggest that prior to your students doing this exercise that they and you read through the Grammar Summary on page 76. Tell them that they can use this for reference as they do the exercise. Ask them to do the exercise on their own and then check with a partner, before you conduct a full class feedback. Tell them to write the contracted forms.

Answers
a I've got a lot of homework tonight.
b Have you got any children?
c Our school's got a library, but it hasn't got any computers.
d My friends have got a CD player.
e I haven't got a Walkman.
f Has your house got a garden?

2 Speaking

This roleplay should be a fun (and not very realistic!) activity. Ask your students to look at the pictures of the king and queen. Ask *What have kings and queens got?* (Getting a few suggestions from the whole class at this stage will be a warmer for the activity.)

Possible answers
palaces
castles
cars
horses
crowns
rings
servants
money

Ask your students to work in pairs, if possible male/female pairs so that one can be queen and the other king. Ask them to think of imaginary names for their countries. (Fairytale names such as Muldavia and Gotalottia can increase the fun with some classes!) Encourage exaggerated stress and intonation as they boast about their possessions! Do the example in the Student's Book first with yourself giving the first line and then in open pairs to illustrate the kind of stress and intonation you want.

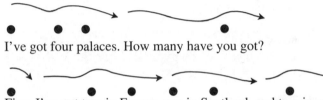

I've got four palaces. How many have you got?

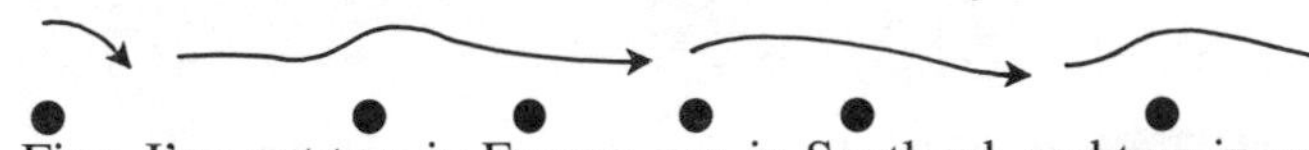

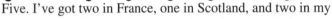

Five. I've got two in France, one in Scotland, and two in my

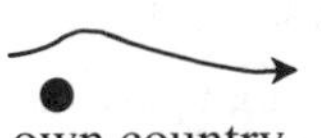

own country.

Give out the rolecards on page 133 of the Teacher's Book and go round the class checking grammar and pronunciation. Only correct where absolutely necessary, in order to encourage fluency. Then get feedback as to who is the richer! (The Queen is.)

Additional material

Workbook Unit 10
Exercises 4–6 These give further practice of *have got*.
Exercise 7 This brings together comparatives and *have got*.

PRESENTATION (3) (SB page 71)

Superlative adjectives

This presentation of superlative adjectives includes revision of comparatives and *have got*.

1 Ask students to look at the pictures of the houses and tell you which they like and why. Here they could be revising *have got*, but don't insist on this, the main aim here is to generate interest in the theme and to take in some of the information about the houses.

Do the examples with the whole class, pointing out the superlative example *the cheapest* but briefly at this stage. Put them into pairs to do the true/false exercise.

Notes

1 This exercise has been specially designed so that *all* the true sentences contain examples of superlative adjectives, thereby providing a means of highlighting the new structure. The false sentences contain examples of comparatives and *have got*.
2 You will have to draw attention to *the* in this construction. It is common for students to omit this.
3 You will have to point out that the superlative *the farthest* is irregular, and the adjective is *far*. (We have purposely avoided using *the furthest*, as we do not want to overload the students. Do not be tempted to include it at this stage! *Farthest* is interchangeable with *furthest* and is more regular.)
4 Either during or at the end of the exercise you will have to draw students' attention to the prepositions in sentences *i* and *j*: *the nearest* ***to***, and *the farthest* ***from***.

Answers

a True.
b False. Seaview is older than Park House/Park House is more modern than Seaview.
c True.
d True.
e False. Park House is bigger than Rose Cottage/Rose cottage is smaller than Park House.
f False. Seaview has got a garage.
g False. Park House has got a smaller garden than Rose cottage/Rose Cottage has got a bigger garden than Park House.
h True.
i True.
j True.

Check through the answers with the whole class and move immediately to the Grammar questions.

● Grammar questions **(SB page 72)**

Ask your class what they notice about all the true sentences. Read out the questions and ask your students to try and supply the rules. Write them up on the board as they do this. Do give them some prompting and guidance if they need it to discover the rules.

Answers

- *the -est* is used with short adjectives such as *cheap, (cheaper), the cheapest.*
- *the most* is used with longer adjectives such as *expensive, (more expensive), the most expensive.*
- some adjectives are irregular, such as *far, (farther) the farthest; good, (better), the best; bad, (worse), the worst.*

You should also use the opportunity to remind them of the comparative forms and write these on the board too, as above.

2 **T 56** This is simply a listen and repeat drill so that your students can practise getting their tongues round the different components of superlative sentences.

Practice **(SB page 72)**

1 Writing and speaking

1 This is a very simple exercise that revises questions needed for part 2 of the activity. Tell your students that each line represents one word. Ask them to fill in the questions on their own and then to check their answers with a partner before you conduct a full class feedback.

Answers

a How much *does it cost*?
b How old *is it*?
c How many bedrooms *has it got*?
d *Has* it *got/does* it *have a* garden?
e How big *is it*?
f How far *is it* from the sea/town centre?

2 Your students should be making use of the questions they have just revised in part 1 of this exercise, but they must also be encouraged to ask further questions (Yes/No questions) themselves about *all* the houses to get practice of the superlative. Make this clear by doing the example in their books first, with you asking the questions and following each question from part 1 with a superlative question. (You could tell them that they should try to *remember* the information on the previous page, and then they can turn to the page to check that they have remembered correctly. In this case they may need to use *I think* in their replies. Encourage them to do it as a memory test only if you feel they can handle it alongside the other practice.)

Sample questions and answers

How old is Rose Cottage?	It's very old.
Is it the oldest?	Yes, (I think) it is.
Is it the cheapest?	No, I don't think so.
Is it near the sea?	Yes, it's very near.
Has it got the biggest garden?	No, it hasn't.
Is it the nearest house to the sea?	Yes, it is.

Go round the class and help and check them as they do the activity. Round it off by asking three pairs to ask questions about a different one of the houses in front of the whole group.

2 Grammar and listening

At last we move away from the houses to different contexts! This is another activity which integrates pronunciation work on stress and intonation.

1 Illustrate the activity by reading aloud the example to them. Then ask students to work on their own to complete the sentences.

Answers

Look at the tapescript on page 119 of the Student's Book.

T 57a Play the tape and ask your students to check their answers. Also tell them to listen carefully to the rhythm/stress and intonation of the sentences.

2 **T 57b** Now ask them to close their books and play the first lines again, pausing after each one so that your students can produce the reply. You could do this in chorus with the whole class, or ask individuals to respond, or mix the two approaches.

Really work hard to encourage good (probably exaggerated) stress and intonation in the replies, with the main stress on the superlative adjective.

Student(s): Yes, it's the oldest house in the village.

Yes, it's the most expensive hotel in London.

The more you work on the stress and intonation the more fun the activity becomes!

3 Speaking

This is a freer speaking activity. It probably will not go on too long.
You could put some words on the blackboard to prompt comparative and superlative sentences: *tall/small; old/young; lives near to school/lives far from school; has a big bag*, etc.
Read the examples with students, then put them into small groups and ask them to look round the room and make sentences about the other students. Then get feedback where the whole class offers comments about each other.

4 Choosing the correct sentence

This exercise brings together all the grammar of the unit. See page 5 of the Teacher's Book for an explanation of this exercise type.
Ask students to work in pairs or small groups to choose the correct sentence. Ask them to work quite quickly, then conduct a full class feedback on which are the correct answers. Try to get students to correct each other and explain any mistakes they hear.

Answers
1 b 2 a 3 b 4 a 5 a 6 a 7 b 8 a

Note
You could read the Grammar Summary on page 76 at this point. Ask students to study it as part of their homework.

Additional material

Workbook Unit 10
Exercises 8–10 These practise comparatives and superlatives together.

● VOCABULARY AND PRONUNCIATION

(SB page 73)

Town and country words

This activity focuses on words related to the theme of the unit, but more particularly it introduces items of vocabulary needed for the following reading texts.

1 Ask students to look at the pictures and the words in the box. Ask them to work in pairs and see how many pictures and words they can match. They can use their dictionaries to help with new words and/or they can ask you about words they don't know. Then ask them to put the words into the correct columns.

Answers

Town	Country	Both
traffic lights	hills	statue (You can find statues in villages and towns.)
factory	farm	bridge (There are rivers in towns and countryside.)
tall buildings	field	swimming pool
pollution	lake	car park
theatre	mountains	river bank
underground	fresh air	
tram	woods	
concert hall	village	
	cottage	

Go through the columns with the whole class. Ask individuals to read out what they have in their columns and see if the others agree. Be prepared for some debate about such things as *pollution*, *traffic lights*, *lakes* as in some cases these could go in the **Both** column. Correct pronunciation as you go.

2 Do this quickly with the whole class. Ask for suggestions and when you have established the correct answer and practised saying it, ask them to write the word in the gap.

Answers
a statue
b mountains
c tram
d traffic lights
e cottage
f tall buildings (skyscrapers!)
g concert hall
h pollution

3 Now focus more particularly on the pronunciation. Do this with the whole class. Illustrate the nature of the activity via the examples, then ask individuals to read out the words and the rest of the class to comment on whether the *r* is pronounced or not.

Note
In standard English the *r* is not pronounced in these words. However there are regional variations such as Scottish English and American English, where they *are* pronounced.

Don't worry! If students ask, just state the differences. They often find this an interesting feature of the language.

Answers

traffic	/træfɪk/	✔
underground	/ʌndəgraʊnd/	✘ ✔
bridge	/brɪdʒ/	✔
tram	/træm/	✔
car park	/kɑ: pɑ:k/	✘ ✘
concert	/kɒnsət/	✘
theatre	/θɪətə/	✘
river	/rɪvə/	✔ ✘

T 58a You could play the tape for your students to listen and repeat or you could model the words yourself.

4 Work on pronunciation continues here with a little more practice of phonetic transcription. Always encourage your students to consult the phonetic chart on the inside back cover when they do an exercise like this. Ask them to do it on their own and then check with a partner before you go through it as a class.

Answers
lake mountains buildings statue village cottage

T 58b You could play the tape for your students to listen and repeat or you could model the words yourself. Ask them to look at the phonetic transcription as they repeat.

Additional material

Workbook Unit 10
Exercises 11 This is a vocabulary exercise which introduces and revises compound nouns connected with town life, such as *department store* and *traffic lights.*
Exercises 13 and 14 There are two writing exercises. The first introduces simple relative pronouns. The second provides a model text about London and gives guidance for students to write a similar piece about their own capital city.

● READING AND SPEAKING (SB page 73)

Two capital cities

Note
This activity is a jigsaw reading. This means that it should result in not only reading practice but also some freer speaking as in Unit 6.

The class divides into two groups and each group reads a different but similar text about a capital city and answers the questions. After this students from the different groups get together to exchange information about the city in their text. This means that they should get some speaking practice whilst their main attention is on the completion of the reading task.

The texts are about two Eastern European cities, Prague and Budapest. These were chosen because there has been so much interest and concern world-wide about events in Eastern Europe in recent years. The information comes from travel articles in newspapers but the texts have been simplified and rewritten to include examples of the grammar taught in this and previous units.

Pre-reading task

These questions are to generate some interest in the topic and hopefully provide some motivation to read the texts.

1 and 2 If you have a world map in your classroom, you could begin the lesson by asking your students to gather round it and show you the countries of Eastern Europe.

You could then reverse the order of the two activities, and first ask your students a general question about changes in Eastern Europe in the 1980s and 1990s as they stand around you. Then ask them to sit down and work in pairs to do Exercise 1. Get feedback as a class.

The main change in all these Eastern European countries is that they have all recently become democracies after being ruled by Communist dictatorships for so long.

Answers
Budapest – Hungary
Sofia – Bulgaria
Prague – The Czech Republic. (Prague was the capital of Czechoslovakia until 1992, when it split into two parts: the Czech Republic and Slovakia. Bratislava is the capital of Slovakia.)
Warsaw – Poland
Bucharest – Romania
Tirana – Albania

Reading

Ask everyone to look at the photographs. Then divide the class into two groups. Tell Group A to read about Budapest and Group B to read about Prague. Allow dictionaries to be used to check new words. Each group has the same questions to answer.

Comprehension check

When they have read the texts, they could either go through the questions on their own and then check with others from the same group, or work with a partner from the same group to answer the questions. The main idea of these questions is to check understanding, therefore short answers are perfectly acceptable.

Answers
Group A – Budapest
1 (see the captions)
2 Over two million people.
3 The River Danube.
4 Six.
5 In 1873 (when Buda and Pest joined).
6 They took control in 1945 after World War II. They lost control in 1989.
7 In 1956. They pulled down a statue of Stalin, and fought the soldiers.
8 By public transport: by underground, bus, tram, taxi.
9 a go to the theatre ✔
b walk in the woods ✔
c walk around the old town ✔
d travel by tram ✔
e travel by underground ✔
f go to a famous music festival ✘
g relax in the spa waters ✔
h see a famous astrological clock ✘

Group B – Prague
1 (see the captions)
2 Over one million people.
3 The River Vltava.
4 Fifteen.
5 In 1918 (when Czechoslovakia became independent).
6 They took control in 1948. They lost control in 1989.
7 In 1968. They fought the soldiers in Wenceslas Square.
8 By underground or on foot/by walking.
9 a go to the theatre ✔
b walk in the woods ✘
c walk around the old town ✔
d travel by tram (?) We don't know.
e travel by underground ✔
f go to a famous music festival ✔
g relax in the spa waters ✘
h see a famous astrological clock ✔

Speaking

1 Tell each student to find a partner from the other group and go through the questions and answers together telling each other about their city.

2 Tell them to read the other text as soon as they have discussed the answers and ask their partner about any new words.

At this point conduct a full class feedback and get answers about both cities, encouraging your students to elaborate on the answers a little and compare the cities as you go. This way you might get some freer use of comparatives and *have got*, but don't force this, just be pleased if it happens! The aim of this feedback is to encourage some fluency practice.

You could end the session by asking *Are there any problems in countries in Eastern Europe now?*

● EVERYDAY ENGLISH (SB page 75)

Directions (2)

1 **T 59a** The listening and the pictures provide the context for the introduction of prepositions of movement.

Establish that your students understand what a *driving lesson* is. Ask *Who can drive? Did you have driving lessons? Do you remember your driving test?*

Then ask them to look at the pictures and play the tape of Robert talking about his driving lesson. Tell them *not* to write at this stage, just to listen, especially for the prepositions he uses. These are all in the box above the pictures.

After playing, ask your students to write the prepositions in the gaps and check their answers with a partner. Play the tape again so they can make a final check.

Answers
Robert drove *out of* the garage, *along* the road and *under* the bridge.
Then he drove *past* the pub, *up* the hill and *down* the hill.
Next he drove *over* the river, *through* the hedge, and *into* the lake!

On the tape Robert uses a few expressions that show his distress at the driving lesson. (See tapescript on page 119). When you ask students to retell the story from the pictures it can be fun to ask them to pretend to be Robert and encourage them to include some of the other things he says, rather than just read out the third person description in the book. This gives better practice of natural stress and intonation. Ask one or two members of the class to do this for the others.

2 **T59b** Ask students to look at the map and find Louisa's school. Play the tape and tell them to mark with a pencil (or a finger) the directions she gives to get to her house from school.

Now ask them to work with a partner to fill the gaps. Play the tape again for a final check.

Answers
Go *out of* the school and turn *left*. Walk *along* Station Road *past* the railway station and the *bank*. Turn *left again* at the *traffic lights* and walk *over* the *bridge* and *up* the *hill*. Turn right *into* Park Avenue. My house is the *first* on the left. It's number *fifty*. It takes ten minutes.

3 You could launch this pairwork by giving some directions yourself to a few places near your school and ask students to call out when they think they know the answer. Go round and help and check as they do it.

GRAMMAR SUMMARY (SB page 76)

Read the Grammar Summary together in class (if you haven't already done this before), and/or ask your students to read it and *learn* the grammar at home.
Encourage them to ask you questions about it.

Don't forget

Workbook Unit 10
Exercise 12 There is an exercise that introduces *everybody*, *nobody*, etc.

Word List
Remind your students of the Word List at the back of their book. Ask them to look at the list for this unit on page 125. Tell them that they could write in the translations, learn them at home and/or write some of the words in their vocabulary notebooks.

Pronunciation Book Unit 10

Video
There are two video sections that can supplement Units 9 and 10 of the Student's Book.
Report (Section 8) *Tea*. This is a mini-documentary about the history of tea and its importance to the British people, in the past and present.
Situation (Section 9) *The Phone Box*. This is a short situation where Paola phones British Airways to book her flight home.

UNIT 11

Present Continuous – *Whose … ? It's mine.* – In a clothes shop

Introduction to the unit

This is the first unit where students encounter the Present Continuous. The Present Simple was introduced and practised much earlier in *Headway Elementary* because it is far more frequently used, but by this stage of the course students should be ready to compare and contrast the two present tenses.
The theme of this unit is 'describing people', and there is a lot of related vocabulary input. There is a song, *Wonderful tonight*, by Eric Clapton.

Language aims

Grammar

Present Continuous

In this unit, we aim to teach the Present Continuous as though the present participle were just another adjective used after the verb *to be*, for example,
She's tall, *pretty*, *hungry* → *She's working*, *cooking*, *thinking*.

Problems
The Present Continuous has no equivalent form in many other languages, which use the present tense to convey the two concepts of 'action which relates to all time' and 'activity happening now'. For example, in French, *il fume dix cigarettes par jour* (he smokes ten cigarettes a day) and *il fume en ce moment* (he is smoking now), the present tense *fume* expresses both ideas.

Students not only confuse the two concepts of the Present Simple and the Present Continuous, they also confuse the forms. When they have seen the *am/is/are* in the Present Continuous, they tend to try to use it in the Present Simple.

Common mistakes
*She's come from Spain.
*I'm come to school by bus.
*What does he doing?
*Where you going out?
*Does he wearing a suit?

Whose … ? It's mine.

Problems
The question *Whose …?* and possessive pronouns present few problems of concept, but learners do confuse *who's* and *whose*. Possessive pronouns simply have to be learnt.

Vocabulary

There is a lot of vocabulary to do with describing people – colours, clothes, adjectives. There is also an exercise on words that rhyme and further practice of the phonetic script.

Everyday English

Language used in a clothes shop is introduced and practised, as is the use of *will* to express a spontaneous decision.

Workbook

The Present Simple and the Present Continuous are further compared and contrasted. The spelling rules for the present participle are presented.
In the vocabulary section, some names for parts of the body are taught. In the writing section, there is more work on linking words, and students are invited to write about two members of their family.

Notes on the unit

PRESENTATION (1) (SB page 77)

Present Continuous

Note
It would save classroom time if you set the vocabulary in Exercises 1 and 2 for homework prior to the lesson.

1 Do Exercises 1 and 2 as a class. Ask students to look around the classroom and find things of these colours. You might need to bring in some pictures if you know that certain colours will not be present. Then students try to find the items of clothing. Again, you might need to bring in some pictures. Ask them to make sentences such as *It's a white T-shirt*, *They're black shoes*, but avoid the Present Continuous at this stage. Remember that students find it puzzling to see that *trousers* and *jeans* are plural in English. You could also mention that we use *a pair of* with these plural nouns.

2 Students look at the pictures and make sentences about the people. Make sure they understand the words. Drill some of the sentences around the class. Do the first two parts of this exercise only (*Who's got …?* and *Who's* + adjective).

Sample answers
1 Isabel's got long brown hair.
2 Becky's got short blond hair. She's good-looking.
3 Amy's got fair hair.
4 John's quite tall and slim. He's good-looking.
5 Emma's got blue eyes. She's pretty.
6 Stacey's got short black hair and brown eyes.
7 Michael's got a moustache. He's handsome.
8 Len isn't very tall.
* You could explain the difference between *good-looking* (general), *handsome* (for men), and *pretty* (for girls/women).

Now look at *Who is smiling? Who is wearing glasses?*, etc. as a class. Again, make sure that students understand the vocabulary. Don't ask them yet to produce sentences containing the Present Continuous – first let them recognize the tense only. Accept answers that are just the name of the person/people.

Sample answers
1 Michael is smiling.
2 Isabel is wearing glasses.
3 Peter is writing.
4 Jack is standing up.
5 Amy is cooking.
6 Jack is holding a dog.
7 Becky is wearing earrings.
8 Peter is sitting down.

Read the information in the Caution Box very carefully. Point out the formation of the negative.

Note
We tell students how the Present Continuous tense is formed and what it means because we don't expect them to know the answers. If you think your class will already have some understanding of this tense, you could make grammar questions to ask them.

What is the name of this tense?
How do you make it?
Is it the same as the Present Simple?

You could put sentences on the board to explore together.

She comes from Spain.	She's wearing jeans.
He works in a bank.	He's smiling.
They speak French.	They're cooking.
I like music.	I'm writing.

Finally, you could ask students to name the two tenses.

So far, students have not produced any sentences containing the Present Continuous. This is because it is important that they understand what it means first. Now is the time to practise it! Look at the sentence at the end of Exercise 2, *Emma's smiling*. Provide a model of this yourself, then drill it. Do the same for one or two more people, using the third person singular only, then invite students to make some sentences of their own, again using only the third person singular.
Now do the same for the third person plural with the sentence *They're standing up*. Now ask students to work in pairs to make two or three sentences about the people.
Jack's got blue eyes and grey hair. He isn't very tall. He's holding a dog.

3

Note
We do not have exercises that specifically practise the negative, inverted question, *wh-* question, or short forms of the Present Continuous. This is because we have introduced it as an extension of the verb *to be*. You might decide that your class would benefit from such isolated practice before moving on to Exercise 3 on page 78. However try not to be so 'thorough' that you slow down the lesson too much.

Do this exercise first as a class so that you can drill the question forms and correct any mistakes. Make sure that students are clear what Yes/No questions are. Ask a student to think of someone in the room, and ask a few questions yourself. Drill these questions. When you feel students are ready, ask them to work in pairs.

Practice (SB page 78)

1 Listening and writing

T60 This aims to practise the difference between the two present tenses, first in a recognition exercise, then in a productive one. Pre-teach, or check that students know, the following vocabulary items.

musician *art gallery* *rich* *cigar* *film producer*

Read the instructions. Students listen and identify the people.

Answers
From left to right: Paul, Kathy, Suzie, Alex, Laura and Ellie.

Ask students to look at the sentences in the Present Continuous and the Present Simple. Do the first sentences about Paul as a class, then ask students to work in pairs to complete the others. Play the tape again to check before you provide the answers.

Answers

	Present Continuous	Present Simple
Paul	He's sitting at the table. *He's talking* to Kathy.	*He works* in LA.
Kathy	*She's wearing a red and white* T-shirt.	*She lives in a beautiful* house.
Suzie	*She's drinking some* wine.	*She writes* books.
Alex	*He's smoking* a cigar.	*He travels all over the* world.
Laura & Ellie	*They're eating* crisps.	*They go to St Mary's* School.

Extra idea
You might want to get some further practice of the two present tenses from this exercise. You could ask questions such as the following:

Where is Paul sitting?
Where does he work?
What is Kathy wearing?
Where does she live?
What is Suzie drinking?
What does she write?
What is Alex smoking?
Where does he travel?
What are Laura and Ellie eating?
What school do they go to?

You could begin by asking a few questions yourself, and then encourage students to ask and answer the other questions in open and/or closed pairs.

2 Grammar

1 Students work in pairs to put the verbs into the Present Continuous tense.

Answers
a Oh, no! It*'s raining*. What a pity!
b I*'m reading* a very good book at the moment.
c We*'re drinking* champagne because it's our wedding anniversary.
d I*'m working* hard because we have exams next week.
e 'What*'s* Peter *doing* on the floor?' 'He*'s looking* for his glasses.'
f 'Why *are* you *running*?' 'Because I*'m going* to a party and I'm late.'
g The photocopier *isn't working*. Phone the engineer.
h I*'m not doing* any more work. I'm tired.

2 You could do this exercise as a class first, as it is quite challenging. Students can then repeat it in pairs.

Answers
a He's a pilot.
b Yes, he is.
c She's an actress.
d No, she isn't.
e She's drinking champagne.
f She's an air stewardess.
g She's serving drinks.
h He's a footballer.
i No, he isn't.
j He's eating.

3 Speaking

You will need to photocopy the pictures on page 134 of the Teacher's Book, enough for half of the class to have picture A and the other half to have picture B. Students should be familiar with such information gap activities by now, but still be careful with instructions. Use L1 if necessary. You could set the activity up by doing one or two examples with them first.
You may need to give students some vocabulary before the exercise, or, if the class is small enough, let them ask you for words when the need arises. (That way you won't give away clues as to what may be missing or different in the pictures beforehand!)

Answers

The ten differences in the pictures:

A	B
Around one table, three people are having a drink.	There are four people.
They are drinking coffee.	They are drinking Coke.
In the pool, two boys are swimming.	Two girls are swimming.
A waiter is carrying out a tray of drinks.	There is no waiter.
There is no man.	A man is diving into the pool.
Three people are sunbathing.	Two people are sunbathing.
There is no gardener.	A gardener is working in the garden.
A man is sitting at another table. He is wearing trousers.	He is wearing shorts.
A woman is sitting at another table. She is reading a book.	She is reading a newspaper.
There is no man or shower.	There is a shower near the pool. A man is having a shower.

Additional material

Workbook Unit 11

Exercises 1–5 Present Continuous

Exercises 6–10 Present Continuous and Present Simple

PRESENTATION (2) (SB page 79)

Whose ...? It's mine.

Note

You might choose to introduce these items yourself and use the coursebook material for further practice and consolidation.

You could use the situation of the classroom for presentation. Take some personal possessions from the students and put them on the floor where everyone can see them. Hold something up and ask *Whose is this? Is it Pedro's? Is it Maria's?* The aim is to convey the concept of possession.

You could use the board and write up the question *Whose is this?*, pointing out that *whose* is not the same as *who's*. Then hold up a possession of your own, and ask *Whose is this?* Teach *It's mine*. Write this on the board. If you can translate the item, do so. Then do the same for the other possessive pronouns, *yours*, *his*, *hers*, *ours*, and *theirs*. You could go to the coursebook for further practice.

1 Read the instructions as a class, and look at the example. Students work in pairs to put a word from the box into each gap.

T 61 Students listen and check their answers.

Answers

a Excuse me! Is this your ball?
No, it isn't mine. It's *his*.

b Is this *yours?*
No, it isn't *mine*. It's *hers*.

c Excuse me! Is this your ball?
No, it isn't *mine*. I think it's *theirs*.

d Hello. Is this yours?
No, it isn't *ours*. It's the dog's!

2 Students ask and answer questions about the things in the picture.

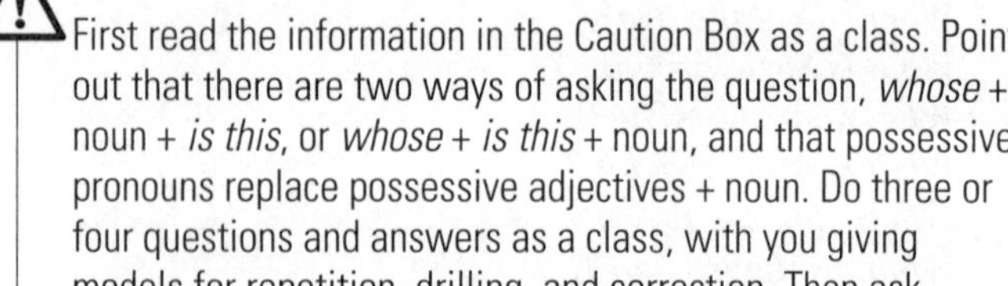

First read the information in the Caution Box as a class. Point out that there are two ways of asking the question, *whose* + noun + *is this*, or *whose* + *is this* + noun, and that possessive pronouns replace possessive adjectives + noun. Do three or four questions and answers as a class, with you giving models for repetition, drilling, and correction. Then ask students to work in pairs.

Answers	
Whose is the/this dog?	It's theirs.
Whose is the/this Walkman?	It's hers.
Whose is the/this T-shirt?	It's hers.
Whose is the/this hat?	It's his.
Whose are the/these crisps?	They're his.
Whose is the/this radio?	It's theirs.
Whose are the/these sunglasses?	They're hers.
Whose is the/this bike?	It's his.

Practice (SB page 80)

1 Grammar

1 Students work in pairs to choose the correct word.

Answers

a Our, theirs	e mine, yours
b their, ours	f Who's
c My, hers	g my
d Her, mine	h Who's

2 **T62** Read the instructions. Students shout out 1 if they think the word is *Whose ...?* and 2 if they think it is *Who's ...?* This is not an easy exercise, so take it slowly, and if a lot of students find it difficult, don't hesitate to explain and clarify.

Answers

a 2 b 2 c 1 d 2 e 1 f 1 g 2 h 2

You might like to play the tape again with students looking at the tapescript.

2 Speaking

Note

This exercise introduces the use of the Present Continuous to refer to arrangements in the near future. You might decide that this use merits a full presentation from you, but you could also decide to downplay it. Students are introduced to the *going to* future in Unit 12. The area of future forms and the concepts that they express in English is very complex, and we do not suggest that you explore it at this level.

It is not such a leap for students to be told that the Present Continuous can be used to describe activities happening in the near future, even though in their own language this concept may be expressed by the equivalent of the Present Simple. You can also mention that to express an arrangement in the near future, the Present Continuous usually needs a future time reference, e.g. *I'm doing my homework (now)* versus *I'm doing my homework tonight.*

1 Read the conversation as a class.

⚠ Read the information in the Caution Box as a class. Use L1 to translate and explain if you can.

2 Students work in pairs to make similar dialogues. Do the first couple as an example with the whole class. It can be good fun to practise the intonation of an exasperated person tidying up!

Answers

a Whose are these football boots?
They're John's.
What are they doing here?
He's playing football later.

b Whose are these ballet shoes?
They're Mary's.
What are they doing here?
She's going dancing tonight.

c Whose is this suitcase?
It's mine.
What's it doing here?
I'm going on holiday tomorrow.

d Whose is this coat?
It's Jane's.
What's it doing here?
She's going for a walk soon.

e Whose is this plane ticket?
It's Jo's.
What's it doing here?
She's flying to Rome this afternoon.

f Whose are all these glasses?
They're ours.
What are they doing here?
We're having a party tonight.

3 Correcting the mistakes

Students work in pairs to correct the mistakes.

Answers

a Alice is tall and she's got long, black *hair.*
b James is *quite* old, about sixty-five.
c I'm wearing jeans.
d Look at Roger. He*'s standing* next to Jeremy.
e He *works* in a bank. He's the manager.
f What *'s Suzie* drinking?
g I*'m not working* any more. I'm tired.
h Where *are* you going tonight?
i What *are you doing* after school today?

Additional material

Workbook Unit 11
Exercises 11 and 12 *Whose ...?* and possessive pronouns

● VOCABULARY AND PRONUNCIATION

(SB page 80)

Words that rhyme

Note
You could do this exercise as it is in the book, or you could put the words in their columns on the board and ask students to do the exercise in pairs or small groups. This makes a nice warmer to do at the beginning of a lesson, as the whole class is focused on the board, and students don't have their 'noses' in the book.

1 The aim of this exercise is to show students once again that English spelling is not phonetic, and so the same sound can be spelled in different ways. Most or all of the vocabulary should be known, but check that students understand it.

Students find the different pronunciations of the spelling *ea* difficult.

steak /eɪ/
head /e/
meat /i:/
wear /ɜə/
heart /a:/
near /ɪə/

The following words often cause problems, too.
lamb (silent *b*)
half (silent *l*)
soap (confused with *soup*)
suit (students often say *sweet*)

Students work in pairs or small groups to match the words that rhyme. Do one or two as a class as an example. Again the pronunciation in the book and on the cassette recording are based on English RP. If, as a native speaker teacher, your accent differs (and some of the pairs don't rhyme for you) then you can point this out to your students.

T63 Students listen and check their answers.

Answers

A and **B**		**C** and **D**		**E** and **F**	
bread	head	soap	hope	meat	feet
steak	wake	when	again	dead	said
lamb	ham	near	beer	hair	wear
lose	shoes	suit	boot	war	door
sign	wine	wait	late	ball	Paul
half	laugh	heart	part	list	kissed

Ask students to practise the words. Do this first as a class so that you can monitor pronunciation. Correct mistakes very carefully! Then students can practise the words again in pairs.

2 Students write one of the words according to the vowel sound. Check first that they know the symbols. They can use the chart at the back of the book. Note that the symbols are in three groups – single sounds, long sounds, and diphthongs.

Answers

a	/e/	bread	head	when	again	dead	said
b	/ɪ/	list	kissed				
c	/æ/	lamb	ham				
d	/a:/	half	laugh	heart	part		
e	/i:/	meat	feet				
f	/ɔ:/	war	ball	door	Paul		
g	/u:/	lose	shoes	suit	boot		
h	/aɪ/	sign	wine				
i	/ɪə/	near	beer				
j	/eɪ/	steak	wake	wait	late		
k	/eə/	hair	wear				
l	/əʊ/	soap	hope				

● LISTENING (SB page 81)

Wonderful tonight

Pre-listening task

Note
You might want to start this activity as suggested with a discussion about going to a party, or you might want to ask your students what they know about Eric Clapton. He is a very famous English blues musician. He sings, composes, and plays the guitar. He has been married once, to Patti Boyd. This song was written for Patti, now his ex-wife, whom he says he still loves. His young son died in a tragic accident a few years ago when he fell out of a window. Eric has been a drug addict and an alcoholic. He still tours and makes records.

1 Discuss the questions as a class or with students in small groups.

2 Read the instructions as a class. Explain that the song is about a husband and wife going to a party together, how they get ready, and what they do at the party.

Students work in pairs to fill the gaps. They will probably need dictionaries to do this. Let them compare their answers in fours before you play the song.

Listening

1 **T64** Play the song. Students check their words.

Answers

Wonderful tonight

It's late in the *evening*
She's wondering what *clothes* to wear.
She *puts* on her make-up,
Then *brushes* her long *blond* hair.
And then she asks me,
'Do I look *all right*?'
And I say, 'Yes,
You *look* wonderful tonight.'
We go to a party
And *everyone* turns to see
This *beautiful* lady
That's *walking* around with me.
And then she asks me,
'Do you feel all right?'
And I say, 'Yes,
I *feel* wonderful tonight.'
I feel wonderful
Because I see
The love light in your *eyes*.
And the wonder of it all
Is that you just don't realize
How much I *love* you.
It's time to go *home* now
And I've got an aching *head*.
So I give her the *car keys*,
She helps me to bed.
And then I tell her
As I turn out the *light*,
I say, ' My *darling*,
You *were* wonderful tonight.'

2 Students work in pairs to find the mistakes in the summary.

Answers

A husband and wife got ready and went to a party. The party started *in the early evening*. (No. It was late in the evening when she got ready.) He thought she looked very pretty, *but he didn't say anything*. (No. He told her she looked wonderful.)
There were *only two or three other people* at the party. (No. *Everyone* sounds like more than two or three people.) *He was angry with his wife*, (No. He loves her very much, and he thinks she is beautiful.) and *she was worried about him*. (No. She asks if he is all right, but not because she is worried about him.) He loves her very much, but *she doesn't love him*. (No. He sees the *love light* in her eyes.)
At the end of the party he didn't feel very well. *He drove the car home*. (No. She drove home.) *He had another drink before he went to bed*. (No. She helped him to bed.)

● EVERYDAY ENGLISH (SB page 82)

In a clothes shop

Note
The final activity in this section works best if you have some props! Try to bring in some clothes so that students can actually try them on.

1 Students look at the lines of conversations in a clothes shop and decide who says them.

You could perhaps do this as a class so that you can sort out any unknown vocabulary. Point out that *I'm afraid* can also mean *I'm sorry*, as it does in this exercise. This is the first time that students may have come across the modal auxiliary verb *will*.

Answers

Can I try it on?	(C)
Mm, that's nice.	(C)
Medium.	(C)
Can I help you?	(A)
Is it the right size?	(A)
How much is it?	(C)
Have you got something bigger?	(C)
By credit card.	(C)
This one's a bit darker.	(A)
What size are you?	(A)
No, thanks. I'm just looking.	(C)
Yes, the changing rooms are over there.	(A)
Blue.	(C)
Yes, it feels fine.	(C)
It's a bit too big/small/long/short.	(C)
£19.99.	(A)
Yes, I'm looking for a jumper.	(C)
No, I don't like the colour.	(C)
What about this one?	(A)
That's the last we've got, I'm afraid.	(A)
I'll have it, please.	(C)
I'll leave it, thanks.	(C)
What colour are you looking for?	(A)
Thank you. How would you like to pay?	(A)

⚠ Read the information in the Caution Box as a class. You might want to translate *decision* into L1.

Note that this concept is often expressed by a present tense in other languages. Students often want to say **I buy it* or **I have it*, but this is a mistake in English.

2 Students try to match some of the lines.

T65 Students listen and compare what they have with the actual dialogues. They might find other lines that match, so do go through and check their alternatives with them after they have listened to the tape.

Answers

a A Can I help you?
C No, thanks. I'm just looking.

b A Can I help you?
C Yes, I'm looking for a jumper.
A What colour are you looking for?
C Blue.
A What size are you?
C Medium.
A What about this one?
C No, I don't like the colour.
A This one's a bit darker.
C Mm, that's nice.
C Can I try it on?
A Yes, the changing rooms are over there.

c A Is it the right size?
C It's a bit too big.

d A Is it the right size?
C Yes, it feels fine.

e C Have you got something bigger?
A That's the last we've got, I'm afraid.
B I'll leave it, thanks.

f C How much is it?
A £19.99.
C I'll have it, please.
A Thank you. How would you like to pay?
C By credit card.

Students practise the dialogues. They can refer to the tapescripts at the back of the book.

3 Students work in pairs to make similar improvised conversations. Use the props! Some interesting dialogues might ensue!

GRAMMAR SUMMARY **(SB page 82)**

Read the Grammar Summary as a class. Encourage students to ask any questions.

Don't forget!

Workbook Unit 11
Exercise 13 Vocabulary of parts of the body
Exercises 14 and 15 There is a writing exercise on linking words and students are invited to write about two people in their family.

Word List
Remind your students of the Word List at the back of their book. Ask them to look at the list for this unit on page 125. Tell them that they could write in the translations, learn them at home, and/or write some of the words in their vocabulary notebooks.

Pronunciation Book Unit 11

UNIT 12

going to – Infinitive of purpose – Suggestions

Introduction to the unit

The theme of this unit is planning the future. We focus on the *going to* future for plans and intentions. We do not at the same time introduce and contrast the Future Simple with *will* (this rather complex distinction is for a later stage of learning), but in the *Everyday English* section we do introduce *will/shall* for suggestions and offers. The second presentation in the unit is the infinitive of purpose, which is relatively simple to operate in English but is often realized differently in other languages. The skills work includes a reading about Catherine Destivelle, a very famous French mountain climber. This provides opportunities to revise the grammar not only of this unit but also of previous units. It is worth noting that the theme of climbers is taken up in the Headway Elementary Video, where there is a short documentary about two climbers, but they don't climb mountains, they climb buildings!

Language aims

Grammar

going to

The learning of the *going to* future is facilitated by the fact that students already know the present forms of the verb *to be*, both on its own and as part of the Present Continuous, which they met in the previous unit, Unit 11. These are, of course, intrinsic parts of this structure. Also, as this is the first future they have encountered (apart from the Present Continuous with future meaning touched on briefly in Unit 11), the problem of when to use it in relation to other future forms (always an area of difficulty for students) is deferred for the time being, and they can simply concentrate on this one. The two uses of *going to* are introduced in the unit: plans and intentions, such as *I'm going to be a photographer*, and making predictions based on present evidence, such as *It's going to rain./He's going to fall.*

Problems

1 With the verbs *go* and *come* we often avoid using the full *going to* future form, and just use the Present Continuous.

She's going to go to Rome next week → She's going to Rome next week.

2 The Present Continuous can be used for future arrangements and is often interchangeable with the *going to* future.
I'm going to see the doctor tomorrow./I'm seeing the doctor tomorrow.

The infinitive of purpose

The infinitive of purpose answers the question *why* in place of *because I wanted to*, e.g.

Why did you go to the shops? Because I wanted to buy a newspaper./To buy a newspaper.

There is often a problem for learners when they attempt to translate this item from their own language and insert *for* which is wrong in English.

Common mistakes
*I went to the shops for to buy a newspaper.
*I went to the shops for buy a newspaper.
*I went to the shops for buying a newspaper.

Vocabulary

Vocabulary to do with weather is introduced, such as *It's sunny/windy/raining* (not *rainy*). The question for description *What ... like?* is presented and practised in dialogues, but only in connection with weather: *What's the weather like?*

Everyday English

A limited selection of the functional exponents for asking for and making suggestions are introduced:

What shall we do?
Let's go to the cinema.

Workbook

All of the auxiliary verbs covered so far – *am/is/are* and *do/does/did* – are brought together and practised.
The vocabulary section focuses on word stress and phonetic transcription of a range of words from previous units.
The writing syllabus continues with work on writing postcards, and provides an opportunity to bring together *going to* with other tenses.

Notes on the unit

PRESENTATION (1) (SB page 83)

going to

1 The context for the presentation of *going to* is future plans not only of a young girl but also of an older woman who is about to retire.

Ask your students to look at the photographs of Gemma /dʒemə/ and Miss Black. Check that they understand the meaning of *grow up* and *retire*. (Note that these *when* clauses with *grow up* and *retire* employ the Present Simple. Sometimes students find it strange that the Present Simple is used to talk about future events, as is the case here. However, try not to go into this with them at this stage.) Make it clear that they are going to read about the future plans of these two people, therefore what they are looking at is a future tense. Put students into pairs to discuss the sentences and put G or B according to who they think is speaking. (Note that the sentences have been selected so that there are a few surprises; it is not always obvious whose the plan might be!)

T 66 Play the tape. Play both Gemma and Miss Black right through, asking students to listen carefully and check if they are right. Tell them that sometimes they both have the same plan, so they must write G & B next to the sentence. At the end ask *Were all your answers right? Were there any surprises?*

Answers

G	I'm going to be a ballet dancer.
G & B	I'm going to travel all over the world.
B	I'm going to learn to drive.
G & B	I'm going to learn Russian.
B	I'm going to write a book.
G	I'm going to open a school.
G	I'm not going to marry until I'm 35.
B	I'm not going to wear skirts and blouses.
B	I'm going to wear jeans and tracksuits all the time.
B	I'm going to become a TV star.

2 This exercise moves from first person to third person, still practising positive (and negative) sentences only. First ask individuals to give you some of Gemma's and Miss Black's plans. This is the time to focus on the pronunciation of *going to* in connected speech. You can practise it in isolation first, and then as part of a full sentence.

going to /gəʊɪŋtə/ or /gəʊɪŋtʊ/

The two plans that are the same are:

They're both going to travel all over the world.
They're both going to learn Russian.

Now put your students into pairs, one to tell the other about Gemma's plans, and the other about Miss Black's. Go round and check as they do this.

● Grammar questions

– In answer to these two questions you could simply ask your class to chorus first the positive and then the negative forms of the verb *to be*.

(Conjugating verbs may be deemed 'old-fashioned' in these communicative days, but it is an effective way of consolidating grammatical forms!)

I am	*I'm not*
You are	*You aren't/You're not*
He is	*He isn't/He's not*
She is	*She isn't/She's not*, etc.

Also this may be a good opportunity to draw your students attention again to the two realizations of the negative of *to be* (see above). Remind them that this is possible in all persons except the first person singular.

– Read out the rule and ask for suggestions to complete it. You could write it up on the blackboard.

Answer
We make the *going to* future with the auxiliary verbs *am, is, are + going to + infinitive/verb.*

3 **T 67a** Now we focus on the formation and pronunciation of the question, which should not cause your students too much difficulty because they are already familiar with the forms of Present Continuous.

Play the tape and ask them to repeat the questions and answers (or you could model them yourself). Encourage them to use falling intonation for the *wh-* questions.

4 Put students into pairs to do this.

Answers
Why is she going to learn French and Russian?
Because she wants to dance in Paris and Moscow.
When is she going to marry? *Not until she's thirty-five.*
How many children is she going to have? *Two.*
How long is she going to work? *Until she's seventy-five.*
What is she going to teach? *Dancing.*

T67b Play the tape for them to check their answers. Then ask them to practise saying the questions and answers in pairs. Go round and help and check as they do this.

Practice (SB page 84)

1 Writing and speaking

1 Now we move away from Gemma and Miss Black and personalize the structure. In this activity the students are talking about themselves.

Do the example with them to illustrate the activity. Then ask them to work on their own. They could write out full sentences if you feel they need more practice in forming the structure, or they could simply put a tick or a cross next to each sentence.

2 Again illustrate the activity first with you asking individuals in the class the sample question and then getting one or two students to question another across the class in open pairs.

Put students into closed pairs to complete the activity and go round and check as they do this.

Round off the activity by asking one or two students to tell the class about their partner, thereby moving from practice of first and second persons to third person. The students in pairs could also tell you if there is anything that they are *both* going to do, thereby using the first person plural *we*.

2 Writing and listening

1 Here we introduce the second use of *going to*, when we can see now that something is sure to happen in the future. Read the introduction to your students. If possible and necessary, use L1 to explain.

Ask them to look at the pictures and write a sentence for each picture using *going to* with *it*, *I*, *we*, etc. Tell them to use their dictionaries to look up new words or to ask you. They could do the activity in pairs so that they can help each other with the vocabulary.

Answers

1 It's going to rain.
2 I'm going to sneeze.
3 We're going to miss the bus.
4 They're going to have a party.
5 I'm going to fail the exam.
6 He's going to pass the exam.
7 You're going to drop the plates!
8 They're going to kiss.

Check through the answers with the class as a whole. Ask individuals to read a sentence aloud.

2 **T68** Ask students to do this on their own or in pairs and then play the tape for them to check their answers. There are some useful little expressions included in the sentences: *Hurry up! Careful! Oh dear! Bless you!* Illustrate the meaning of these when you go through the exercise and get the class to repeat them. It can also be interesting and fun to discuss what is said in the students' own language(s) when someone sneezes, and to express disgust as in *Yuk!* in sentence *g*.

They can then practise saying the sentences with a partner and have fun practising the stress and intonation in the expressions.

Answers

a Take an umbrella. *It's going to rain.*
b Hurry up! *We're going to miss the bus.*
c I'm very worried about this exam. I know *I'm going to fail.*
d Jack is studying very hard. I know *he's going to pass the exam.*
e Careful! *You're going to drop the plates*!
f Look at all that wine and food! *They're going to have a party.*
g There's my sister and her boyfriend! Yuk! *They're going to kiss.*
h 'Oh dear, *I'm going to sneeze.* Aaattishooo!' 'Bless you!'

Additional material

Workbook Unit 12
Exercises 1–5 These consolidate and practise all aspects of the *going to* future.

PRESENTATION (2) (SB page 84)

Infinitive of purpose

1 The aim of this activity is to set the scene and check the vocabulary needed for the presentation dialogue in part 2.

First ask your students to look at the postcards and ask them which places they recognize. The pictures will also help to check some of the vocabulary needed for the matching exercise.

Put them into pairs to match a country or city with an activity, and a postcard if possible. Then check quickly through the exercise with the whole class.

Answers
Holland – see the tulips
Norway – see the midnight sun
Moscow – walk in Red Square
Spain – watch a bullfight
Egypt – visit the pyramids
Kenya – take photographs of the lions
India – visit the Taj Mahal
China – walk along the Great Wall
USA – drive through the Grand Canyon
Rio – sunbathe on Copacabana beach

2 This is the same Miss Black from the first presentation. She is now planning all the countries she will visit on her travels.

Note
Miss Black's dialogue with her friend, Arthur, incorporates revision of *going to* but some additional information is introduced: the fact that with the verb *go* we do not usually say *going to go*, but simply use the Present Continuous. The Caution Box beneath spells this out in more detail. You could read this with your students either after they first read the dialogue, or after they have listened to check the answer.

Do the dialogue with the whole class. Ask one student to read Miss Black's lines and another Arthur's. See if they can complete Miss Black's final line.

Answer
Miss Black: Well, then I'm going to Norway to *see the midnight sun*.

T 69 Play the tape for your students, not only to check the line, but also to get a good model for stress and intonation in the dialogue.

Read through the Caution Box with the class (if you have not done so earlier).

Grammar question

Read out the question and the sentences.

Answer
Yes, the sentences do mean the same.
(If possible you could explain in L1 that the infinitive can be used in answer to a *why* question when the answer means *because I want to*, in other words, expresses purpose.)

Practice (SB page 85)

1 Speaking

1 This is a controlled practice roleplay, where students work in pairs and take the roles of Miss Black and Arthur, and ask and answer questions about the places on page 84. Do the example in the book in open pairs across the class to illustrate the activity. Then put your students into closed pairs to complete it. Go round and check as they do it.

2 This is just to round off the previous activity. You could cut it and move to the personalized activity in 3 if you feel it is unnecessary for your students.

Do it with the whole class and ask four individual students to take turns to tell *part* of Miss Black's planned journey. Try not to let this activity go on too long otherwise it will become tedious, only do it with one set of four students. Be prepared to have to feed in the adverbs *then*, *next*, *after that*, etc.

Sample answer
Student 1: First she's going to Holland to see the tulips. Then she's going to Norway to see the midnight sun.
Student 2: Next she's going to Moscow to walk in Red Square and then to Spain to see a bullfight, and after that to Egypt to visit the pyramids.
Student 3: Next she's going to Kenya to take photos of the lions, and then to India to see the Taj Mahal and to China to walk along the Great Wall.
Student 4: After that she's going to America to drive through the Grand Canyon, and finally to Rio to sunbathe on Copacabana beach.

3 This activity personalizes the infinitive of purpose. It also moves away from practising the structure with *going to*, and revises the Past Simple.

You could introduce the activity by just going through the example in the book with them, but it is much more interesting if *you* say some names of places *you* visited last year, then get them to ask you why you went there, and tell them the purpose of your visit.

Example
Teacher: I went to London.
Student(s): Why did you go?
Teacher: To visit an English friend and to practise my English. When I was there I went to the British Museum.
Student(s): Why did you go there?
Teacher: To work in the reading room.

Ask your students to write down the names of some places they visited *last year*. These could be countries, cities, towns, villages, or any places of interest. Then put them into pairs to ask each other questions about the places. Let this go on for as long as they are interested if you have time.

Round the activity off by asking one or two individuals to give feedback to the class about their partner.

Sample answer
Last year Thomas went to England to learn English and to visit his penfriend.

2 Grammar

Students could do this exercise for homework but it is also good immediate consolidation if done in class. Ask students to work on their own to do it and then check their answers with a partner before you conduct feedback with the whole class.

Answers
- a He went to the station to catch the train.
- b She turned on the TV to watch the film.
- c Are you going to the pub to have a beer?
- d Did you open the door to get some fresh air?
- e I phoned Bill to tell him the news.
- f Are you learning English to get a better job?
- g They're studying hard to pass their exams.
- h I'm going home early to finish my homework.

3 Choosing the correct sentence

This exercise is a general revision exercise, bringing together not only structures from this unit, but also from previous units. It should take very little time to do. Ask your students to do it on their own as quickly as possible, then check their answers with a partner before you conduct feedback with the whole class.

Answers
1 b 2 b 3 a 4 b 5 a 6 a 7 a 8 a

Additional material

Workbook Unit 12
Exercises 6 and 7 These consolidate and practise the infinitive of purpose.

● READING AND SPEAKING (SB page 86)

The Rock Star!

Note
This is overall quite a challenging reading text, but the tasks have been carefully selected and staged to help students cope with it. However you may feel on reading the text that you would like to pre-teach more items of vocabulary than is suggested in the Pre-reading task. You can be the judge of this according to your students' capabilities.

Pre-reading task

1 This activity is to set the scene for the reading about a dangerous sport, and hopefully motivate students to read the text.

First ask your students to work on their own and number the list according to which sports they think are the most dangerous. Make it clear that 1 is the *most* dangerous. Obviously there are no right or wrong answers to this. Encourage them to give reasons for decisions in the feedback, both with a partner and with the whole class. With luck some free speaking might result if there is disagreement.

Finally establish with everyone where *mountain climbing* came on their lists. Ask if anyone goes mountain climbing/would like to go mountain climbing.

2 This is to check vocabulary needed in the text. Ask students to identify the things in the photographs. Talk a little about the photos and also introduce them to the climber, Catherine Destivelle. Tell them that they are going to read about her.

Reading

Ask your students to read through the text as quickly as they can, then to work in pairs to answer the two questions. These questions are quite challenging so they may need some help when you go through the answers with the whole class. Ask them first to tell you what the title *Rock Star* means in relation to the text, and next for its other meaning.

Answer
1 Catherine Destivelle is a *rock star* because she is famous for climbing rocks and mountains.
A *rock star* is also someone who is famous for singing or playing rock music. This is also the normal use of the term.
(Ask your class to give you examples of rock stars that they know.)

2 Go from the text to the letters when you go through this, so that you are all looking at the paragraphs in the order that they appear. Ask your students to give you reasons for their decisions. Don't worry too much how they express themselves in English in this, as long as they get their message across.

Answers

1 c **How did she begin?**
(Because it talks about when she started climbing at the age of five.)

2 d **Her best climb**
(Because it describes a new route that she found.)

3 a **Why does she climb?**
(Because the paragraph begins with *People always ask her this question* and then it talks about her love of climbing.)

4 b **Her future**
(Because it talks about what she is going to do.)

Ask your students to write in the correct headings. (If the book belongs to them and is not part of a class set!)

Comprehension check

Make it clear to your students that in this exercise *all* the sentences are *false*, and they have to correct them. Ask your students to read the article again and then to work in pairs to do the exercise. Do the example with them to illustrate the type of exercise it is. (It is quite a linguistically challenging exercise, because they have to get the correct negative short reply in the first part of their answers, but the second part can usually be taken directly from the text.)
When they have finished go through it as a class, getting individuals to read out their answers.

Answers

1 No, she isn't. She's good at climbing mountains and rocks.
2 No, she isn't. She's famous because she often climbs without ropes.
3 No, she didn't. She started climbing when she was five.
4 No, she didn't. She climbed better and more quickly than the older members.
5 No, it didn't. It took eleven days.
6 No, she didn't. She slept and ate in a bivouac.
7 No, they didn't. They tried to follow her route, but they failed.
8 No, she doesn't. She likes reading the face of the rock.
9 No, she isn't. She's going to climb a mountain in Pakistan.
10 No, it isn't. It's going to take longer to climb.

Language work

This provides revision of some of the grammar covered in the book so far.
Ask students to work on their own and underline the examples they find, then check with a partner before you go through with the whole class.

Answers

Present Simple
Three of the following:
She *loves* rock …
… she often *climbs* without ropes.
She *climbs* in many countries …
… Chamonix, where she *lives*.
People always *ask* her this question.
She *says* 'I *climb* because …
I like touching the rock … I *like* it a lot.
I *feel* comfortable …
I *prepare* well before I *go* …
Catherine *chooses* new mountains …
I *see* a nice mountain and I *go* to climb it.

Past of *can*
… the snow was so heavy that she *could* not move.

Past Simple
Four of the following:
She *started* climbing near her home in Paris …
… she *joined* the French Alpine Club …
… she *climbed* better and more quickly …
She *won* her first competition in Italy …
Three years ago she *found* a new route …
The climb *took* eleven days …
She *slept* and *ate* in a bivouac …
… other climbers *tried* to follow the new Destivelle route, but they *failed*.

Future plans
They *are going to try* again this year.
She *is going* there next month.
… it*'s going to take* longer to climb.
… Jeff Lowe *is coming* with me to help.

Comparative or Superlative
She is probably *the most famous* woman climber in the world …
… she climbed *better and more quickly than* the *older* members …
It's *much bigger than* the Dru …

(Note that your students will probably also underline 'most often' in paragraph 1. Give them credit for this even though it is in fact an adverb. However, don't be tempted to give them the grammatical explanation!)

Speaking

Roleplay

Divide your class into As and Bs and tell them that the As are journalists and the Bs are Catherine Destivelle.
Ask the As to get together in small groups to plan some of the questions they are going to ask her. Tell them to plan 6–10 questions only, otherwise the activity may go on too long.
Ask the Bs to reread the text, particularly the headings, and think about how to answer questions as Catherine about her life.
Give them about ten minutes to prepare and then put an A with a B to enact the roleplay. Tell them to begin it according to the example in the book.
Go round and listen as they do this, helping only if all communication breaks down.
Finally ask a couple of pairs to act out their interview to the whole class. It would be a lovely idea to tape some of the roleplays if possible and play them back to the whole class for them to comment on and correct. This is often a very productive and satisfying thing to do.

Additional material

Video

Report (Section 10) This is a short documentary about two climbers, but they don't climb mountains, they climb buildings. The documentary shows them climbing Coventry Cathedral.

● VOCABULARY (SB page 88)

The weather

Note

Before the lesson, you need to photocopy the World Weather Reports on page 135 of this book to give to Student B for the information gap activity.

1 Ask your students to look at the weather symbols. Check if anyone in the class knows any of the symbols already, in which case practise those they know.

Ask them to work in pairs, and use their dictionaries to look up the other words and write them in. Go through the answers with the class.

Problem

We say : *it's sunny/cloudy/windy/foggy*, but *it's raining/snowing*. Although the adjectives *rainy* and *snowy* exist, these are usually used with a noun: *it's a rainy/snowy day.* Make sure that you draw your students' attention to the different endings, but do not be tempted to mention *rainy* and *snowy* at this stage.

Answers

cloudy, windy, sunny, foggy, raining, snowing

The next part of this exercise is to practise which *pairs* of adjectives *commonly* go together to describe weather. This will vary in different countries according to the climate, for example it can be *warm and windy* in many climates but is only rarely so in Britain.

Ask your class to give you their ideas about British weather. (Everyone always has something to say about British weather!)

Cultural notes

1 Despite London's reputation, the last big fog/smog (smoke + fog) was in 1957 when the Clean Air Act was passed!
2 There are lots of jokes about British weather. Can your students understand this one?
If you don't like English weather, wait ten minutes!

You could have a mini-discussion comparing which pairs they think will often go together in Britain (if you think it's useful to them) and which for the climate of their own country.

Sample answers (for Britain)
cold and cloudy
dry and cloudy
wet and windy
cold and windy
warm and sunny
hot and sunny
cold and foggy
cold and raining
cold and snowing

Also you often hear the pairs *warm and dry*, *cold and wet* together.

2 **T 70** Indicate out of the window to the weather outside, and either play the tape or model the question yourself.

Problem

What … like? for descriptions always creates some difficulty because of the different use of *like*. You need to make two things very clear to your students:
1 It has nothing to do with the verb *like*. The Caution Box will help you do this.
2 The answer does *not* contain the word like.
What's the weather like? It's sunny.
NOT *It's like sunny.

Ask your students to listen and write in the weather for today and yesterday. Check their answers.

 Read through the Caution Box with them.

Practise the questions and answers in open pairs across the class. Encourage falling intonation in these *wh-* questions.

3 This is an information gap activity.

Ask your students to work in pairs. Tell Student A to look at the World Weather on page 88 of the Student's Book and give Student B the one you have photocopied from page 135 of the Teacher's Book. (It is repeated to reduce photocopying.)

Illustrate the activity by doing the first questions and answers about Athens and Berlin with them across the class. This is a good time to feed in the modifier *quite*, if you feel your students can cope with it. (Make sure they realize that this is *yesterday's* weather and therefore they need to use *was* in the questions and answers.)

Student A: *What was the weather like in Athens?*
Student B: *It was sunny and (quite) warm. Eighteen degrees Celsius.*

Get them to continue the activity in closed pairs. Go round and check as they do it.

Answers

World Weather
noon yesterday

		°C	**It was:**
Athens	S	18	sunny and warm
Berlin	R	7	wet/raining and cold
Bombay	R	31	raining and hot
Edinburgh	C	5	cloudy and cold
Geneva	C	12	cloudy and (quite) cold
Hong Kong	S	29	sunny and hot
Lisbon	C	19	cloudy and warm
London	R	10	wet/raining and (quite) cold
Los Angeles	Fg	21	foggy and warm
Luxor	S	40	sunny and very hot
Milan	Fg	19	foggy and warm
Moscow	Sn	–1	snowing and cold
Oslo	Sn	2	snowing and cold

S = sunny C = cloudy Fg = foggy
R = raining Sn = snowing

Round off the activity with the questions about the weather report.

Answers
Luxor was the hottest. (Ask your students if they know where this is. It's in Egypt.)
Moscow was the coldest.
The month is in fact March. (Encourage a bit of discussion about this, because obviously it could be other months, but clearly, in Europe anyway, the season is either winter or early spring.)

Additional material

Workbook
Exercise 12 This writing activity is writing postcards and fits nicely after this vocabulary as it includes information about the weather. It could be done in class or for homework.

● EVERYDAY ENGLISH (SB page 88)

Making suggestions

Notes
We restrict the exponents for making suggestions to: *shall* to ask for suggestions and *Let's* to make them.
We also revise *will* for immediate decisions, which was introduced in the Everyday English in the previous unit.

1 Ask your students to write the two lists in pairs or on their own and then compare their lists with a partner's. Ask for some feedback from the whole class and tell them that they will need their lists later.

2 **T71** Tell them that they are going to hear the beginnings of two conversations, one for good weather and one for bad. Ask them to read and listen at the same time. Then get them in chorus, first to practise the question, then to practise the answer. Encourage good stress and intonation.

What shall we do?	/wɒt ʃəl wɪ dʊ/
Let's play tennis.	/lets pleɪ tenɪs/

Ask your students to work in pairs and practise the conversations.

⚠ You could read through the Caution Box either after the pairs practice or before it. You decide when is best for your class. In a monolingual class you could ask them to translate the sentences.

3 Ask your students to work in pairs. Ask them first to find the 'good weather' lines and then the 'bad weather' lines. Then ask them to put each set in order to complete the conversations.

T72 Play the tape for them not only to check their answers but to get a good model for stress and intonation. They can then practise these conversations for a short time.

4 Still in their pairs, ask them to look at the lists they made earlier. They then use these to substitute activities in the dialogues. Go round and listen as they do this. To round off the activity you could either ask a couple of pairs to do their dialogues for the whole class, or record a few

dialogues and play them to the class for them to correct any mistakes in the language and the pronunciation.

5 This is a freer speaking activity still in pairs. You need to photocopy the list of TV programmes on page 136 of the Teacher's Book and give a copy to each pair. Tell them that they live together in a flat with only one TV and to decide what to watch together during the evening. Read the example together. You will have to practise the question *What's on TV tonight?* Then let them do the activity and go round and listen as they do this. Round off the activity by asking a few of the pairs to tell the rest of the class about their evening's viewing: *We're going to watch … and then …*, etc.

GRAMMAR SUMMARY (SB page 89)

Read the Grammar Summary together in class, and/or ask your students to read it and *learn* the grammar at home. Encourage them to ask you questions about it.

Don't forget

Workbook Unit 12
Exercises 8 and 9 These bring together all the auxiliary verbs covered so far.
Exercises 10 and 11 These revise many items of vocabulary covered so far. They focus on word stress and phonetic transcription.

Word List
Remind your students of the Word List at the back of their book. Ask them to look at the list for this unit on page 126. Tell them that they could write in the translations, learn them at home, and/or write some of the words in their vocabulary notebooks.

Pronunciation Book Unit 12

Video
There are two video sections that can supplement Units 11 and 12 of the Student's Book.
Report (Section 10) *Climbers.* (You may have done this already after the reading.) It is a mini-documentary about people who climb buildings.
Situation (Section 11) *The Dinner Party.* This is a short situation where Paola and David go to dinner at their friends' house.

EXTRA IDEAS Units 9–12

On page 137 of the Teacher's Book there is an additional reading text: *The Garden that Moved House!*
If you have time and feel that your students would benefit from it, you can photocopy it and use it in class. The reading exercise revises all the units so far, particularly Units 9–12. It could also be done for homework.
Activities and exercises to exploit the reading are provided on page 137 and the answers are below.

Answers to the reading
Vocabulary

Flowers	**Colours**
tulip	pink
rose	yellow
daffodil	orange
snowdrop	brown
primrose	grey
	red
	gold
	white

(Note that *pink* is also a flower, a type of carnation, but it is not necessary to mention this.)

Comprehension check
a She's an artist. Her hobby is gardening.
b To make her garden beautiful. / Because she wanted to make her garden beautiful.
c Summer, because there were hundreds of red, white, and pink roses.
d Because she wanted a bigger house.
e Yes, they did. (They fell in love with it immediately.)
f Because there was no garden, just a brown field with some stones and rocks. Also there weren't any flowers or trees.
g £1,000.
h She's going to plant all the flowers and trees again and she's going to have a pond with some goldfish.
i They're going to see their solicitor.

Language work
1 b Which was the prettiest season?
c Why did a lot of people come to the village?
d Was the cottage easy to sell?
e Why did Mr and Mrs Grey want to move from London?
f When did they move?
g What was the garden like?
h Has Verena got a bigger house (now)?
i What is she going to do (with it)?
j Who are Mr and Mrs Grey going to see?

2 a ***have got***
Present
I've got a much bigger garden
Past
She had flowers and plants for every season
... *we didn't have* a garden there.

b **comparative**
It was *more beautiful than* the park.
... she would like to move to a *bigger* house.
...I'm going to make it even *more beautiful than* my first garden.

c **superlative**
Summer was *the prettiest season of all.*

d **irregular past**
spent, had, grew, bought, came, fell, left, (*was/were*).

e **future**
I'm going to make it even more beautiful than my first garden
I'm going to plant all the flowers and trees again.
I'm going to have a pond.
We're going to see a solicitor.

f **infinitive of purpose**
She spent ten years and thousands of pounds *to make* her garden there beautiful.
A lot of people came to the village especially *to see* Verena's garden.
Mr and Mrs Grey came *to see* it.

g ***some***
There was a brown field with *some stones and rocks.*
I'm going to have a pond with *some goldfish.*

h ***any***
There weren't *any flowers* or trees and there wasn't *any grass*!

STOP AND CHECK Units 9–12

There is a Stop and Check revision section after each quarter of the Student's Book. The idea is that your students pause to check their progress so far. Each test is out of 100. There is a Stop and Check Answer Key on page 142 of the Teacher's Book. You could set it in class as an informal progress test or you could use the following procedure.

1 Give your students the Stop and Check to do for homework, preferably when they have more time, such as at the weekend.
2 In the next lesson ask them to go over their answers in small groups, trying to agree on the right answer. Allow enough time for this. It can be very productive for students to try and persuade their peers of the right answer. Many previous lessons are recalled.
3 Go over it with the whole class, reminding students of the language items covered.

After all the group discussion everyone *should* have a reasonably high score!

UNIT 13

Question forms – Adverbs – At the railway station

Introduction to the unit

Unit 13 marks the beginning of the last quarter of *Headway Elementary*. Question forms are the main target language. This is not a particularly new language area, as question forms have been introduced and practised throughout the book, but focusing on question forms allows a lot of language areas, especially tenses, to be pulled together and revised.

The theme of the unit is general knowledge, and reading simplified stories. In the reading section, students read an abridged version of *The Girl with Green Eyes*, from a book of short stories in the *Oxford Bookworm Series*. If you haven't already encouraged your students to read simplified stories, now is the time to start! Reading is one of the easiest, cheapest, and most pleasurable ways of learning a foreign language.

Language aims

Grammar

Question forms

All the *wh-* questions (*when*, *where*, *who*, *what*, *why*, *which*) except *whose*, and questions with *how* + adjective (e.g. *How old …?*) and *how* + adverb (e.g. *How far …?*) are revised. *What* + noun (*What languages …?/What sort of …?*) is also practised.

We 'drop in' three subject questions, *Who won …?*, *What happens …?* and *What happened …?* in Presentation (1). The first of these is 'dropped in' in case students want to make such a question in Exercise 3, where they are asked to think up some general knowledge questions of their own. The second two are 'dropped in' because they are needed to talk about stories in the Vocabulary section and the Reading section. We suggest that you do not embark on a detailed presentation of the difference between subject and object question forms. If students wonder (very sensibly) why *do/does/did* is not used in these questions, try to mollify them with a quick explanation. Put on the board the sentences *Joe likes Betty. Betty likes Tim.* Ask these questions: *Who likes Betty? (Joe does.) Who does Betty like? (She likes Tim.)* to show them that the first queston refers to the subject of the sentence, while the second one asks about the object of the sentence. Then tell them not to worry about it at this stage! In our experience, it would not further students to go too deeply into it at this level, or at all, unless they ask about it.

Adverbs

Regular and irregular adverbs are presented and practised.

Vocabulary

The vocabulary introduced in this unit is not a specific lexical area, but is on the general topic of talking about a book.

Everyday English

The situation of *At the railway station* is explored. This picks up on the reading *The Girl with Green Eyes*.

Workbook

Which one …? is introduced and practised. Noun and adjective suffixes are introduced, as are *-ed* and *-ing* adjectives (*interested/interesting*). In the writing section, adjectives and adverbs are further practised, and students are invited to write a story.

Notes on the unit

PRESENTATION (1) (SB page 92)

Question forms

Ask students questions about the photographs, e.g. *Who's this?*, *What's this?*, *What's happening here?* to create interest and also to check that the various people, etc., are familiar to them. Be careful, however, not to pre-empt the general knowledge questions themselves!

1 Students work in groups to answer the general knowledge quiz. Ask for feedback before you play the tape, and encourage discussion if/when students disagree about the answers.

Answers (and tapescript)

1 A When did the Berlin Wall come down?
B 1989.
2 A When did the first American walk on the moon?
B 1969.
3 A Where are the Andes mountains?
B In South America.
4 A Who did the actress Elizabeth Taylor marry twice?
B Richard Burton.
5 A Who won the 100 metres in the Seoul Olympics?
B Carl Lewis.
6 A How many countries are there in the EC?
B Twelve.
7 A How much does an African elephant weigh?
B Five to seven tonnes.
8 A How fast does Concorde fly?
B 2500 kilometres an hour.
9 A How far is it from London to New York?
B Six thousand kilometres.
10 A How old was Charlie Chaplin when he died?
B Eighty-eight.
11 A What languages do Swiss people speak?
B German, French, Italian, and Romansch.
12 A What did Columbus discover in 1492?
B America.
13 A What sort of music did Elvis Presley play?
B Rock 'n' roll.
14 A What happens at the end of the story *Cinderella*?
B She marries the prince.
15 A What happened in Chernobyl in 1986?
B There was a nuclear explosion.
16 A Why do birds migrate?
B Because the winter is cold.
17 A Which newspaper does Queen Elizabeth read?
B *The Times*.
18 A Which language has the most words?
B English.

2 **T73** Students listen and check their answers. Play some of the questions again and ask students to focus on the intonation of the questions. Drill them around the class.

● Grammar question

Ask students to underline the question words, and to say which questions are in the Past Simple and which are in the Present Simple.

Answers

1	*When ...?*	Past Simple
2	*When ...?*	Past Simple
3	*Where ...?*	Present Simple
4	*Who ...?*	Past Simple
5	*Who ...?*	Past Simple
6	*How many ...?*	Present Simple
7	*How much ...?*	Present Simple
8	*How fast ...?*	Present Simple
9	*How far ...?*	Present Simple
10	*How old ...?*	Past Simple
11	*What ...?*	Present Simple
12	*What ...?*	Past Simple
13	*What sort ...?*	Past Simple
14	*What ...?*	Present Simple
15	*What ...?*	Past Simple
16	*Why ...?*	Present Simple
17	*Which ...?*	Present Simple
18	*Which ...?*	Present Simple

3 Students work in groups to write some more general knowledge questions. Allow adequate time for this. It might take students a while to get started. Go round the groups to ensure that the questions are well formed.

When they have a reasonable number of questions, ask the groups to put the questions to the rest of the class. You could make this activity into a team game, if time allows.

Practice (SB page 93)

1 Question words

Students work in pairs to match a question word in A with an answer in B. Ask for feedback before you give the answers.

Answers

A	B
When?	Last Saturday.
Where?	To the cinema.
Who?	Jenny.
How?	By bus.
How many?	Five.
How much?	60p.
What?	A book.
Why?	Because I need it for my job.
Which one?	The new one in the High Street.

2 Grammar

1 Students work in pairs to put the words in the correct order. They then choose the correct answers from column B in Exercise 1.

Answers

a How many cigarettes do you smoke a day?
Five.
b Where did you go last night?
To the cinema.
c How much does a litre of petrol cost?
60p.
d When did you last go shopping?
Last Saturday.
e Which restaurant did you go to?
The new one in the High Street.
f How did you come to school today?
By bus.
g What did you buy at the shops?
A book.
h Who did you speak to at the party?
Jenny.
i Why do you want to learn English?
Because I need it for my job.

Practise the questions and answers in open pairs. Make sure that students start high when asking questions.

2 In pairs, students ask and answer the questions about themselves. Not all the questions will apply, for example, they will not necessarily have an answer for questions e, g, and h.

3 Listening and pronunciation

T74 Students listen and tick the sentence they hear. Let students check in pairs before you give the answers.

Answers

1 b 2 a 3 b 4 b 5 a 6 b 7 a 8 a

4 Speaking

You will need to photocopy the Student A and Student B information on page 138 of the Teacher's Book.
Students should be familiar with the principles of an information gap activity by now, but still use L1 for instructions if you think this would help.
First of all ask students to look at the photo and tell you what they know about the characters. Read the introduction and the examples as a class. Give out the relevant information. Do one or two questions yourself as a further example, and to make sure that students remember how to form questions in the Past Simple. As students are asking and answering questions, go round the pairs and monitor carefully.
When students have finished, ask for the questions again and correct any mistakes.

Answers

Student A's questions

a Where did they meet? (Hollywood)
c When did they stop making films? (1952)
e What did they win for their film *The Music Box*? (an Oscar)
g Where was Stan Laurel born? (England)
i When did he go to America? (1910)
k How many times did he marry? (Four)
m When did he die? (1965)
o Where was Oliver Hardy born? (Atlanta, Georgia)
q When did he go to Hollywood? (1911)
s How many times did he marry? (Once)
u What did he like doing in his free time? (Playing golf, going to horse races)
w Where did he die? (California)

Student B's questions

b When did they meet? (1926)
d How many films did they make? (200)
f When did they win an Oscar? (1932)
h When was Stan Laurel born? (1890)
j When did Stan Laurel make his first film? (1917)
l How many children did he have? (One daughter)
n Where did he die? (California)
p When was Oliver Hardy born? (1892)
r When did he make his first film? (1913)
t How many children did he have? (None)
v How much money did he lose in one day? ($12,000)
x When did he die? (1957)

Additional material

Workbook Unit 13
Exercises 1–4 Question forms
Exercises 5 and 6 *Which …?*
Exercise 7 Questions and short answers

PRESENTATION (2) (SB page 94)

Adverbs

1 Read the explanation about adjectives and adverbs as a class.

2 Students work in pairs to decide if the word in italics is an adjective or an adverb.

Answers

a adjective	g adverb (point out that *well* is the irregular adverb of *good*)
b adverb	h adjective
c adverb	i adjective
d adjective	j adverb (This question is difficult, as *hard* is irregular.)
e adjective	
f adverb	

● Grammar questions

Look at the Grammar questions as a class.

Answers

– We make regular adverbs by adding *-ly* to the adjective. If the adjective ends in *-y*, it changes to *-ily*.
– *well* and *hard* are irregular.

Practice (SB page 94)

1 Listening and speaking

1 Students check the meaning of the adverbs in their dictionary. To save time, you could translate them.

2 Ask students to look at the picture. What can they see?

T 75 Students listen to the story and put the adverbs in the correct order.

Answers

6 quickly	2 slowly
3 carefully	1 suddenly
4 quietly	5 immediately

3 In pairs, students retell the story either one sentence at a time each, or one student first, then the other.

2 Grammar

1 Students match a verb or phrase in A with an adverb in B.

Answers

run fast
work hard/carefully
get up early
speak two languages fluently
do your homework carefully/early/fast

2 Students put the word in brackets in the right place in the sentences, changing the adjective to an adverb if necessary. Students can work in pairs, or alone and then check with a partner.

Note

We do not overtly give the rules for the order of adverbs (front position, mid position, end position), because the rules are rather complicated. We do not suggest that you try to go into them at this stage. You could perhaps point out that adverbs usually follow the verb and object if there is one, whereas adjectives go before the noun (unlike many other languages). Otherwise let students see how they get on without rules, and simply correct any mistakes.

Answers

a We had a holiday in Spain, but unfortunately we had *terrible* weather.
b Maria dances *well*.
c When I saw the accident, I phoned the police *immediately* (or I *immediately* phoned …).
d Don't worry. Justin is a *careful* driver.
e Jean-Pierre is a *typical* Frenchman. He loves food, wine, and rugby.
f Please speak *slowly*. I can't understand you.
g We had an *easy* test today.
h We all passed *easily*.
i You speak *good* English./You speak English *well*.

3 Correcting the mistakes

Students work in pairs to correct the mistakes.

Answers

a Where does Anna's sister live?
b What sort of music do you like?
c What does *scream* mean?
d Did they go out last night?
e Can you help me, please?
f When is Peter going on holiday?
g Last night I went to the cinema. / I went to the cinema last night.
h Do your homework very carefully.
i You drive too fast! Slow down!
j You're a beautiful dancer!

Additional material

Workbook Unit 13
Exercises 10 and 11 Adverbs

● VOCABULARY (SB page 95)

Talking about a book

Note
There are many good series of simplified readers. Oxford University Press have one called *The Oxford Bookworm Series*. Your students should be able to cope with levels 1 and 2. Encourage your students to read as much as possible.

1 Read the introduction as a class. You will need to pre-teach the following words. Do this quickly.

monkey *paw* *title* *main characters* *recommend* *accident* *horror story* *magic* (adj) *wish* (n)

Students work in pairs to match a question about the book with Maria's answers.

Answers
1 d 2 e 3 c 4 g 5 a 6 f 7 b

Note
Notice that in this exercise, and in the Comprehension questions about *The Girl with Green Eyes*, a lot of the questions are in the Present Simple, not the Past Simple. This use of the Present Simple is called the Historic Present, and it is common when talking about stories, films, etc. We do not suggest that you point this out to students, and don't worry too much if students want to reply using the Past Simple.

T76 Students listen to Maria and check their answers.

2 Ask students to look at the four book covers. What can they see? Ask them to match a book cover in A with a text in B and a type of book in C. There will no doubt be quite a few unknown words, but tell students not to worry about them. They should be able to do the exercise despite the presence of new words.

Answers
The President's Murderer – d – an adventure story
Sherlock Holmes Short Stories – c – a detective story
The Love of a King – b – a romance/biography
Voodoo Island – a – a horror story

You could practise the questions in part 1 further and get some considerable speaking practice if you ask students to talk about books they have read recently.

● READING AND LISTENING (SB page 96)

A short story

Read the introduction as a class. Make sure students understand *one-way ticket*.

Pre-reading

1 Discuss the question as a class.

2 Discuss the question as a class. Ask students to look at picture 1. Who are friends? Who are strangers? Who are husband and wife? Of course, students won't know the answers for sure, but they can speculate.

Sample answer
Perhaps the woman with long hair is married to the man opposite. The man with the hat is a friend of the man opposite, because they're laughing together. The woman with the children is married to the man with the hat.

3 Students look at the other pictures and say what they think happens in the story.

Reading and listening

Note
We suggest that students read and listen at the same time to discourage students from worrying too much about unknown vocabulary. The only item of vocabulary that might cause problems in part 1 is *bored*, so check this. You might want to do Exercise 9 in the Workbook of this unit, which introduces and practises *-ed/-ing* adjectives.

However, you might decide that you want students to read in silence, in which case you could play the tape afterwards.

1 **T77** Students read and listen to part 1 of the story and check their ideas about picture 1. They then answer the questions in pairs or small groups.

Answers
a Julie and Bill are husband and wife. There is a mother and her two children.
b The man next to the window is the tall dark man. The woman opposite is Julie. The young man next to her is Bill. The woman beside the man in the brown hat is the mother of the two children.
c Perhaps she thinks he's boring.
d (Various answers)

2 Students read and listen to part 2 and answer the questions.

Answers

e Bill talks to the man in the brown hat. The tall dark man reads his newspaper.
f Because she is bored and doesn't want to listen to Bill and the other man.
g The first time, no; the second time, yes.
h She probably thinks he's attractive.

3 Students read and listen to part 3 and answer the questions.

Answers

i The tall dark man gets off the train, and a lot of people get on. Julie gets off too, while her husband is in a different part of the train, buying something to eat and drink.
j The little girl and the mother.
k Perhaps Julie and the man fell in love without actually speaking to each other.
l Perhaps because she thinks her husband is boring, and the tall dark man looks so exciting.

Vocabulary

Students find words to do with parts of the body.

Answers

eyes hair mouth hands

There is a lot of mention of eyes. This is partly because Julie has very beautiful eyes, but mainly because it is only through looking into each other's eyes that Julie and the man fall in love, and Julie decides to leave Bill without ever talking to the tall dark man.

Speaking

1 Students work in groups of three to practise the dialogue from '*Where's Julie?*'. You could ask them to work in groups of four and have a narrator, if you want. Encourage students to put a lot of expression into their voices. Play the tape again to act as a model.

2 Students ask and answer the questions.

Answers

1 What's the title of the story? *The Girl with Green Eyes.*
2 What sort of story is it? *A romance.*
3 Who are the main characters? *Julie, her husband Bill, and a tall dark man.*
4 What's it about?
It's about a young woman called Julie, and her husband, Bill. Julie thinks that her husband is boring. They're on a train with five other people, and Julie falls in love with the tall dark man.
5 What happens in the end? *When the tall dark man gets off the train, Julie goes with him. She leaves her husband!*
6 Did you enjoy it? (Various answers)
7 Do you recommend it? (Various answers)

Students retell the story in the Past Simple (but don't worry if they switch to the Present). You could do this at the beginning of the next lesson if you think students have had enough of the story.

● EVERYDAY ENGLISH (SB page 97)

Catching a train

1 Read the introduction as a class. (Newcastle is a town in the north-east of England. King's Cross is a railway station in London.) If you have a map of Britain in your classroom it would be a nice idea to show your students where Newcastle is in relation to London.

T 78a Students listen and complete the timetable.

Answers

Departure time from King's Cross	Arrival time in Newcastle
0700	1005
0840	1130
0950	1245
1130	1437
1200	1455

2 **T 78b** Students listen to the conversation and complete it. Play it all through first, then bit by bit so students have time to write.

Answers

A Good morning. (a) *Can you tell me* the times of trains (b) *back from* Newcastle, please?
B Afternoon, evening? When (c) *do you want to come back*?
A About 5 o' clock this afternoon.
B About (d) *5 o'clock*. Right. Let's have a look. There's a train that (e) *leaves at* 4.45, and there's (f) *another one* at 5.25.
A And (g) *what time do they* get in?
B Back at King's Cross at 7.15 and (h) *8. 20.*
A Thanks a lot.

Students can practise the dialogue in pairs.

3 Students work in pairs to put the dialogue in the right order.

T 78c They listen and check.

Answers
A Hello. I'd like a ticket to Newcastle, please.
C Single or return?
A Return, please.
C Day return or period return?
A I want to come back this evening, so a day return.
C How do you want to pay?
A Cash, please.
C Forty-eight pounds fifty, please.
A Twenty, forty, sixty pounds.
C Here's your change and your ticket.
A Thank you.

Students close their books and try to remember the conversations.

4 **T 78d** Students listen and correct the notice boards.

Answers

ARRIVALS

From	**Platform**	**Time**	**Remark**
Edinburgh	*8*	0830	On time
Hertford	6	0835	On time
Newcastle	15	0845	Delay *40* mins
Darlington	9	*0855*	On time

DEPARTURES

Destination	**Platform**	**Time**	**Remark**
Peterborough	12	0825	Ready
Newcastle	*17*	0840	Ready
York	5	*0900*	

GRAMMAR SUMMARY (SB page 98)

Read the Grammar Summary as a class. Encourage students to ask any questions.

Don't forget!

Workbook Unit 13
Exercises 8 and 9 Noun and adjective suffixes, and *-ed/-ing* adjectives
Exercise 12 Adverbs and adjectives, and students read a fairy story. They are then invited to write a story of their own.

Word List
Remind your students of the Word List at the back of the book.

Pronunciation Book Unit 13

UNIT 14

Present Perfect – Telephoning

Introduction to the unit

This unit sees the introduction of one of the most difficult tenses for students of English to learn, for the reasons outlined below. The Present Perfect is one of the most commonly used tenses in English, especially spoken English, but its presentation has been deferred until Unit 14 because until students have understood the concept that the Past Simple refers to the definite past, they will not be able to grasp the idea that the Present Perfect refers to the indefinite past.

The theme of this unit is 'In my life', and various people's experiences in life are explored. There is a jigsaw reading activity where students read about three amazing grandmothers.

Language aims

Grammar

Present Perfect

In this unit we introduce only one main use of the Present Perfect, that is, to refer to an experience some time in one's life. We touch on another use (to refer to the present result of a past action) only briefly, with the adverbs *yet* and *just*. We do not introduce at all the third main use of the Present Perfect, which is to refer to unfinished past (*I have been a teacher for ten years*), nor do we teach the Present Perfect Continuous.

The aim of this unit is to provide an introduction to the Present Perfect, but do not expect your students to master the area quickly! It takes a long time (and a lot of mistakes, correction, and re-teaching) before students feel at all confident with this tense.

Problems

The Present Perfect tense presents students with problems mainly because a similar form of auxiliary verb *have* + past participle exists in many European languages, but it is used in a very different way. In English, the Present Perfect expresses the concept of an action happening at an indefinite time *before now*, and so it cannot be used when a definite time is given. The following sentences are examples of incorrect usage.

Common mistakes

* I have seen him last week.
* When have you been to the States?
* Did you ever try Chinese food?
* In my life I went to most countries in Europe, but I never went to Greece.

Note that American English can use the Past Simple with *just* and *yet*.

Did you do your homework yet?
I just did it.

Vocabulary

There is quite a lot of vocabulary introduced in the three reading texts on pages 102 and 103. In the Vocabulary section there is another 'odd one out' activity, which revises a lot of the words in the unit and adds some more.

Everyday English

Language useful for making phone calls is introduced and practised.

Workbook

The difference between *been* and *gone* is presented. In the Vocabulary section, various nouns are revised or introduced. In the Writing section, students are given help with form filling.

Notes on the Unit

PRESENTATION (1) (SB page 99)

Present Perfect + *ever* and *never*

Note

1 Students find the difference between *He's been to the States* and *He's gone to the States* quite confusing. This is dealt with in Exercise 9 of the Workbook. We do not suggest that you attempt to sort this out at this stage of the presentation.

2 The approach to the grammar in this unit is slightly different from other units in *Headway Elementary*. Students are exposed to the form of the Present Perfect in Exercises 1 and 2. In Exercise 3 they see the Present Perfect contrasted with the Past Simple. We do not ask any Grammar questions because we feel that students will not know the answer at this stage. With so little exposure to and understanding of the Present Perfect, students are unlikely to be able to infer any rules. Instead, we give some basic rules regarding Past Simple to refer to definite time and Present Perfect to refer to indefinite time in the Caution Box.

3 Students have already seen a Present Perfect form with the structure *have got*, but we do not suggest that you mention this at all. It would be very confusing for students, as *have got* expresses an essentially present-time concept.

1 Students look at the countries and tick or write down those they have visited at some time in their life. Translate this instruction if you can. Don't draw students' attention to the Present Perfect at this stage. Practise the pronunciation of the countries.

2 **T 79a** Students read and listen to the sentences. Remember that they will probably never have seen the Present Perfect tense before, and *been* will be unfamiliar. Using L1 if possible, explain that *been* is the past participle of the verb *to be*, and that *have been* is an example of the Present Perfect tense. Don't try to explain the meaning yet. For the time being, you are 'imposing' the form on them. You could keep stressing the idea of 'some time in your life'.

Ask students to repeat the sentences on tape (not worrying whether they are true for them or not). Do this chorally and individually, and correct mistakes carefully.

Now ask students to make similar sentences, saying which countries they have/haven't been to. Do this first as a class, so you can check students' utterances. Students then do the same in groups or pairs.

3 **T 79b** Students read and listen to the conversation. They can practise saying each sentence, either after the tape or with you modelling each one. With this exercise and the information in the Caution Box, you begin to explore the meaning of the Present Perfect, and how it differs from the Past Simple. Don't rush this stage, and remember that the ideas you are exploring are really quite complicated and subtle.

Draw students' attention to the question form of the Present Perfect, then to *When did you go?* and ask what tense this is.

⚠ Read the information in the Caution Box carefully. Translate *definite past time* and *indefinite past time* if you can, otherwise students can check the meaning in their dictionary.

If your students have a similar tense form in their language, and if you can use L1, you might like to make a brief comparison between the way L1 and English use the auxiliary verb *have* + past participle. Be careful, however! Keep it short, and as simple as possible, because it would be very easy to overload students with too much information at this early stage of their exposure to the Present Perfect.

Before you move on, ask students to ask you questions about countries you have been to, exactly as in Exercise 3. Encourage them to ask *When did you go?* and tell them.

Then in open pairs, students can have similar dialogues about countries they have been to, and when. This might sound repetitive and laborious, but remember you are introducing students to a very new concept with the Present Perfect tense and they need practice with forming questions, answers and negatives.

4 Students write down the names of four capital cities and in pairs make similar dialogues. Go round and check as they do this.

5 Ask three or four students to talk about their partners. This practises the third person singular for the first time, so make sure they remember to change *have* to *has*.

Practice (SB page 100)

1 Grammar

Students write in the infinitives. All the verbs are used in exercises that come later in this unit.

Answers

visited	*visit*	seen	*see*	taken	*take*
eaten	*eat*	met	*meet*	driven	*drive*
drunk	*drink*	cooked	*cook*	lived	*live*
stayed	*stay*	flown	*fly*	bought	*buy*
won	*win*	written	*write*	had	*have*
made	*make*	sent	*send*	done	*do*

The four regular verbs are *visit*, *cook*, *live*, and *stay*.

Students can check/revise the Past Simple form of the irregular verbs by looking at the list in Appendix 1 on page 127.

2 Listening and speaking

1 Read the introduction as a class. Go through the list first, making sure students understand all the vocabulary. You will probably need to check the following:

company *jumbo jet* *play* *tractor* *competition*

There are one or two words that might be new on the tape. Check the following:

flight *boy scout* *beans* (These are often cooked in a tomato sauce, and are sold in tins.)

T 80 Students listen and tick the things Roger has done.

Answers

lived in a foreign country	✔
worked for a big company	✘
stayed in an expensive hotel	✘
flown in a jumbo jet	✔
cooked a meal for ten (or more) people	✔
met a famous person	✘
seen a play by Shakespeare	✔
driven a tractor	✔
been to hospital	✔
won a competition	✘

Ask students to check in pairs before they give you the answers.

2 First ask students to go through the questionnaire to produce some sentences about Roger. This is to further practise the third person singular. Get some positive sentences first, then some negative ones. Drill them around the class, correcting carefully.

Read the instructions for this exercise. Ask for the positive sentences again. This time you will ask further questions in the Past Simple, which students will answer in the Past Simple. (You might want to play the tape again before you do this to remind students of the information about Roger.) Although these questions and answers practise the Past Simple, you are also indirectly practising the Present Perfect, because you are showing students when the Present Perfect isn't applicable. In order to know what a grammatical item is, one also needs to know what it isn't.

Your questions (and the students' answers)
Which city did he live in? (Osaka.)
Did he enjoy it? (Yes, he did.)
Did he like the food? (Yes, he did.)

When did he fly in a jumbo jet? (When he went to Japan.)
Where did the plane stop? (In Moscow.)
How long was the flight? (About twelve or thirteen hours.)

When did he cook a meal for more than 10 people? (When he was a boy scout.)
What did he cook? (Beans on toast.)

What play did he see? (*Hamlet*.)
When did he see *Hamlet*? (When he was at school.)

When did he drive a tractor? (When he worked on a farm.)
When did he work on a farm? (When he was seventeen.)

Why did he go to hospital? (Because he broke his leg.)
When did he break his leg? (When he was six.)
What happened when he was twenty-two? (He had a car accident.)

3 Students ask you the same questions. Make sure they remember to include *ever*. (Look at the examples with the students first.) Answer their questions.

4 Students ask a partner the same questions, then report back to the class.

3 Choosing the correct sentence

This exercise revises the grammar just learnt. Students work in pairs to choose the correct sentence.

Answers
1 a 2 b 3 a 4 b 5 b 6 a 7 b 8 a

Additional material

Workbook Unit 14
Exercises 1–4 Past Simple and Present Perfect
Exercise 5 Past time expressions

PRESENTATION (2) **(SB page 100)**

Present Perfect + *yet* and *just*

Note

1 The concepts expressed by *yet* and *just* are very subtle and they are realized by different structures in different languages. We do not ask any Grammar questions that test concept (only form), because the language required would be more complex than the target item itself. We rely on context, but mainly translation and/or dictionaries, to convey the meaning of the two adverbs.

2 It might be a good idea to do Exercise 9 of the Workbook on *been* versus *gone* before you do Presentation (2), as these structures occur in this presentation.

1 Read the introduction and the list as a class. Explain that New York is known as *the Big Apple* (but we have no idea why!). Make sure that students understand vocabulary items such as the following:

show *climb* *Statue of Liberty* *helicopter tour*

Careful with the pronunciation of Greenwich /grenɪtʃ/!

2 **T81** Read the instructions as a class. Either translate *yet* or ask students to look it up in their dictionary. Students listen to the tape and put a tick or a cross beside the activities.

Answers

see a show on Broadway	✘
climb the Empire State Building	✔
see the Statue of Liberty	✔
go to Greenwich Village	✘
walk in Central Park	✔
go to Chinatown	✘
take a helicopter tour	✔

3 Play the conversation again. Ask students to complete the sentences.

Answers

a We *haven't* been to Greenwich Village yet.
b Have you *seen* the Statue of Liberty yet?
c We've just *had* a helicopter tour.

Play the conversation again for students to check. Ask students to find two more examples of *yet*.

Answers

Have you seen a show on Broadway yet?
… we haven't decided what to see yet.

● Grammar questions

Note

1 Remember that these questions focus on the form of *yet* and *just*, not the concept, because any questions that tested students' understanding of these items would be more complex than the items themselves. You need to make sure, probably via translation if possible, that students have understood them. Explain that *(not) yet* means *(not) before now* whereas *just* means *a short time before now*, using examples from the text or putting examples on the board.

2 These Grammar questions are quite difficult, so don't be surprised if students find them hard to answer. If you have to prompt a lot, it doesn't really matter.

Look at the Grammar questions as a class.

Answers

- *yet* comes at the end of a sentence.
- *just* comes before the past participle.
- We do not use *yet* in positive sentences, only in *questions* and *negatives*.

Practice **(SB page 101)**

1 Speaking

1 Students haven't practised the sentences in the Present Perfect with *yet*, so now's the time to do it! Read the instructions as a class, and ask for some sentences. Correct any mistakes carefully.

Answers

They've been for a walk in Central Park.
They've climbed the Empire State Building.
They've seen the Statue of Liberty.
They've taken/had a helicopter tour.
They haven't been to Greenwich Village yet.
They haven't been to Chinatown yet.
They haven't seen a show on Broadway yet.

2 Students work in pairs to make questions with *yet* and answers with *just*. This is a very straightforward drill that tests the form of the Present Perfect with the two adverbs.

Answers

a Have you finished your homework yet?
Yes, I've just done/finished it.
b Have you washed your hair yet?
Yes, I've just done/washed it.
c Have you cleaned the car yet?
Yes, I've just done/cleaned it.
d Have you met the new student yet?
Yes, I've just met him/her.
e Have you made the dinner yet?
Yes, I've just made it.
f Have you done the shopping yet?
Yes, I've just done it.
g Have you talked to the teacher yet?
Yes, I've just talked to her/him.
h Have you bought your plane ticket yet?
Yes, I've just bought it.

2 Reading

Students work in pairs to complete the story and put the verbs into the Present Perfect or the Past Simple. Make sure students understand *safari*. Careful with the pronunciation of *psychiatrist* /saɪkaɪətrɪst/! Ask for feedback before you give the answers.

Answers

A Sad Story of a Sad Man

One Sunday evening two men (a) *met* in a London pub. One of them was very unhappy.

'Life is terrible, everything in the world is really boring,' he said.

'Don't say that,' said the other man. 'Life is marvellous! The world is so exciting! Think about Italy. It's a wonderful country. (b) *Have* you ever *been* there?'

'Oh yes. I (c) *went* there last year and I (d) *didn't like* it.'

'Well, (e) *have* you *been* to Norway? (f) *Have* you ever *seen* the midnight sun?'

'Oh yes. I (g) *went* in 1984 and I (h) *saw* the midnight sun. I (i) *didn't enjoy* it.'

'Well, I (j) *have* just *returned* from a safari in Africa. (k) *Have* you *visited* Africa yet?'

'Yes, I (l) *went* on safari in Africa last year and I (m) *climbed* Mount Kilimanjaro. It was really boring.'

'Well,' said the other man, 'I think that you're very ill. Only the best psychiatrist can help you. Go to see Dr Greenbaum in Harley Street.'

'I am Dr Greenbaum,' answered the man sadly.

You could ask two students to take the parts of the two men and read the completed story aloud with you or a third student as the narrator. Encourage them to make the sad man sound *very* sad and his companion cheerful and enthusiastic.

3 Grammar

Students work in pairs to complete the sentences with a word from the box. Point out that thank-you letters are written after the receipt of a present, such as a birthday present or a Christmas present. They are especially written by children upon exhortation from their parents!

Answers

a *Did* you go to America *last* year?
b '*Has* he *ever* been to India?' 'Yes, he *has*.'
c '*Have* you *ever* met the Queen?' 'No, I *haven't*.'
d 'When *did* you meet your husband?' 'Ten years *ago*.'
e I *have just* finished my homework. Now I can watch TV.
f '*Have* you finished your homework *yet*?'
'No, I *haven't*.'
g 'I *didn't* play tennis *last* weekend because it was wet.'
h Kate *hasn't* written her thank-you letters *yet*.
i We *have* been to Spain but we *have never* been to Portugal.
j '*Have* they moved to their new house *yet*?'
'Yes, they moved three days *ago*.'

Additional material

Workbook Unit 14
Exercise 6 Choosing the correct adverb
Exercises 7 and 8 *yet* and *just*

● READING AND SPEAKING (SB page 102)

Three amazing grandmas

Pre-reading task

Note
It would be a nice idea if you could bring in some photos of your grandmother(s). It would be even nicer if students could also bring in some photos of *their* grandmother(s)!

1 Students work in pairs to answer the questions. Ask for some feedback as a class. This could go on for quite a while, especially if students have brought some photos.

2 Students check the new words in their dictionary.

Reading

Students divide into three groups.

Group A reads about Dorothy Moriarty.
Group B reads about Kitty Currie.
Group C reads about Alice Hyde.

They answer the questions in the Comprehension Check. Note that Florence Nightingale was a famous nurse in England in the nineteenth century. She worked in the Crimean War (1853–56).

Answers

Dorothy Moriarty

a 102.
b Because she has just written her first book at the age of 102.
c Yes. She worked as a nurse at the beginning of the century.
d In 1922.
e Yes. She has lived in Egypt.
f Yes. When she started working as a nurse conditions were very difficult. Her husband had a drink problem and finally died.
g *cockroach civilian military*

Alice Hyde

a 97.
b She was the first Miss World in 1911.
c Yes. She had an antique shop.
d In 1912.
e Yes. She has lived in Spain.
f Possibly. She wanted to go to Hollywood, but her parents said she couldn't.
g *active antique shop (do) exercises regret*

Kitty Currie

a 68.
b She robbed a bank.
c No, she hasn't.
d When she was sixteen.
e No, she hasn't.
f No, until she went to prison!
g *cardigan gun knit stocking toy*

Speaking

1 Students find someone from the other two groups to compare answers and tell each other about their old ladies.

2 Students read the other two texts and answer the true/false questions.

Answers

a Alice Hyde is the oldest. ✗
b They are all widows. ✗
c They have all been famous at some time in their lives. ✓
d Dorothy and Alice have both written books about their lives. ✗
e In the First World War military hospitals got more money than other hospitals. ✓
f Kitty Currie robbed the bank because she was bored with her life. ✓
g Charlie Chaplin wanted to marry Alice. ✗
h Kitty and Alice both have five children. ✗
i They all have plans for the future. ✓
(Dorothy is planning her next book; Alice is going to Spain; Kitty isn't going to rob another bank.)

Discussion

1 Discuss the questions as a class.

Sample answers
Alice says that she has had a wonderful life.
Dorothy says that she has had a difficult life.
Dorothy says that she has had an interesting life.

2 Have a class discussion about grandmothers. That is, if you haven't already exhausted the subject at the beginning of the lesson!

● VOCABULARY AND PRONUNCIATION

(SB page 104)

Odd one out

> **Note**
> This vocabulary activity revises a lot of words from Unit 14 and previous units. It also further practises recognition of the phonetic script.

1 Students work in pairs or small groups to decide which word is the odd one out. They should use dictionaries. (Note also that the new or least familiar vocabulary is illustrated, so you could ask them to match some words with the pictures.) They might well come up with alternative answers, which is fine as long as they can justify them.

Answers

a *nephew*, because the others refer to women.
b *gloves*, because the others go over feet or legs.
c *sailed*, because the others are irregular verbs. (This is difficult.)
d *customer*, because the others are about hospitals.
e *letter*, because the others are machines.
f *T-shirt*, because the others go over legs.
g *wrote*, because the others are past participles. (This is difficult.)
h *foot*, because the others are at the top of the body!
i *boring*, because the others are positive.
j *plays*, because the others are auxiliary verbs.
k *cat*, because the others express the idea of a young animal.

2 Students work in pairs to practise saying the words.

Answers

a gloves	g amazing
b tights	h widow
c patient	i nephew
d jeans	j nurse
e shorts	k puppy
f foot	l trousers

3 Students work in pairs to put one of the words from Exercise 1 into each gap. Tell the students that all of the words needed are the odd ones out from Exercise 1.

Answers

a Have you seen my *gloves*? My hands are really cold!
b Mary Moss has written ten novels. She *wrote Love in the Sun* two years ago.
c I have three nieces and one *nephew*.
d John thought the film was marvellous but I thought it was *boring*.
e I haven't seen my grandmother recently. I think I'll send her a *letter*.
f Our *cat* has had four kittens!
g That *customer* has tried on every dress in the shop and she doesn't like any of them!
h John has just bought a guitar. He *plays* it all the time.
i Ruth hates flying so she *sailed* to New York.
j Bobby has hurt his *foot* because he kicked the ball so hard.
k When I was in London I bought a *T-shirt* with *I had tea with the Queen* on the front!

● EVERYDAY ENGLISH **(SB page 104)**

Telephoning

1 **T82a** Listen to the three British telephone tones. Students might well have no idea which tone means what!

Answers

1 This means 'The number is engaged'.
2 This means 'You can dial'.
3 This means 'The number is ringing'.

2 Students work in pairs to complete the three telephone conversations. Make sure they understand the following:

get someone (as in *fetch*) *message* *Great!*
Never mind *put you through*

After students have done the exercise, you could also point out to students the use of *I'll* to express a decision made at the time of speaking, e.g. *I'll ring back later,* as first introduced in Unit 12, Everyday English.

Answers

1

A Hello. 276694.
B Hello. Can I speak to Jo, please?
A *This is Jo speaking.*
B Oh! Hi Jo. This is Pat. I'm just ringing to check that Sunday is still OK for tennis.
A Yes. That's fine.
B *Great! See you on Sunday at 10. Bye!*
A Bye!

2

A Hello. Chesswood 4576.
B Hello. Is that Liz?
A *No, it isn't. I'll just get her.*
C Hello. Liz here.
B Hi, Liz. It's Tom. Listen! *I'm having a party on Saturday. Can you come?*
C Oh sorry, Tom. I can't. I'm going to my cousin's wedding.
B *Never mind. Perhaps next time. Bye!*
C Bye!

3

A Hello. Barclays Bank, Chesswood.
B Hello. *Can I speak to the manager, please?*
A Hold on. I'll put you through ... I'm afraid Mr Smith isn't in his office. *Can I take a message*?
B Don't worry. *I'll ring back later.*
A All right. Goodbye.
B Goodbye.

T 82b Students listen and check. In pairs, they memorize one of the conversations and practise saying it. Learning something by heart sounds boring, but students often enjoy doing it.

3 Read the introduction as a class.

T 82c Students listen and answer the operator's questions. Do this as a class activity, asking one student to answer the questions.

Answers

Directory Enquiries. Which town, please? Harrogate.
Can I have the surname, please? Duncan.
And the initial? J.
What's the address? 42, Collier Lane.
Thank you. The number you want is 0423 287221.

Students work in pairs to roleplay the operator and someone wanting a number. You could write the following information on bits of paper to give the operators, or simply write it on the board.

Ian Macdonald's phone number is 0738 644321.

Donna Vale's phone number is 0101 416 7896533, and her fax number is 0101 416 7865443.

GRAMMAR SUMMARY (SB page 105)

Read the Grammar Summary as a class. Encourage students to ask any questions.

Don't forget!

Workbook Unit 14
Exercise 10 Various nouns
Exercise 11 Filling in a form

Word List
Remind your students of the Word List at the back of their book. Ask them to look at the list for this unit on page 126. Tell them that they could write in the translations, learn them at home and/or write some of the words in their vocabulary notebooks.

Video There is a final section 12 called *Cappuccino* which can be used after this unit or the next one, in which Paula spends her last day with David in Bath, before she goes back to Italy.

Pronunciation Book Unit 14

UNIT 15

Verb patterns – *say* and *tell* – Problems with officials

Introduction to the unit

The theme of this unit is 'Thank you and goodbye', and it marks the final unit of Headway Elementary. There is a general idea of conclusion as students come to the end of the book! Students listen to a song, *She's Leaving Home*, and there is a discussion about parents and teenagers.

Language aims

Grammar

Verb patterns

It is a feature of English that when one verb follows another, various patterns are possible. The most common patterns are verb + *-ing* (*enjoy doing*), verb + *to* + infinitive (*want to do*), and verb + infinitive without *to* (*can do*). There are few rules, and students simply have to learn the possible patterns. There is a list of verb patterns on page 127 of the Student's Book.
Similarly, there are certain adjectives that are followed by an infinitive, and these too have to be learnt (*easy to do*).

say* and *tell

The verbs *say* and *tell* are introduced, not so much as part of reported speech, but rather as a part of verb patterns. That is, *say* is often not followed by an indirect object, whereas *tell* is nearly always followed by a direct object.
She said (to me) that she liked curry.
She told me she liked curry.
We do not introduce or practise any of the tense shifts that are commonly associated with reported speech in this unit. Everything is in the Past Simple, which is fine here.

Vocabulary

We formally introduce multi-word verbs for the first time (they are often known as phrasal verbs). A few of them have occurred before, for example *take off* and *try on*, but they are such an important area of the language that they need introducing, albeit at a very basic level.

Everyday English

We end the Everyday English sections with 'Problems with officials', and drop in *have to* to express obligation. This is not a major presentation, but it is useful for students and interesting for them to see the verb *have* being used in a very different way.

Workbook

There is an exercise that practises *have to* for obligation.
In the vocabulary section, the noun suffix *-ion*, and words that are nouns and verbs are practised.
In the writing section, students practise dividing a letter into paragraphs, and they write a thank-you letter.

Notes on the unit

PRESENTATION (1) (SB page 106)

Verb patterns

1 Ask students to look at the picture and say what they can see.

They read the thank-you letter. They probably won't realize until they do Presentation (2) that Barbara isn't being entirely honest about her reactions to the dinner party! If students raise an eyebrow when they read about the interesting evening talking about dogs and dishwashers, just wait before you tell them the joke!

Ask a student to read out the letter. Be careful with the pronunciation of recipe /resɪpɪ/. You could ask students what they think of duck and banana curry, and if the evening sounds good fun!

2 Students complete the answers.

Answers

a Because she wants *to thank* Margo and Dennis for the dinner party.
b 'Is it possible *to send* me the recipe?'
'Is the curry expensive *to make*?'
c She says that she has decided *to cook* the curry.
d She says that they enjoyed *meeting* them.
They hope *to meet* them again one day.
e She says that they loved *hearing* about their house and dishwasher.

Ask students to look at all the words they wrote in. Check they remember the word *infinitive*. It's probably best to call words such as *meeting* verb + *-ing* rather than gerunds.

⚠ Read the information in the Caution Box as a class. You might want to look at the list of verb patterns on page 127.

Practice (SB page 107)

1 Grammar

1 Students read the letter again and underline the examples of infinitives and *-ing* forms.

Answers

Mon. March 7th

Dear Margo and Dennis,

I want *to thank* you very much for the lovely dinner party last Saturday evening. Raymond and I had a wonderful time. The food was delicious! Is it possible *to send* me the recipe for the Duck and Banana Curry? We really enjoyed it, especially with the pink champagne. Is it expensive *to make*? I have decided *to cook* it for my next dinner party.

Also we enjoyed *meeting* your friends Betty and Oswald. We enjoyed *hearing* about their big house, their car, their dog, their holiday in Corfu, and their new dishwasher. It was very interesting. We hope *to meet* them again one day.

Thank you again. See you soon.

Love Barbara and Raymond

2 Students complete the sentences with the verbs from the box.

Answers

a Do you think English is difficult *to learn*?
b My mother has promised *to buy* me a new coat for my birthday.
c How do you do? It's very nice *to meet* you.
d John hates *flying*, but I love planes.
e I need *to talk* to somebody about my problem.
f We stopped *playing* tennis because it started *to rain/raining*.
g I don't like *driving* big cars, I prefer *riding* my bike.
h Bob's finished *painting* the bathroom doors.
i Did you enjoy *visiting* the British Museum?
j Please don't forget *to post* my letter.

Additional material

Workbook Unit 15
Exercises 1–4 Verb patterns

PRESENTATION (2) (SB page 107)

say and *tell*

T 83 Students listen to Barbara talking to a friend about the dinner party. They should see the joke now!
First ask students to listen and read, but not write. When they have heard the complete conversation, they can work in pairs to fill the gaps.
Play the tape again to check.

Answers
A Hi Barbara! Did you and Raymond enjoy Margo's dinner party?
B No, we *didn't*. It *was awful*!
A What about the food?
B Oh, the food *was disgusting!* We *hated* it. We *had* Duck and Banana Curry!
A Duck and what?! Ugh!
B I know. I *don't like* duck and Ray *doesn't like* bananas!
A And their friends? Tell me about their friends. Were they nice?
B Oh, Alice! They were friendly, but they were so *boring!* They talked for three hours about their *house* and their *dog* and their *dishwasher*! And they *didn't ask* one question about us. We *said* very little, only 'Yes?' and 'No!'
A Oh dear! What a terrible evening!

⚠ Read the information in the Caution Box as a class. Remember that we introduce *say* and *tell* mainly as verbs with certain patterns rather than as examples of reported speech, so we don't suggest you say anything about reported speech.

● Grammar questions

These grammar questions are difficult, even though the information is virtually in the Caution Box above, so don't worry if you have to prompt a lot.

Answers
- We use *say* with or without *that*, usually without the person/indirect object.
- We use *tell* with or without *that*, usually with the person/indirect object.
- Both are possible.

Practice (SB page 108)

1 Speaking

Students work in pairs to compare Barbara's letter and her conversation.

Sample answers
In the letter she said the food was delicious, but she told Alice they hated it.
She said she enjoyed meeting their friends, but she told Alice they were boring.

2 Writing and speaking

Students work in pairs to write a dialogue about a good dinner party. They act it out, then other students make sentences with *say* and *tell*.

3 Correcting the mistakes

Students work in pairs to correct the mistakes which are all to do with verb patterns.

Answers
a I started to smoke when I was sixteen years old.
b We'd like you to come for dinner.
c She told me the restaurant was next to the cinema. (*Or* She said the restaurant ...)
d Jeremy has never told me about his trip to Paris.
e It's difficult for me to learn Portuguese.
f I've been to the post office to buy some stamps.
g Do you want to meet the manager?
h Money can't buy love.

● VOCABULARY (SB page 108)

Multi-word verbs

Note
Multi-word verbs, also known as phrasal verbs, cause students a lot of problems because they can be used literally and idiomatically. It is by no means obvious which adverb or preposition to use, and there are four types, some intransitive and some transitive. See a grammar book for more information.

However, at this stage of your students' English learning career, they probably won't be worrying about these things yet! This exercise simply gives some dictionary extracts, revises some multi-word verbs that have already appeared in *Headway Elementary*, and practises a few more. Note that *break down*, *go out with*, and *get on* are taught as they are used in the reading and listening exercises which follow on page 109.

1 Read the explanation as a class. Check that students understand *literal* and *idiomatic*. Translate if you can, they can check in their dictionaries.

2 Students use the multi-word verbs to complete the sentences. Read the extracts as a class. Students might want to check the words in their dictionary, and they might have problems in finding the correct entry and the correct definition, so be prepared to help with this.

Answers
a My neighbours are away on holiday so I*'m looking after* their cat.
b The plane is delayed. It *hasn't taken off* yet.
c Please can you *turn off* the radio. That music is too loud.
d My husband wants *to give up* smoking, but he can't.
e Have you heard? Rita*'s going out* with Rick. They met at Ann's party.
f '*Do* you *get on* well with your husband's parents?' 'No, I don't.'
g The journey took ten hours because our car *broke down* on the motorway.
h Mary *broke down* when Roger told her that he was in love with another girl.

Additional material

Workbook Unit 15
Exercise 6 *say* and *tell*
Exercise 9 Multi-word verbs

● READING AND SPEAKING (SB page 109)

Leaving home

The letter on this page not only sets the scene for the Beatles' song *She's Leaving Home* on the next page, but it also introduces some vocabulary necessary to understand it.

Pre-reading task

First try to get your class to talk about themselves in relation to the topic. This is often a good way to generate interest. You could begin by telling your students a little about yourself and if/when you left home. Then ask:

How many of you still live at home with your parents? Do you like it?
Who has left home? When/why did you leave? Where do you live now?

Read out the questions in the book and ask your students to work in groups of three or four to discuss them. Then get some feedback from the class and encourage a short discussion.

Cultural note
In Britain it is quite common to leave home at about eighteen and go away from home for further education, either at university or college. However recent cuts in government grants now means that fewer students leave home, because they can't afford it. They go instead to their nearest university or college.

In some families there is conflict between teenagers and parents, and children leave home at sixteen or even younger. They often go to the big cities, particularly London, and try to find work, but because this is often difficult they end up homeless and living on the streets.

This problem has grown in recent years.

Reading

You will need to pre-teach *It was a struggle*. You can say that it means the same as *It was difficult.* (The word is used in the letter because it appears in the song.)
Ask them to read the letter quite quickly and then discuss the questions with a partner.

Answers
Paula has written the letter.
She wrote it at four o'clock in the morning, on a Wednesday in June.
She wrote it because she wanted to tell her parents that she is leaving home.
You could also ask: *How old do you think she is?*

Comprehension check

Ask students to work in pairs to do this. Then go through the answers with the whole class.

Don't just ask them to say *true* or *false*, but encourage them to tell you why.

Answers
a False. (She is telling them that she is going to get married, but she is not inviting them to the wedding.)
b True. (They wanted to plan her life. They tried to choose her friends, her job, and her clothes.)
c False. (They *don't* like Martin because he is a car salesman. They think he isn't good enough for their daughter.)
d False. (It was difficult to buy toys, clothes, and an expensive education because they didn't have much money.)
e True. (They bought her toys and clothes.)
f False. (Paula loves her parents, but she wants to be free/independent and they don't like Martin.)
g False. (She's an only child.)
h False. (She is going to write. She promises to write at the end of the letter.)

Note
If you have time and you feel it would not stop the flow of the lesson, you could include a quick language focus at this point and ask your students to find and underline the three multi-word verbs in the letter. These are revision of some of the ones covered in the vocabulary section on page 108. They are:

You didn't want me *to go out with* him.
I'd love us all *to get on* well together.
Look after each other.

Listening

T84 Your students should be prepared now to listen to the song. *She's Leaving Home* is from the Beatles album *Sergeant Pepper's Lonely Hearts Club Band.*
Before you play it ask them to look at the pictures on the page, and check some of the vocabulary through these. For example *dressing gown, clutch, snore.*
(If you want, you could first play it right through and tell your class to close their books, relax and enjoy it, and not worry about understanding all the words at this stage.)
Ask them to work in pairs and read the first verse and choose the best word to fill the gaps. They can use their dictionaries to check any other new words. Play the verse for them to check their answers. Continue like this through all the verses.

Answers
See the tapescript on page 122 for the answers.

Play the song for a final time and ask them to read and listen. They should be able to understand it all.

Discussion
Ask your students for their opinion on the situation in the song. Was Paula right to leave home, or not? Who do they feel sorry for – Paula or her parents?

● EVERYDAY ENGLISH (SB page 111)

Problems with officials

Additional material
Workbook Unit 15
Exercise 5 This introduces *have to* for strong obligation. It may be a good idea to do this with your class before you do this Everyday English, as it is used in the activity.

1 Most people have tales to tell about confrontation with officialdom and red tape. It would be nice if you could begin by telling your class about a time when *you* had such a problem. Then ask them in pairs or small groups to tell each other any similar stories.

Get feedback from the whole class. (Make a note of any interesting stories so that you can choose those students to act out with a partner at the end of the session [see 4].)

2 Still in their pairs or groups, ask them to study the sentences and say who they think is speaking and where they are. Go through the answers as a class.

Answers
a A clerk in a post office.
b A customer in a clothes shop.
c This could be a barman/maid in a pub asking for proof of age and identity, or a shop assistant asking for proof of identity for a cheque over £100. (Note that in Britain we do not have identity cards.)
d A shop assistant in a shop. (Be careful with the pronunciation of *receipt* /rɪsiːt/)
e An immigration/passport officer at an airport or at any point of entry into another country.
f A shop assistant in a shop.
g A clerk in a post office or an airport official.
h An immigration officer at an airport or at any point of entry into another country.

⚠ Read through the Caution Box with your students. It is a little explanation of the use of *have to.*

3 **T85** Ask students to do this in pairs. Then play the tape for them to check their answers.

Answers

1 A Can I help you?
  B Yes. Can I change this jumper please? *I bought it last week and it's too small.*
  A Have you got the receipt?
  B No. I'm sorry, I've lost it.
  A Oh dear! *You have to give us the receipt. We can't change anything without a receipt.*
  B But …!

2 A Can I send this parcel to Greece, please?
  B Yes, of course. That's £3.50. Thank you. *Have you filled in the customs form?*
  A Customs form? What customs form?
  B *You have to fill in a customs form when you send a parcel overseas.*
  A Can you give me a form then, please?
  B No, I don't have any. They're over there on that table.
  A Sorry? Where?
  B Over there. They're the green forms.

3 A That's £104.50 altogether. How do you want to pay?
  B Can I pay by cheque?
  A Yes, but have you got any identification? *You have to show identification with cheques over £100.*
  B Oh dear! Let me see. I've got a photo of me and my aunt at the seaside.
  A No, no, no. *Have you got a passport or a driving licence*?
  B No, I haven't.
  A Then I'm afraid we can't take your cheque.
  B But …!

4 A *What's the purpose of your visit?*
  B Oh – I'm going to study English and have a holiday.
  A And how long are you staying?
  B For a month.
  A And where are you going to stay? What's your address?
  B I'm not sure. The language school is going to find me somewhere to stay.
  A Mmm! *You have to give us an address. You can't enter the country without an address!*
  B But …!

4 Ask a few pairs to act out some of the more interesting problems they talked about at the beginning of the session.

GRAMMAR SUMMARY (SB page 111)

Read the Grammar Summary together in class, and/or ask your students to read it and *learn* the grammar at home. Encourage them to ask you questions about it. Remind them of the list of verb patterns in Appendix 2 on page 127 of their books.

Don't forget

Workbook Unit 15
Exercises 7 and 8 These revise many items of vocabulary covered so far. They focus on noun and verb forms.
Exercise 10 The writing activity is another informal letter. This is a thank-you letter written by Paola (from Unit 2 and the video) to her English family.

Word List
Remind your students of the Word List at the back of their book. Ask them to look at the list for this unit on page126. Tell them that they could write in the translations, learn them at home and/or write some of the words in their vocabulary notebooks.

Pronunciation Book Unit 15

Video
There is a video section that can supplement this unit and the last one: **Finale** (section 12), *Cappuccino*. It is the last day of Paola's visit to David in Bath before she goes back to Italy, and she and David have become rather fond of each other!

EXTRA IDEAS Units 13–15

On page 139 of the Teacher's Book there is an additional reading text about the actress Liza Minnelli.
If you have time and feel that your students would benefit from it, you can photocopy it and use it in class. The reading exercise revises the input of Units 13–15. It could also be done for homework.
Activities and exercises to exploit the reading are provided on page 139 and the answers are below.

Answers to the reading

Reading

a visiting	f told
b watching	g to go
c said	h immediately
d only	i unfortunately
e to be	j to produce

Comprehension check

1 March 12, 1946.
2 Judy Garland.
3 Her parents divorced.
4 MGM.
5 Two and a half.
6 Six.
7 1963.
8 No, she hasn't. She has been married three times and she has had problems with alcohol and drugs.

Language work

1 a How many children did her mother have?
b What was her father's job?
c How many times did her mother marry?
d What did she win in 1973?
e How many films has she made?
f When did she make *Stepping Out*?

2 Past Simple
was, divorced, spent, liked, enjoyed, learned, said, went, practised, appeared, danced, knew, wanted, saw, looked, told, decided, won

Present Perfect
has won, has made, has had, has (not) been, have lasted

STOP AND CHECK Units 13–15

There is a Stop and Check revision section after each quarter of the Student's Book. The idea is that your students pause to check their progress so far. Each test is out of 100. There is a Stop and Check Answer Key on page 143 of the Teacher's Book. You could set it in class as an informal progress test or you could use the following procedure.

1 Give your students the Stop and Check to do for homework, preferably when they have more time, such as at the weekend.

2 In the next lesson ask them to go over their answers in small groups, trying to agree on the right answer. Allow enough time for this. It can be very productive for students to try and persuade their peers of the right answer. Many previous lessons are recalled.

3 Go over it with the whole class, reminding students of the language items covered.

After all the group discussion everyone *should* have a reasonably high score!

PHOTOCOPIABLE MATERIAL

Oxford University Press
Walton Street, Oxford OX2 6DP

Student B's information for Practice Speaking Exercise 1 on page 13 of the Student's Book.

Surname	
First name	*Martin*
Country	
Job	*Policeman*
Address	
Phone number	*061 755 6439*
Age	
Married?	*Yes*

Surname	
First name	*Martin*
Country	
Job	*Policeman*
Address	
Phone number	*061 755 6439*
Age	
Married?	*Yes*

Surname	
First name	*Martin*
Country	
Job	*Policeman*
Address	
Phone number	*061 755 6439*
Age	
Married?	*Yes*

Surname	
First name	*Martin*
Country	
Job	*Policeman*
Address	
Phone number	*061 755 6439*
Age	
Married?	*Yes*

Forms for Practice Speaking Exercise 3 on page 13 of the Student's Book.

Student 1

Name ____________________

Country/town ____________________

Age ____________________

Job ____________________

Phone number ____________________

Married? ____________________

Student 2

Name ____________________

Country/town ____________________

Age ____________________

Job ____________________

Phone number ____________________

Married? ____________________

Student 1

Name ____________________

Country/town ____________________

Age ____________________

Job ____________________

Phone number ____________________

Married? ____________________

Student 2

Name ____________________

Country/town ____________________

Age ____________________

Job ____________________

Phone number ____________________

Married? ____________________

Reading

1 A magazine called *Weekend* interviewed a politician, Roberta Tomlinson. Read about her.

Weekend goes to the Houses of Parliament to interview an MP.

2 Complete the questions or answers in the interview with Roberta Tomlinson.

a A What's your name?
  B Roberta Tomlinson.
b A ______________________________ ?
  B T – O – M – L – I – N – S – O – N.
c A Where are you from?
  B ______________________________ .
d A ______________________________ ?
  B I'm forty-three.
e A Are you married?
  B ______________________________ .
f A ______________________________ ?
  B Andrew.
g A What does your husband do?
  B ______________________________ .
h A Do you have any children?
  B ______________________________ .
i A ______________________________ ?
  B Yes. I have two brothers.
j A Do you enjoy your work?
  B ______________________________ .
k A ______________________________ ?
  B Because I meet a lot of people.
l A Where do you live?
  B ______________________________ .
m A Do you have a garden?
  B ______________________________ .
n A ______________________________ in your free time?
  B Having friends for dinner, going to the theatre, and listening to music.

Meet... ROBERTA TOMLINSON

■ Me and my family ■

I'm from Glasgow, in Scotland, and I'm forty-three years old. I'm married, and my husband's name is Andrew. He's a teacher in a school for blind children. We have three children – two boys and a girl. I have two brothers. They still live in Scotland.

■ Me and my work ■

I'm a Member of Parliament, so I work in London for part of the week and in Scotland for the rest. I enjoy my work very much. I like it because I meet a lot of people and it is my job to help them. I work about fifty or sixty hours a week.

■ Me and my home ■

We have a flat in London, but my home is Glasgow, and we have a large house there. There are about twelve rooms, and the house is like a hotel. So many people come and go! We have a garden where we grow fruit and vegetables.

■ Me and my free time ■

Well, I have very little free time, but when I can, I like having friends for dinner. We sit, eat, drink, and talk for hours! I also enjoy the theatre, and I love the Edinburgh Festival, which takes place in August. I like all kinds of music but especially folk music.

EXTRA IDEAS UNITS 1–4 Revision

Listening

(You can find this song after the tapescripts for Unit 4 on the Class Cassette.)

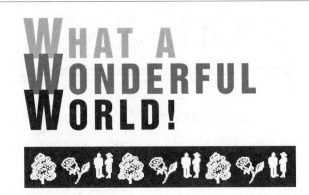

WHAT A WONDERFUL WORLD!

Louis Armstrong

I see trees of green
Red roses too
I see them bloom for me and you
And I think to myself
what a wonderful world.
I see skies of blue
and clouds of white,
the beautiful day
and the beautiful night,
and I think to myself
what a wonderful world.
The colours of the rainbow
so pretty in the sky
are also on the faces
of the people going by.
I see friends shaking hands
saying How do you do?
They're really saying
I love you.
I hear babies cry.
I watch them grow.
They learn much more
than they ever know
and I think to myself
what a wonderful world.
Yes, I think to myself
what a wonderful world.

WHAT A WONDERFUL WORLD!

Louis Armstrong

I see trees of green
Red roses too
I see them bloom for me and you
And I think to myself
what a wonderful world.
I see skies of blue
and clouds of white,
the beautiful day
and the beautiful night,
and I think to myself
what a wonderful world.
The colours of the rainbow
so pretty in the sky
are also on the faces
of the people going by.
I see friends shaking hands
saying How do you do?
They're really saying
I love you.
I hear babies cry.
I watch them grow.
They learn much more
than they ever know
and I think to myself
what a wonderful world.
Yes, I think to myself
what a wonderful world.

Pictures for Student A and Student B in Practice Speaking Exercise 1 on page 35 of the Student's Book.

Picture A

Picture B

Alternative gapped interview to Roleplay on page 44 of the Student's Book.

Alternative to roleplay

A = Interviewer   B = Ivan *or* Jaya

A Hello, __________ ! Can I __________ you a few questions?
B Yes, of course.
A First of all, how old __________ you?
B I'm __________ .
A And where do you __________ to school?
B I __________ go to school. I …
A And __________ do you live?
B I live in New York with …
A __________ you born in New York?
B No, I __________ . I …
A That's interesting. And were you clever when you __________ very young?
B Well, perhaps. You see I could …
A I can't believe it! Tell me, do you __________ any friends in America?
B No, I __________ .
A Oh! So what do you do in your __________ time?
B Well, I …
A Thank you very much. It's all very interesting. Good luck in the future!

Alternative to roleplay

A = Interviewer   B = Ivan *or* Jaya

A Hello, __________ ! Can I __________ you a few questions?
B Yes, of course.
A First of all, how old __________ you?
B I'm __________ .
A And where do you __________ to school?
B I __________ go to school. I …
A And __________ do you live?
B I live in New York with …
A __________ you born in New York?
B No, I __________ . I …
A That's interesting. And were you clever when you __________ very young?
B Well, perhaps. You see I could …
A I can't believe it! Tell me, do you __________ any friends in America?
B No, I __________ .
A Oh! So what do you do in your __________ time?
B Well, I …
A Thank you very much. It's all very interesting. Good luck in the future!

Alternative to roleplay

A = Interviewer   B = Ivan *or* Jaya

A Hello, __________ ! Can I __________ you a few questions?
B Yes, of course.
A First of all, how old __________ you?
B I'm __________ .
A And where do you __________ to school?
B I __________ go to school. I …
A And __________ do you live?
B I live in New York with …
A __________ you born in New York?
B No, I __________ . I …
A That's interesting. And were you clever when you __________ very young?
B Well, perhaps. You see I could …
A I can't believe it! Tell me, do you __________ any friends in America?
B No, I __________ .
A Oh! So what do you do in your __________ time?
B Well, I …
A Thank you very much. It's all very interesting. Good luck in the future!

Alternative to roleplay

A = Interviewer   B = Ivan *or* Jaya

A Hello, __________ ! Can I __________ you a few questions?
B Yes, of course.
A First of all, how old __________ you?
B I'm __________ .
A And where do you __________ to school?
B I __________ go to school. I …
A And __________ do you live?
B I live in New York with …
A __________ you born in New York?
B No, I __________ . I …
A That's interesting. And were you clever when you __________ very young?
B Well, perhaps. You see I could …
A I can't believe it! Tell me, do you __________ any friends in America?
B No, I __________ .
A Oh! So what do you do in your __________ time?
B Well, I …
A Thank you very much. It's all very interesting. Good luck in the future!

Information for Student A and Student B for Practice Speaking Exercise 1 on page 49 of the Student's Book.

Student A

Prince Albert was German, and they married in ____________ (*Where?*) in 1840.

Soon after they married, they visited the French king, Louis Philippe. They visited him in ____________ (*When?*).

Unfortunately, Prince Albert died in 1861 when he was only ____________ (*How old?*). Queen Victoria was terribly unhappy, and she never lived in London again. She lived in Windsor and Scotland. She loved Scotland because ______________________________ ____________(*Why?*).

She died in 1901. She was ____________ (*How old?*).

Student B

Prince Albert was ____________(*What nationality?*), and they married in London in 1840.

Soon after they married, they visited ________________________ (*Who?*). They visited him in 1843.

Unfortunately, Prince Albert died in _________ (*When?*) when he was only 42. Queen Victoria was terribly unhappy, and she never lived in London again. She lived in __________________ (*Where?*). She loved Scotland because she often went there on holiday with her family.

She died in _________ (*When?*). She was 81.

Student A

Prince Albert was German, and they married in ____________ (*Where?*) in 1840.

Soon after they married, they visited the French king, Louis Philippe. They visited him in ____________ (*When?*).

Unfortunately, Prince Albert died in 1861 when he was only ____________ (*How old?*). Queen Victoria was terribly unhappy, and she never lived in London again. She lived in Windsor and Scotland. She loved Scotland because ______________________________ ____________(*Why?*).

She died in 1901. She was ____________ (*How old?*).

Student B

Prince Albert was ____________(*What nationality?*), and they married in London in 1840.

Soon after they married, they visited ________________________ (*Who?*). They visited him in 1843.

Unfortunately, Prince Albert died in _________ (*When?*) when he was only 42. Queen Victoria was terribly unhappy, and she never lived in London again. She lived in __________________ (*Where?*). She loved Scotland because she often went there on holiday with her family.

She died in _________ (*When?*). She was 81.

Information for Student A and Student B for Practice Listening and pronunciation Exercise 2 on page 55 of the Student's Book.

Student A

Did you know that ...?

... Vincent van Gogh sold only two of his paintings while he was alive.

... the actress Shirley Temple was a millionaire before she was ten.

... Shakespeare spelled his name in eleven different ways.

... in 1979 it snowed in the Sahara Desert.

... King Louis XIV of France had a bath only three times in his life.

... the American President George Washington grew marijuana in his garden.

Student B

Did you know that ...?

... it took 1,700 years to build the Great Wall of China.

... King Henry VIII of England had six wives.

... Walt Disney used his own voice for the character of Mickey Mouse.

... Shakespeare and the Spanish novelist Cervantes both died on the same day, 23 April 1616.

... King Francis I of France bought the painting *The Mona Lisa* to put in his bathroom.

... when Shakespeare was alive, there were no actresses, only male actors.

Student A

Did you know that ...?

... Vincent van Gogh sold only two of his paintings while he was alive.

... the actress Shirley Temple was a millionaire before she was ten.

... Shakespeare spelled his name in eleven different ways.

... in 1979 it snowed in the Sahara Desert.

... King Louis XIV of France had a bath only three times in his life.

... the American President George Washington grew marijuana in his garden.

Student B

Did you know that ...?

... it took 1,700 years to build the Great Wall of China.

... King Henry VIII of England had six wives.

... Walt Disney used his own voice for the character of Mickey Mouse.

... Shakespeare and the Spanish novelist Cervantes both died on the same day, 23 April 1616.

... King Francis I of France bought the painting *The Mona Lisa* to put in his bathroom.

... when Shakespeare was alive, there were no actresses, only male actors.

EXTRA IDEAS UNITS 5–8 Revision

Reading and speaking

1 Work in groups.
How good is your memory? Answer the questions.
1 When is your parents' wedding anniversary?
2 What did you have to eat last night?
3 Where were you ten days ago? What did you do that day?
4 Where were the Olympic Games in 1992?
5 When was your mother born?
6 How many phone numbers can you remember?

2 Read the newspaper article about Dominic O'Leary, the man with the best memory in the world.

3 Answer the questions.
a What are some of the things Dominic can remember?
b How did he become world champion?
c Was he good at school? Why not?
d What did his teachers say about him?
e When did he start to improve his memory? What did he see?
f Why isn't he popular with casino managers?
g How many clubs did he visit with the interviewers?
h How many clubs did he play in? Why?
i What do you think of Dominic's suggestions for a good memory?

Try his ideas to remember some words in English!

4 Here are the answers to some questions. Write in the questions.

a ______________________________?
Wednesday.

b ______________________________?
Last October.

c ______________________________?
Eight hundred pounds a day.

d ______________________________?
She's a clothes designer.

e ______________________________?
Seven hundred and fifty pounds.

f ______________________________?
He likes number games, crosswords, writing music, and playing the piano.

5 There are a lot of numbers in the article. What do these numbers refer to?

Example

1876 *April 21, 1876 was a Wednesday.*

a 35 b 34 c £1,000
d 7 e £1,250 f 5

WORLD CHAMPION MEMORY MAN

THIS IS DOMINIC O'LEARY, the man with the best memory in the world. He can tell you the day of any date in any year. What day was April 21, 1876? 'Wednesday,' says Dominic. He can remember the teams and the scores of every football match in every World Cup. And he became world champion memory man when he remembered the order of thirty-five packs of playing cards!

At school, Dominic was a pupil who couldn't remember his lessons. 'My Maths and English teachers said I was stupid because I could never remember what they taught me.' But four years ago he saw a programme on television which showed people how to improve their memory, and last October he became world champion. 'I remembered the order of thirty-five packs of cards,' said Dominic. 'It was quite easy.'

Dominic, 34, can earn £800 a day on European TV programmes. He lives with his wife, Alison, a clothes designer, in a small village near Bath, and he is the manager of an office cleaning company.

How to improve your memory

Dominic says anyone can have a good memory. These are his suggestions.

1 When you go to bed, remember everything you did that day.
2 Remember things in pictures, not words. 'Words are difficult to remember, but pictures are easy.' For example, if you want to remember the name Kate, think of a cat. For the number 8814, think of two snowmen, a tree and a bird.
3 If you forget something, remember where you were when you *could* remember it.

WINNING

Casino managers don't want Dominic to visit their casinos, because he can remember every card. 'I played as a professional gambler for a few months, and I won £1,000 a night, but then the managers asked me to leave.'

We went with Dominic to seven clubs in London and Brighton. He started with £500, and four hours later, he had £1,250 in his pocket. He won £750.

He played in just three clubs for four hours. The other four clubs knew his face and didn't want him to play.

In his free time, Dominic loves number games and crosswords, writing music, and playing the piano. He says children can learn to improve their memory from the age of five. 'Then they can do anything,' says Dominic.

EXTRA IDEAS UNITS 5–8 Revision

Listening

(You can find this song after the tapescript for Unit 8 on the Class Cassette.)

All the way from America

by Joan Armatrading

You called all the way from America
And said 'Hold on to love, girl.'
But the weeks and the months and the tears passed by
And my eyes couldn't stand the pain
Of that promised love
All the way from America.
You called all the way from America
And said 'I'll soon be home, girl.'
But the years and the tears and the fears passed by,
And my heart couldn't stand the pain
Of that promised love
All the way from America.
I stayed all alone and I waited nights
For you to knock at my door
But the knock never came and no ring at all
And now I sit and wonder why
You made that first call
All the way from America.
I don't believe I'll stay here
I don't think I want to wait here any more
And if you look for me, baby
You'd better bring some more love than you declared,
All the way from America.
All the way from America
All the way from America.

All the way from America

by Joan Armatrading

You called all the way from America
And said 'Hold on to love, girl.'
But the weeks and the months and the tears passed by
And my eyes couldn't stand the pain
Of that promised love
All the way from America.
You called all the way from America
And said 'I'll soon be home, girl.'
But the years and the tears and the fears passed by,
And my heart couldn't stand the pain
Of that promised love
All the way from America.
I stayed all alone and I waited nights
For you to knock at my door
But the knock never came and no ring at all
And now I sit and wonder why
You made that first call
All the way from America.
I don't believe I'll stay here
I don't think I want to wait here any more
And if you look for me, baby
You'd better bring some more love than you declared,
All the way from America.
All the way from America
All the way from America.

Rolecards for Speaking Exercise 2 of the Student's Book on page 71.

The King

6 castles – 2 in Scotland, 1 in Romania, and 3 in own country

20 cars – 10 Jaguars and 10 Porsches

150 Arab horses

3 gold crowns

50 gold and diamond rings

500 servants

5 million dollars

The Queen

6 castles – 3 in Scotland and 3 in own country

30 cars – 10 Lambourghinis, 10 Mercedes-Benz, and 10 Rolls Royces

100 Arab horses

5 gold crowns

80 platinum rings

500 servants

5 million pounds

The King

6 castles – 2 in Scotland, 1 in Romania, and 3 in own country

20 cars – 10 Jaguars and 10 Porsches

150 Arab horses

3 gold crowns

50 gold and diamond rings

500 servants

5 million dollars

The Queen

6 castles – 3 in Scotland and 3 in own country

30 cars – 10 Lambourghinis, 10 Mercedes-Benz, and 10 Rolls Royces

100 Arab horses

5 gold crowns

80 platinum rings

500 servants

5 million pounds

The King

6 castles – 2 in Scotland, 1 in Romania, and 3 in own country

20 cars – 10 Jaguars and 10 Porsches

150 Arab horses

3 gold crowns

50 gold and diamond rings

500 servants

5 million dollars

The Queen

6 castles – 3 in Scotland and 3 in own country

30 cars – 10 Lambourghinis, 10 Mercedes-Benz, and 10 Rolls Royces

100 Arab horses

5 gold crowns

80 platinum rings

500 servants

5 million pounds

Pictures for Student A and Student B for Practice Speaking Exercise 3 on page 79 of the Student's Book.

Picture A

Picture B

Student B's information for Speaking Activity Exercise 3 on page 88 of the Student's Book.

World Weather
noon yesterday

		°C
Athens	S	18
Berlin	____	____
Bombay	R	31
Edinburgh	____	____
Geneva	C	12
Hong Kong	____	____
Lisbon	C	19
London	____	____
Los Angeles	Fg	21
Luxor	____	____
Milan	Fg	19
Moscow	____	____
Oslo	Sn	2

S = sunny C = cloudy
Fg = foggy R = raining
Sn = snowing

World Weather
noon yesterday

		°C
Athens	S	18
Berlin	____	____
Bombay	R	31
Edinburgh	____	____
Geneva	C	12
Hong Kong	____	____
Lisbon	C	19
London	____	____
Los Angeles	Fg	21
Luxor	____	____
Milan	Fg	19
Moscow	____	____
Oslo	Sn	2

S = sunny C = cloudy
Fg = foggy R = raining
Sn = snowing

World Weather
noon yesterday

		°C
Athens	S	18
Berlin	____	____
Bombay	R	31
Edinburgh	____	____
Geneva	C	12
Hong Kong	____	____
Lisbon	C	19
London	____	____
Los Angeles	Fg	21
Luxor	____	____
Milan	Fg	19
Moscow	____	____
Oslo	Sn	2

S = sunny C = cloudy
Fg = foggy R = raining
Sn = snowing

World Weather
noon yesterday

		°C
Athens	S	18
Berlin	____	____
Bombay	R	31
Edinburgh	____	____
Geneva	C	12
Hong Kong	____	____
Lisbon	C	19
London	____	____
Los Angeles	Fg	21
Luxor	____	____
Milan	Fg	19
Moscow	____	____
Oslo	Sn	2

S = sunny C = cloudy
Fg = foggy R = raining
Sn = snowing

World Weather
noon yesterday

		°C
Athens	S	18
Berlin	____	____
Bombay	R	31
Edinburgh	____	____
Geneva	C	12
Hong Kong	____	____
Lisbon	C	19
London	____	____
Los Angeles	Fg	21
Luxor	____	____
Milan	Fg	19
Moscow	____	____
Oslo	Sn	2

S = sunny C = cloudy
Fg = foggy R = raining
Sn = snowing

World Weather
noon yesterday

		°C
Athens	S	18
Berlin	____	____
Bombay	R	31
Edinburgh	____	____
Geneva	C	12
Hong Kong	____	____
Lisbon	C	19
London	____	____
Los Angeles	Fg	21
Luxor	____	____
Milan	Fg	19
Moscow	____	____
Oslo	Sn	2

S = sunny C = cloudy
Fg = foggy R = raining
Sn = snowing

TV programme information for Everyday English Exercise 5 on page 89 of the Student's Book.

BBC 1

8.00 Utopia House
The story of Bob & Flo's marriage problems continues.
8.30 The Big Match
Moments from football's big night: Liverpool v. Arsenal
9.00 News & weather
9.40 Play Murder in our Village:
Can Detective Dixon help?
10.15 QED
This week: Divorce. Is it too easy?

BBC 2

8.00 Nature
Animals and birds in Siberia.
8.50 Points Of View
Your opinions of BBC programmes.
9.00 Star Trek
Travel through time again with Captain Kirk and his spaceship.
9.30 Hollywood
Norman Barry talks about new films.
10.30 Newsnight
Today's news and views from experts.

ITV

8.00 Happy Families
A quiz show for all the family.
8.30 Film
Ghostbusters 4
10.00 News & weather
10.30 The World of Money
Louisa Scott helps you with your money problems.
10.40 The Clothes Show
Fashions from Rome and Paris.

CHANNEL 4

8.00 The Food Programme
Chinese cooking
8.30 Today In Parliament
Politics and people.
8.55 Roseanne
American family comedy: The Diet!
9.25 Art in 15th Century Italy
Florence in the Renaissance.
10.20 Ice-skating
World championships from Prague.

BBC 1

8.00 Utopia House
The story of Bob & Flo's marriage problems continues.
8.30 The Big Match
Moments from football's big night: Liverpool v. Arsenal
9.00 News & weather
9.40 Play Murder in our Village:
Can Detective Dixon help?
10.15 QED
This week: Divorce. Is it too easy?

BBC 2

8.00 Nature
Animals and birds in Siberia.
8.50 Points Of View
Your opinions of BBC programmes.
9.00 Star Trek
Travel through time again with Captain Kirk and his spaceship.
9.30 Hollywood
Norman Barry talks about new films.
10.30 Newsnight
Today's news and views from experts.

ITV

8.00 Happy Families
A quiz show for all the family.
8.30 Film
Ghostbusters 4
10.00 News & weather
10.30 The World of Money
Louisa Scott helps you with your money problems.
10.40 The Clothes Show
Fashions from Rome and Paris.

CHANNEL 4

8.00 The Food Programme
Chinese cooking
8.30 Today In Parliament
Politics and people.
8.55 Roseanne
American family comedy: The Diet!
9.25 Art in 15th Century Italy
Florence in the Renaissance.
10.20 Ice-skating
World championships from Prague.

BBC 1

8.00 Utopia House
The story of Bob & Flo's marriage problems continues.
8.30 The Big Match
Moments from football's big night: Liverpool v. Arsenal
9.00 News & weather
9.40 Play Murder in our Village:
Can Detective Dixon help?
10.15 QED
This week: Divorce. Is it too easy?

BBC 2

8.00 Nature
Animals and birds in Siberia.
8.50 Points Of View
Your opinions of BBC programmes.
9.00 Star Trek
Travel through time again with Captain Kirk and his spaceship.
9.30 Hollywood
Norman Barry talks about new films.
10.30 Newsnight
Today's news and views from experts.

ITV

8.00 Happy Families
A quiz show for all the family.
8.30 Film
Ghostbusters 4
10.00 News & weather
10.30 The World of Money
Louisa Scott helps you with your money problems.
10.40 The Clothes Show
Fashions from Rome and Paris.

CHANNEL 4

8.00 The Food Programme
Chinese cooking
8.30 Today In Parliament
Politics and people.
8.55 Roseanne
American family comedy: The Diet!
9.25 Art in 15th Century Italy
Florence in the Renaissance.
10.20 Ice-skating
World championships from Prague.

EXTRA IDEAS UNITS 9–12 Revision

Pre-reading task

Vocabulary

The following words are either flowers or colours. Put them into the correct column. Use your dictionary to check new words.

tulip pink orange daffodil grey rose red
gold white snowdrop yellow primrose brown

Flowers	Colours

Reading

Read the text and answer the questions. Use your dictionary to help with new words.

THE GARDEN THAT MOVED HOUSE!

■ **Artist Verena Devoy loves gardening.** It is her passion. Until three days ago she lived in a lovely little thatched cottage in a village near Cambridge. She spent ten years and thousands of pounds to make her garden there beautiful. She had flowers and plants for every season of the year.

■ **In autumn, big orange chrysanthemums grew** next to the gold of the trees and bushes. In winter, little white snowdrops grew in the grass and under the trees. In spring there were bright yellow daffodils all over her front lawn and tulips and primroses next to the path. And summer! Summer was the prettiest season of all! She bought hundreds of roses to fill every part of the garden: she bought climbing roses to put round the windows and doors, pink roses for the front garden, and red and white roses for the back. A lot of people came to the village especially to see Verena's garden. It was more beautiful than the park.

■ **Then last summer** she decided that she would like to move to a bigger house. It was easy to sell her beautiful cottage. Mr and Mrs Grey from London came to see it.

■ **'We fell in love with it immediately,** especially the garden – we couldn't believe the colours of the roses. We wanted to move from London because we didn't have a garden there.'

■ **Of course Mr and Mrs Grey bought the cottage** and at the end of the summer they moved from London. They arrived at the cottage.

'There was *no* garden! There was a brown field with some stones and rocks. There weren't any flowers or trees and there wasn't any grass! It looked terrible! We couldn't believe our eyes!'

■ **But it was true!** Verena Devoy loved her garden so much that she took it with her when she left. Five large lorries carried all the flowers, trees, and plants to her new house five miles away. It cost £1,000! She says:

■ **'I've got a much bigger garden now** and I'm going to make it even more beautiful than my first garden. I'm going to plant all the flowers and trees again and this time I'm going to have a pond with some goldfish.'

■ **And Mr and Mrs Grey?** What do they say? 'She can't do this! We bought the garden with the house! We're going to see our solicitor!'

Comprehension check

a What is Verena's job? What is her hobby?
b Why did she spend thousands of pounds?
c Which was the most colourful season in her garden?
d Why did Verena want to move?
e Did Mr and Mrs Grey like the cottage when they first saw it?
f Why were they shocked when they arrived at the cottage?
g How much did Verena pay to move her garden?
h What are her plans for her new garden?
i What are Mr and Mrs Grey going to do?

Language work

1 Here are some answers. Complete the questions.

a How much *did she spend to make her garden beautiful*?
Thousands of pounds.

b Which was ______________________?
Summer. Because of all the roses.

c Why ______________________?
To see Verena's garden.

d Was ______________________?
Yes, it was. Very easy.

e Why ______________________?
Because they wanted to have a garden.

f When ______________________?
At the end of the summer.

g What ______________________ like?
It looked terrible. There weren't any flowers, just stones and rocks.

h Has Verena ______________________ now?
Yes, she has. It's much bigger.

i What ______________________ ?
She's going to make it even more beautiful and she's going to have a pond.

j Who ______________________ ?
Their solicitor.

2 Find examples of the following in the text. Underline them.

a The present and past of *have got*
b a comparative sentence
c a superlative sentence
d three irregular past tenses
e three sentences about the future
f an infinitive of purpose
g a sentence with *some*
h a sentence with *any*

Information for Student A and Student B for Practice Speaking Exercise 4 on page 93 of the Student's Book.

Student A

Laurel and Hardy, the comedy duo

They met in (a) ________ (*Where?*) in 1926, and they stopped making films together in (c) ________ (*When?*). They made about two hundred films. They won (e) ________ (*What?*) for their film *The Music Box* in 1932.

Stan Laurel, the thin one, was born in (g) ________ (*Where?*) in 1890. He went to America in (i) ________ (*When?*), and made his first film in 1917.

He married (k) ________ (*How many times?*), and had one daughter. He wrote the scripts and directed most of their films. He died in (m) ________ (*When?*) in California.

Oliver Hardy, the fat one, was born in (o) ________ (*Where?*) in 1892. He went to Hollywood in (q) ________ (*When?*), and made his first film in 1913.

He married (s) ________ (*How many times?*). He didn't have any children. In his free time, he liked (u) ________ (*What?*) and going to horse races. In one day he lost $12,000. He died in (w) ________ (*Where?*) in 1957.

Student B

Laurel and Hardy, the comedy duo

They met in Hollywood in (b) ________ (*When?*), and they stopped making films together in 1952. They made about (d) ________ films (*How many?*). They won an Oscar for their film *The Music Box* in (f) ________ (*When?*).

Stan Laurel, the thin one, was born in England in (h) ________ (*When?*). He went to America in 1910, and made his first film in (j) ________ (*When?*). He married four times, and had (l) ________ (*How many children?*). He wrote the scripts and directed most of their films. He died in 1965 in (n) ________ (*Where?*)

Oliver Hardy, the fat one, was born in Atlanta, Georgia, in (p) ________ (*When?*) . He went to Hollywood in 1911, and made his first film in (r) ________ (*When?*).

He married once. He (t) ________ children (*How many?*). In his free time, he liked playing golf and going to horse races. In one day he lost (v) ________ dollars (*How much money?*). He died in California in (x) ________ (*When?*).

Student A

Laurel and Hardy, the comedy duo

They met in (a) ________ (*Where?*) in 1926, and they stopped making films together in (c) ________ (*When?*). They made about two hundred films. They won (e) ________ (*What?*) for their film *The Music Box* in 1932.

Stan Laurel, the thin one, was born in (g) ________ (*Where?*) in 1890. He went to America in (i) ________ (*When?*), and made his first film in 1917.

He married (k) ________ (*How many times?*), and had one daughter. He wrote the scripts and directed most of their films. He died in (m) ________ (*When?*) in California.

Oliver Hardy, the fat one, was born in (o) ________ (*Where?*) in 1892. He went to Hollywood in (q) ________ (*When?*), and made his first film in 1913.

He married (s) ________ (*How many times?*). He didn't have any children. In his free time, he liked (u) ________ (*What?*) and going to horse races. In one day he lost $12,000. He died in (w) ________ (*Where?*) in 1957.

Student B

Laurel and Hardy, the comedy duo

They met in Hollywood in (b) ________ (*When?*), and they stopped making films together in 1952. They made about (d) ________ films (*How many?*). They won an Oscar for their film *The Music Box* in (f) ________ (*When?*).

Stan Laurel, the thin one, was born in England in (h) ________ (*When?*). He went to America in 1910, and made his first film in (j) ________ (*When?*). He married four times, and had (l) ________ (*How many children?*). He wrote the scripts and directed most of their films. He died in 1965 in (n) ________ (*Where?*)

Oliver Hardy, the fat one, was born in Atlanta, Georgia, in (p) ________ (*When?*) . He went to Hollywood in 1911, and made his first film in (r) ________ (*When?*).

He married once. He (t) ________ children (*How many?*). In his free time, he liked playing golf and going to horse races. In one day he lost (v) ________ dollars (*How much money?*). He died in California in (x) ________ (*When?*).

EXTRA IDEAS UNITS 13–15 Revision

Pre-reading task

What films have you seen recently?
What's your favourite film?
Who are your favourite films stars?

Reading

Read the text about Liza Minnelli. Put one of the words or phrases from the box into each gap.

told to be visiting said to produce watching immediately unfortunately only to go

Liza Minnelli,
Actress, Singer, Dancer...

Liza Minnelli was born on March 12, 1946, in Hollywood, California. She is the oldest of her mother's three children. Her mother, of course, was Judy Garland and her father was the film director, Vincente Minnelli. He was the second of Miss Garland's five husbands. In 1951 Liza's parents divorced.

Liza spent most of her childhood in Hollywood, and she often liked (a) ________ her mother's or father's film sets at the MGM Studios. She was interested in everything to do with making films, but she especially enjoyed (b) ________ dancers such as Fred Astaire, Gene Kelly, and Cyd Charisse. 'I learned all their dances,' Liza Minnelli (c) ________ in an interview in 1972, 'and I went home and practised them all in front of the mirror.' When she was (d) ________ two and a half years old she appeared in her first movie, called *In the Good Old Summertime*, and five years later she danced on the stage of the Palace Theatre in New York.

She knew that she wanted (e) ________ a professional actress when she saw a musical on Broadway in 1960. 'The kids on stage looked fantastic,' she (f) ________ her biographer, Jenny Craig, 'so I decided (g) ________ to drama school (h) ________.'

She won her first award when she was nineteen for her performance in a musical called *Flora, the Red Menace*, and since then she has won five more awards. She won an Oscar in 1973 as Sally Bowles in *Cabaret*. She has made more than fifteen films and recorded eight albums. She made her first album, *Liza! Liza!* in 1963.

She has had an interesting life, but it has not always been easy for her. She was an alcoholic for many years and has also had problems with drugs. In 1984 she went to the Betty Ford Center in California and she has been much happier since then.
She has been married three times, but (i) ________ none of the marriages have lasted very long. In 1991 she made a film called *Stepping Out*, which was about a group of people who find happiness and a purpose in life through dancing. 'Next year I'd like (j) ________ a film about my mother,' she said, 'and I hope to start writing it soon.'

Comprehension check

Answer the questions about Liza Minnelli.

1 When was she born?
2 Who was her mother?
3 What happened to Liza in 1951?
4 Which studio did her mother and father work for?
5 How old was she when she first appeared in a film?
6 How many awards has she won?
7 When did she make her first album?
8 Has she had an easy life? Why/why not?

Language work

1 Put the words in the right order to form a question.

a children mother many did her how have

________________________?

Three.

b job what father's was her

________________________?

He was a film director.

c times did marry how mother her many

________________________?

Five times.

d 1973 win what in she did

________________________?

An Oscar.

e films many she has how made?

________________________?

More than fifteen.

f did make *Stepping Out* she when

________________________?

In 1991.

2 Find five verbs in the Past Simple, and five in the Present Perfect.

KEY

Stop and Check

UNITS 1–4

1 Correcting the mistakes

a London is a very big city.
b My mother works in a hotel. She's a receptionist. *or* My mother is a receptionist in a hotel.
c My father watches TV in the evening.
d He likes watching football.
e On Sundays we go to a restaurant.
f Hans is a businessman.
g Your family is very nice.
h I like listening to music.
i Our school has a lot of students.
j The children go to school near here.
k We have dinner at 7.00.
l Buses in London are red.
m My brother doesn't have a job.
n Do you want an ice-cream?
o My flat is near here.

2 Word order

a John is a policeman from New York.
b Is your sister married?
c My sister goes skiing in the mountains.
d English coffee isn't very nice.
e What is your teacher's name?
f How do you spell your surname?
g I often go swimming at weekends./I go swimming often at weekends.

3 Choosing the correct sentence

1 b 2 c 3 a 4 b 5 c 6 a 7 b 8 c

4 Questions

1 What do you do at weekends?
Where do you go on holiday?
What time do you go to bed?
Who do you sit next to?
How much is a cup of coffee and a sandwich?
How many languages do you speak?

2 a What time does Peter start work?
b Where do Sylvie and Jacques come from?
c What's your wife's name?
d How many children do you have?
e Do you like gardening?

5 Prepositions

James lives (a) *in* Cambridge. He lives (b) *with* two other boys who are students (c) *at* Cambridge University. They work hard during the week, but (d) *at* weekends they invite a lot of friends to their house. They cook a meal (e) *for* their friends, and then they go out (f) *to* the pub (g) *for* a drink, or they stay (h) *at* home and listen (i) *to* music.

James has two jobs. (j) *On* Mondays, Tuesdays and Wednesdays he works (k) *in* a hospital, where he helps to look (l) *after* children who are ill. He goes to the hospital (m) *by* bus. He starts(n) *at* ten o'clock and works until quarter (o) *to* five. On Thursdays and Fridays he works (p) *at* home. He has a word processor (q) *in* his bedroom, and he writes stories. (r) *In* the evening, one of the boys cooks a meal. (s) *After* dinner, they look in the newspaper to see what's on TV, or they talk (t) *about* their day. They usually go to bed at about midnight.

6 Vocabulary

(five points for each column)

Things to read	**Professions**	**Things to eat**
map	actor	cheese
notebook	dentist	toast
dictionary	journalist	ham
magazine	interpreter	chicken
newspaper	engineer	orange
Places	**Verbs**	**Adjectives**
palace	arrive	favourite
village	want	easy
night club	bring	expensive
beach	leave	friendly
office	listen	funny

7 *am/is/do/does (not)*

a Vienna *is* in Austria.
b Where *are* you from?
c I *'m not* on holiday. I'm at work.
d My teacher *is/isn't* very funny.
e What time *does/is* the bank open?
f My sister *doesn't* eat meat because she *doesn't* like it.
g I *'m* hungry. How much *is* a cheese sandwich?
h Where *do* you usually go on holiday?
i Daddy, we *don't* want to go to bed. We *aren't* tired.
j Learning English *isn't* boring! It's interesting!

Translate

The idea behind this is that students begin to be aware of similarities and differences between English and L1. Emphasize that they must not translate word by word. Obviously it will only be possible to check their answers in a monolingual class but even in a multilingual class students can discuss their answers together in nationality groups.

UNITS 5–8

1 Correcting the mistakes

a My brother goes to university.
b English is an international language.
c I don't like swimming.
d I arrived at Heathrow airport at ten o'clock last night.
e She could speak three languages when she was ten.
f Where did you go last night?
g I saw Jeremy's wife at the shops.
h I can't go out because I have a lot of homework.
i There is a table in the kitchen.
j I went to the cinema last weekend.
k My children like their school very much.
l I bought a new video.
m Did you watch the football on TV last night/yesterday evening?
n Italian people are very artistic.
o I like cities because I can go to the theatre.

2 *can/could/was/were (not)*

a Our teacher *wasn't* at school last week because she *was* ill.
b Leonardo *was* a student in Florence. He *could* draw, write music and design buildings.
c We *can* see the Mona Lisa in the Louvre in Paris.
d 'Where *were* you last night? You *weren't* at home. I phoned you, but there *was* no answer.'
'I *couldn't* get into my flat because I lost my keys. I *was* at a friend's house.'

3 Irregular verbs

a	give	*gave*	f	make	*made*
b	leave	*left*	g	break	*broke*
c	sell	*sold*	h	meet	*met*
d	speak	*spoke*	i	win	*won*
e	lose	*lost*	j	take	*took*

4 Past Simple

He was a student in Florence, where he (a) *studied* painting, sculpture and design. He (b) *began* a lot of paintings, but he (c) *didn't finish* many of them. His picture of the Mona Lisa is the most famous portrait in the world.

Leonardo (d) *was* interested in many things. He (e) *wanted* to know about everything he saw. He examined the human body. He (f) *thought* that the sun (g) *didn't go* round the earth. He (h) *wrote* music. He designed a flying machine four hundred years before the first one flew. Many people (i) *didn't understand* his ideas. It is difficult to think that one man (j) *could* do so much.

5 *a/an* or nothing?

a	I have toast for breakfast.	✔
b	My sister works ~~in office~~.	*in an office*
c	Do you like Indian food?	✔
d	Is there ~~Indian restaurant~~ near here?	*an Indian restaurant*
e	Have ~~nice weekend~~!	*a nice weekend*
f	There's ~~good library~~ near my house.	*a good library*
g	Meat is expensive.	✔
h	My grandfather is ~~engineer~~.	*an engineer*

6 *some/any/a/an*

a Did Charles Dickens have *any* children?
b I bought *a* newspaper and *some* magazines.
c Jane lives in *an* old house in France.
d There are *some* trees in my garden, but there aren't *any* flowers.
e Do you have *any* books by Gabriel García Márquez?
f There are *some* letters for you on the table.

7 Vocabulary – connections

(Students might come up with alternative answers to those suggested. Do award points for anything sensible!)

Easter Day – egg
cupboard – kitchen
wallet – money
library – borrow
check-in desk – luggage
smell – nose
Welcome to Britain! – arrival hall
son – sun
Congratulations! – wedding
recipe – chef
soldier – war

8 Vocabulary – opposites

wonderful – horrible	clean – dirty
win – lose	late – early
king – queen	begin – finish
abroad – at home	interesting – boring
before – after	difficult – easy

Translate

The idea behind this is that students begin to be aware of similarities and differences between English and L1. Emphasize that they must not translate word by word. Obviously it will only be possible to check their answers in a monolingual class but even in a multilingual class students can discuss their answers together in nationality groups.

UNITS 9–12

1 Correcting the mistakes

a It's very hot today – would you like something to drink?
b Peter's got a lot of books because he likes reading.
c How many children have you got/do you have?
d How much money has he got?
e Whose is that new car?
f I'm going home now because it's late.
g Last night I went to a cafe to meet my friends.
h We're going to have a test next week.
i I'm wearing old clothes because I'm going to clean the car.
j Pierre is French, he comes from Paris.
k What are you doing tonight?
l My sister is older than me.
m I think it is going to rain.
n Your house is bigger than mine.
o Who is the richest person in the world?

2 Questions and answers

Whose is this coat? – It's Jane's.
How many cats have you got? – Three.
How much did your bike cost? – £100.
Could you help me, please? – Yes, of course. What can I do for you?
Would you like some more to eat? – No, thanks. I'm full.
Do you like Henry? – Yes. I think he's very nice.
Where are you going on holiday? – To Turkey.
Why are you going to the chemist's? – To buy some toothpaste.
What did you do last night? – I stayed at home.
Who's the new teacher? – Her name's Mrs Taylor.

3 Comparatives and superlatives

Adjective	Comparative	Superlative
big	bigger	biggest
beautiful	more beautiful	most beautiful
bad	worse	worst
exciting	more exciting	most exciting
noisy	noisier	noisiest

4 Comparing hotels

1 a The Strand is bigger than the Ritz.
b The Ritz is more expensive than the Strand.
c The Strand is nearer the sea than the Ritz.
d The Strand is farther from the town centre than the Ritz.
e The Strand is more modern than the Ritz.

2 a The Strand is the biggest.
b The Star is the most expensive.
c The Star is the nearest to the sea.
d The Strand is the farthest from the town centre.
e The Strand is the most modern.

5 *some* and *any*

a Would you like *a* cup of tea?
b You have *some* lovely pictures on the walls!
c Is there *any* water in the fridge?
d Can I have *some* grapes, please?
e I'd like *a* hamburger and *some* chips, please.
f Do you want *a* sandwich?
g The shop doesn't have *any* eggs, peas or bread.
h There are *some* eggs in the cupboard, but there isn't *any* sugar.

6 Present Simple or Present Continuous

a Pierre *smokes* twenty cigarettes a day, but he *isn't smoking* now because he's in class.
b Alice and Peter *are looking* for a new house. They *don't like* living in London.
c I always *wear* nice clothes for work. Today I*'m wearing* a blue jacket and skirt.
d 'Why *are* you *going* to bed? It's only 10.00.' 'I always *go* to bed early.'
e Jane *works* in a bank, but today she's at home. She*'s writing* letters.

7 going to

a Peter *is going to buy* some bread *at the baker's*.
b I *am going to borrow* some books from *the library*.
c We *are going to see* a play at *the theatre*.
d They *are going to have* a holiday in *Florida*.
e I *am going to write* a letter to *my friend*.

8 Vocabulary

(five points for each column)

Clothes shop	Food	Chemist's
a dress	fruit	a film
a suit	mushrooms	toothpaste
a shirt	rice	aspirin
jumper	cheese	soap
shorts	cereal	shampoo

Translate

The idea behind this is that students begin to be aware of similarities and differences between English and L1. Emphasize that they must not translate word by word. Obviously it will only possible to check their answers in a monolingual class, but even in a multilingual class students can discuss their answers together in nationality groups.

UNITS 13–15

1 Correcting the mistakes

a Why do you want to learn Portuguese?
b She hasn't ever been to Madrid./She has never been to Madrid.
c I've written to her three times and she hasn't answered yet.
d We'd like to invite you to dinner at our house.
e How many times have you been to Greece?
f I have just finished doing my homework.
g We met two years ago in New York.
h Tell me when you want to stop for lunch.
i What sort of books do you like reading?
j Have you ever been to Ireland?

2 Questions and tenses

a Anna's tired.	Why *is she tired*?
b I don't go to work by car.	How *do* you *go to work*?
c This pen isn't mine.	Whose *is this pen*?
d I met a famous actress.	Who *did* you *meet*?
e Sarah's bought a new car.	What sort *of car did she buy*?
f We saw Bill yesterday.	Where *did* you *see him*?
g Sue's watching television.	What *is she watching*?
h They're going on holiday.	Where *are they going*?
i Peter's left the party.	Why *did he leave*?
j She drank a lot of wine.	How much *wine did she drink*?

3 Past Simple and Present Perfect

a I ***met****/have met* Anna ten years ago.
b My sister *did never go/****has never been*** to France.
c I'm sorry. I *didn't finish /****haven't finished*** my work yet.
d I ***ate****/have eaten* a lot of ice cream when I was a child.
e They ***climbed****/have climbed* Everest in 1953.

4 Adverb or adjective?

a Our village is always very ***quiet****/quietly.* Nothing happens.
b Please speak more *slow/****slowly****.* I can't understand you.
c She's a very ***good****/well* driver.
d He doesn't drive very *good/****well****.*
e My grandparents are very strong and ***healthy****/ healthily* for their age.

5 Infinitive or *-ing*?

a Both my husband and I enjoy *cooking* very much.
b Our new neighbours are difficult *to get* on with.
c We've decided *to move* to the countryside.
d Have you finished *painting* the kitchen yet?
e My uncle needs *to see* a doctor about his leg.

6 Word order

a How many cousins have you got?
b They have just arrived in Rome.
c Jane gave up smoking three years ago.
d The man walked quickly along the road.
e Have you ever seen a play by Shakespeare?
f Has Mary decided to go to the party?
g My teacher says that English is easy to learn.
h Did you enjoy meeting Bob's parents? *or* Did Bob's parents enjoy meeting you?
i How many people are you going to invite to your party?
j They told us about their new car.

7 Auxiliaries

a Look at those children. They *are* smoking cigarettes!
b *Does* your daughter speak French well?
c *Did* you learn German when you were at school?
d *Has* Ben ever been to India?
e We *have* never played volleyball.
f I *am* going to give up smoking soon.
g *Do* Mark and Jane live near you?
h *Is* John going to phone you tomorrow?
i When *did* you learn to drive? A long time ago?
j *Have* you written to thank Sue and Bill yet?

8 Vocabulary – word groups

(five points for each column)

Travel	**Parts of the body**	**Telephoning**	**Books**
jumbo jet	head	engaged	a detective story
platform	neck	dial	title
journey	nose	ringing	a horror story
passenger	hands	operator	characters
helicopter	face	call	dictionary
take off	mouth	biography	
station	foot		
timetable			
train			
arrival			
departure			
return ticket			

9 Prepositions

a I'm reading a book *about* the history of France.
b *Oliver Twist* is a book *by* Charles Dickens.
c Is it far *from* your house to the station?
d Is Mexico City the biggest city *in* the world?
e Jane's worried *about* her exam.
f What's *on* television tonight?
g Are you interested *in* politics?
h She works *for* a big company.
i Can I speak *to* you for a moment?
j He drove *out of* the garage and down the street.

Translate

The idea behind this is that students begin to be aware of similarities and differences between English and L1. Emphasize that they must not translate word by word. Obviously it will only be possible to check their answers in a monolingual class but even in a multilingual class students can discuss their answers together in nationality groups.

PROGRESS TESTS

Note to the teacher

There are three tests in this booklet

Progress Test One covers the work done in Units 1–5
Progress Test Two covers the work done in Units 6–10
Progress Test Three covers the work done in Units 11–15

Each test carries with it a total possible score of 100 marks.

Oxford University Press
Walton Street, Oxford OX2 6DP

UNITS 1-5

Progress Test One

GRAMMAR

Exercise 1 Asking about people

Surname	Smith
First name	John
Country	Britain
Age	30
Address	94 East St, Oxford OX1 9HJ
Job	Teacher
Place of work	School in Oxford
Married	No
Free time	Football

Read the information about John Smith. Write the questions.

Example *What's his first name?*
His first name's John.

a ______________________________
His surname is Smith.

b ______________________________
He's from Britain.

c ______________________________
He's 30.

d ______________________________
94 East St, Oxford OX1 9HJ.

e ______________________________
He's a teacher.

f ______________________________
In a school in Oxford.

g ______________________________
No, he isn't. He's single.

h ______________________________
He plays football.

Total 8

Exercise 2 Word order

Put the words in the correct order.

Example you from are Where
Where are you from?

a do at What weekends you do
______________________________?

b work she does Where
______________________________?

c a television There photo is the on
____

d near there chemist's a Is here
______________________________?

e Coke please I a Can have
______________________________?

f children How they do have many
______________________________?

g skiing in Hans Switzerland teaches
____

h any Is milk the there fridge in
______________________________?

i not work Rosy go by does to car
____

j Sue going Dave and the opera like to
____

Total 10

Exercise 3 Questions

Match a line in A with a line in B to make a question. Then find an answer in C.

A	B	C
Who	do you do on Sundays?	At seven o'clock.
How much	do you meet on Saturday evenings?	To the theatre.
What	do you go on Friday evenings?	My friends, Dave and Paul.
Where	do you get up?	I play tennis.
How	is a ham sandwich?	By bus.
What time	do you travel to work?	£1.30.

Total 5

Exercise 4 *some, any, a,* and *an*

Put *some*, *any*, *a*, or *an* into the gaps.

Example There are _some_ flowers in the garden.

a There are ______ pictures on the wall.
b Can I have ______ apple, please?
c Are there ______ books in the living room?
d There aren't ______ good restaurants in our town.
e There's ______ newsagent's opposite the post office.
f John has ______ trees in his garden.
g Are there ______ Japanese students in your class?
h There's ______ orange on the table.
i There aren't ______ photographs on the wall.
j There are ______ plates next to the sink.

Total 10

Exercise 5 Present Simple

Put the verbs in brackets into the correct form.

I (a) ______ (have) two brothers, Simon and Chris. They (b) ______ (live) in London. Simon (c) ______ (be) a pilot and Chris (d) ______ (work) in a garage. Simon (e) ______ (like) flying, but Chris (f) ______ ______ (not like) mending cars. At weekends I (g) ______ (go) to London and I (h) ______ (stay) with them. We (i) ______ (go) to the theatre or to the cinema on Saturday evening, and on Sunday we (j) ______ (walk) in Hyde Park.

Total 10

Exercise 6 *be* and *do*

Put a verb from the box into each gap.

Example Peter _is_ a teacher.

am / am not	does / does not
is / is not	do / do not
are / are not	

a I ______ hungry. Can I have an apple?
b How ______ you travel to work?
c Rome ______ in Spain. It ______ in Italy.
d Mary and Sarah ______ like milk.
e ______ James have two jobs?
f Ben ______ like travelling by bus.
g We aren't from Spain – we ______ from Portugal.
h '______ you like ice cream?' 'No, I ______.'

Total 9

Exercise 7 *a, an, the,* or nothing

Put *a*, *an*, *the*, or nothing in the gaps.

Example Madonna is _a_ singer.

a I have ______ breakfast at eight o'clock.
b I read ______ Times every day.
c Peter goes to ______ school by bus.
d Can I have ______ chicken sandwich, please.
e Please close ______ window. It's cold!
f What time do you go to ______ bed?
g Paul Newman is ______ actor.
h I like playing volleyball on ______ beach.
i Sylvia doesn't go to work by ______ car.
j David has ______ house in London.

Total 10

Exercise 8 Prepositions

Write the correct preposition in the gaps. Write one word on each line.

a There are two chairs ______ the living room.

b The sofa is ______ ______ the table.

c There's a lamp ______ the sofa.

d There's a picture ______ the wall.

e The chair is ______ the television.

f There's a cat ______ ______ ______ the fire.

g The telephone is ______ the table.

Total 7

Exercise 9 Choose the correct sentence

One sentence is correct, one sentence is wrong. Tick (✔) the correct sentence.

Example Let's go to home.
Let's go home. ✔

a Kate and Ann are students in Cambridge University.
Kate and Ann are students at Cambridge University.

b Let's go out to the pub!
Let's go out at the pub!

c On Thursdays I get home at six o'clock.
In Thursdays I get home at six o'clock.

d Richard lives at London.
Richard lives in London.

e To weekends I go swimming.
At weekends I go swimming.

Total 5

VOCABULARY

Exercise 10 Which one is different?

Underline the different word.

Example Cambridge London Oxford Rome

a	magazine	pen	newspaper	book
b	milk	apple	ice-cream	ham
c	house	palace	street	flat
d	actor	dentist	policeman	teach
e	boring	interesting	like	funny
f	father	sister	mother	man
g	house	bathroom	kitchen	living room
h	often	near	next to	opposite
i	France	England	American	Hungary
j	my	we	his	your

Total 10

Exercise 11 Adjectives

Match the opposites.

Example small – *big*

difficult	cheap
expensive	horrible
hot	right
lovely	easy
wrong	left
old	young
new	cold
right	old

Total 8

Exercise 12 Words that go together

Match a verb in A with a line in B.

A	B
drive	football
play	a train
go	tea
speak	television
drink	a car
travel	to music
catch	windsurfing
listen	by bus
watch	French

Total 8

Score

Exercise 1	_____	out of 8
Exercise 2	_____	out of 10
Exercise 3	_____	out of 5
Exercise 4	_____	out of 10
Exercise 5	_____	out of 10
Exercise 6	_____	out of 9
Exercise 7	_____	out of 10
Exercise 8	_____	out of 7
Exercise 9	_____	out of 5
Exercise 10	_____	out of 10
Exercise 11	_____	out of 8
Exercise 12	_____	out of 8
Total	_____	**out of 100**

UNITS 6-10

Progress Test Two

GRAMMAR

Exercise 1 The past tense of the verb *to be*

What are the past tense forms of the verb *to be*?

	Positive	Negative
Example I	*was*	*wasn't*
a you	______	______
b he/she/it	______	______
c we	______	______
d they	______	______

Total 8

Exercise 2 *can* and *can't*

Read the information, then complete the sentences with *can* or *can't* and a verb.

	swim	play tennis	speak German	speak Italian
Sylvia	✔	✘	✔	✔
Linda	✔	✔	✘	✔
Marianne	✘	✘	✔	✔

Example Linda *can swim* and she *can play tennis.*

a Sylvia can swim, but she ________________ .

b Marianne ________________ and she ________________.

c Linda ________________ , but Sylvia and Marianne can.

d Everybody ________________ .

e Only Linda ________________ .

f Sylvia and Linda ________________ , but Marianne can't.

Total 7

Exercise 3 Past Simple

Write the Past Simple of these verbs.

Regular	Irregular
a work ______	f have ______
b live ______	g come ______
c earn ______	h give ______
d move ______	i go ______
e stay ______	j buy ______

Total 10

Exercise 4 Past Simple and Present Simple

Put the verbs in brackets into the correct tense and form: the Past Simple or the Present Simple.

My friend Jack is 40. He (a) ______ (leave) Britain when he was 20 and (b) ______ (go) to Italy. He (c) ______ (work) in Naples for ten years, then he (d) ______ (move) to Rome. There he (e) ______ (meet) Antonella. They (f) ______ (get) married in 1982 and now they (g) ______ (live) in Florence. Jack (h) ______ (teach) English in a language school. And what (i) ______ (do) Antonella do? She (j) ______ (sell) computer software.

Total 10

Exercise 5 Past Simple: negative

Make these positive sentences negative.

Example He bought a new shirt.
He didn't buy a new shirt.

a We enjoyed the film.

____

b I took a photograph of my sister.

____

c Angela wrote a letter to her friend.

____

d Charles Dickens became a journalist when he was 18.

____

e Germany won the World Cup in 1986.

____

f Her father died when she was 14.

____

g I lost £10 last night.

____

h People flew by plane 100 years ago.

____

i That book was very interesting.

____

j We arrived at school at eight o'clock.

____

Total 10

Exercise 6 *would like*

Choose the correct sentence.

Example A Would you like / Do you like | a drink? ✔ ✘
B No thanks, I'm not thirsty.

a A Would you like / Do you like | some fruit?
B Yes. An apple, please.

b A Would you like / Do you like | windsurfing?
B Yes, but I prefer swimming.

c A What | do you like / would you like | for dinner this evening?
B Steak and chips.

d A Would you like / Do you like | Mr Brown?
B No. He's not very nice.

e A Can I help you?
B Yes. | I like / I'd like | a bottle of mineral water, please.

Total 5

Exercise 7 Countable and uncountable

Write C next to the countable nouns and U next to the uncountable nouns.

Example book *C*
rice *U*

a pencil ____
b music ____
c rain ____
d flower ____
e apple ____
f money ____
g bread ____

Total 7

Exercise 8 *some, any,* or *a*

Write *some*, *any*, or *a* in the gaps.

Example Do you have __*any*__ rice?

a I've got ______ pens in the office.
b Can I have ______ can of Coke, please?
c There isn't ______ sugar in the dining room.
d Have you got ______ photographs of Jim?
e I'd like ______ shampoo, please.
f Peter put ______ water and ______ glasses on the table.
g There wasn't ______ petrol or oil in the car.

Total 8

Exercise 9 *How much* and *How many*

Complete the questions with *How much* or *How many.*

a ____________ soap is there in the bathroom?
b ____________ stamps do you need?
c ____________ oranges and apples are there on the table?
d ____________ Coke is there in the kitchen?
e ____________ money did you take to France?

Total 5

Exercise 10 Comparatives and superlatives 1

Read about the castles.

Abergoran Castle
Price: £200,000
Built: 1072
Rooms: 0

Footleby Castle
Price: £10 million
Built: 1835
Rooms: 160

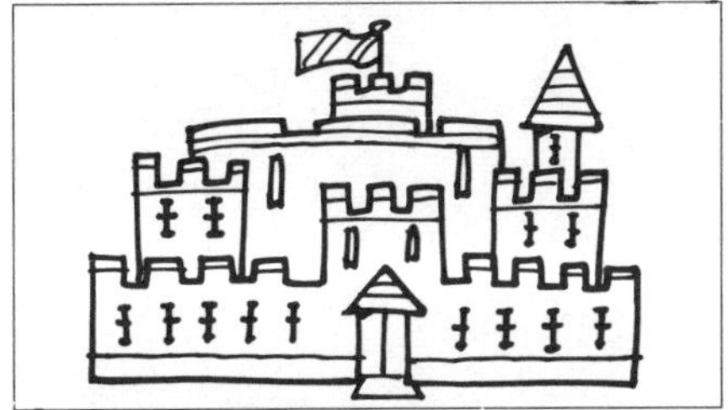

Haywood Castle
Price: £2 million
Built: 1450
Rooms: 20

These sentences are false. Correct them.

Example Haywood Castle is more modern than Abergoran Castle.
No, it isn't. It's older.

a Footleby Castle is cheaper than Haywood Castle.

____

b Abergoran Castle is bigger than Footleby Castle.

____

c Abergoran Castle is the biggest.

____

d Abergoran Castle is more expensive than Footleby Castle.

____

e Footleby Castle is the cheapest.

____

f Footleby Castle is older than Haywood Castle.

____

g Abergoran Castle is the most modern.

____

Total 7

Exercise 11 Comparatives and superlatives 2

Complete this chart.

Adjective	Comparative	Superlative
______	more dangerous	______
______	______	best
bad	______	______
interesting	______	______

Total 8

VOCABULARY

Exercise 12 Ordinal numbers

Write the ordinal numbers in words.

Example 6th *sixth*

a 1st _____
b 2nd _____
c 3rd _____
d 12th _____
e 20th _____

Total 5

Exercise 13 Opposites

Choose a word from the box and write it next to its opposite.

Example big *small*

interesting	old	buy	before	start
quiet	east	day	new	same

a boring ______
b stop ______
c night ______
d sell ______
e different ______
f noisy ______
g old ______
h modern ______
i west ______
j after ______

Total 10

Score

Exercise 1	_____	out of 8
Exercise 2	_____	out of 7
Exercise 3	_____	out of 10
Exercise 4	_____	out of 10
Exercise 5	_____	out of 10
Exercise 6	_____	out of 5
Exercise 7	_____	out of 7
Exercise 8	_____	out of 8
Exercise 9	_____	out of 5
Exercise 10	_____	out of 7
Exercise 11	_____	out of 8
Exercise 12	_____	out of 5
Exercise 13	_____	out of 10
Total	_____	**out of 100**

UNITS 11-15

Progress Test Three

GRAMMAR

Exercise 1 Present continuous: *-ing* form

Write the correct *-ing* form.

Example walk *walking*
smoke *smoking*

a drive __________
b stop __________
c work __________
d use __________
e look __________
f get __________
g buy __________
h think __________
i swim __________
j cry __________

Total 10

Exercise 2 Present continuous

Put the verbs in brackets into the Present Continuous.

Example Julie *is wearing* earrings. (wear)

a I __________ on holiday tomorrow. (not go)
b 'Why __________ you __________ ?' (smile)
'Because Mr Black didn't give us any homework.'
c 'Who's Richard?'
'He __________ next to Jane.' (stand)
d Tom __________ at his desk. (not sit)
e 'What __________ Sue __________ ?' (eat)
'A tuna sandwich.'
f 'What __________ you __________ ?' (do)
'I __________ my shoes.' (clean)
g I can't phone my wife. The telephone __________ . (not work)

Total 8

Exercise 3 Present Simple and Present Continuous

Put the verb into the correct tense: the Present Simple or the Present Continuous.

Example 'Be quiet! I *'m watching* (watch) this film!'

a We usually __________ (take) the bus to town, but today we __________ (go) by car.
b 'Where ______ you usually __________ (go) on Friday evenings?'
'To a disco.'
c 'It's 11.30. Why ______ you __________ (work) so late?'
'Because I __________ (have) a lot of homework.'
d 'Where ______ your parents __________ ?' (live)
'In a small village near Oxford.'
'______ they __________ (like) living in the country?'
'Yes, they do.'
e 'What ______ you usually __________ (have) for breakfast?'
'Toast. But today I __________ (have) some fruit because there isn't any bread.'
f 'The telephone __________ (ring). Can you answer it?'
'OK.'

Total 10

Exercise 4 Possessive pronouns

Write the sentences using a possessive pronoun.

Example It's my pen. *It's mine.*
They're her socks. *They're hers.*

a It's your newspaper.

____

b They're his books.

____

c It's her T-shirt.

____

d They're our videos.

____

e This is their house.

____

Total 5

Exercise 5 *going to*

Make positive sentences, negative sentences, and questions using *going to.*

Examples she / pilot
She's going to be a pilot.

he / not / bus driver
He isn't going to be a bus driver.

you / hairdresser?
Are you going to be a hairdresser?

a they / architects

____

b he / not / ballet dancer

____

c you / pilot?

____

d I / not / policeman

____

e we / athletes

____

f she / not / chef

____

g he / vet?

____

h I / actress

____

i he / not / travel agent

____

j you / English teacher?

____

Total 10

Exercise 6 Infinitive of purpose

Rewrite these sentences using the infinitive of purpose.

Example I went to Holland because I wanted to see the tulips.
I went to Holland to see the tulips.

a I'm going to Moscow because I want to see the Kremlin.

____

b Paul is going to London because he wants to buy some clothes.

____

c Roger went to India because he wanted to visit the Taj Mahal.

____

d Tracey often goes to the disco because she wants to dance.

____

e Tim is going to America because he wants to see the Niagara Falls.

____

f Frank is learning French because he wants to get a better job.

____

g Peter is saving money because he wants to buy a car.

____

h Henry went to Japan because he wanted to visit Kyoto.

____

i Chris went to the newsagent's because he wanted to buy a newspaper.

____

j Brian and Jane are going to Paris because they want to climb the Eiffel Tower.

Total 10

Exercise 7 Adverbs

Write the adverbs next to the adjectives.

Example quick *quickly*

a slow ______
b early ______
c careful ______
d good ______
e hard ______
f sudden ______
g fast ______
h bad ______

Total 8

Exercise 8 Question words

Complete the questions with a word from the box.

Example '*How* tall is your sister?'
'1m 52.'

Where Which Why How Who What When

a '______ often do you go to the cinema?'
'About once a month.'

b '______ time does the programme start?'
'At nine o'clock.'

c '______ did you close the window?'
'Because I'm cold.'

d '______ colour is Angela's new car?'
'Red.'

e '______ did you go to town with?'
'Jim and Lucy.'

f '______ newspaper do you want – the Italian one or the English one?'
'The English one.'

g '______ is Edinburgh?'
'It's in Scotland.'

h '______ are you going to clean your room?"
'When this film has finished.'

i '______ is your favourite season?'
'I like summer best.'

Total 9

Exercise 9 Past Simple and Present Perfect

Write the Past Simple and the Past Participle of these verbs.

Example stay *stayed* *stayed*
sing *sang* *sung*

a eat ______ ______
b win ______ ______
c live ______ ______
d have ______ ______
e do ______ ______
f cook ______ ______
g go ______ ______
h drive ______ ______

Total 8

Exercise 10 Present Perfect and Past Simple

Choose the correct sentence.

a I went to London last week.
I have been to London last week.

b Have you ever been to France?
Did you ever go to France?

c Kate has finished her homework two hours ago.
Kate finished her homework two hours ago.

d Did he go to the dentist last week or the week before?
Has he been to the dentist last week or the week before?

e I haven't seen that film yet.
I didn't see that film yet.

f I've just bought my plane ticket to Paris – here it is!
I just bought my plane ticket to Paris – here it is!

g Jim and Cathy won £1,000 last month.
Jim and Cathy have won £1,000 last month.

Total 7

VOCABULARY

Exercise 11 Word groups

Put these words into the correct columns.

blue T-shirt foggy green jumper
tie sunny brown cloudy snowing
pink suit skirt yellow windy

Colours	Clothes	Weather

Total 15

Score

Exercise 1 _____ out of 10
Exercise 2 _____ out of 8
Exercise 3 _____ out of 10
Exercise 4 _____ out of 5
Exercise 5 _____ out of 10
Exercise 6 _____ out of 10
Exercise 7 _____ out of 8
Exercise 8 _____ out of 9
Exercise 9 _____ out of 8
Exercise 10 _____ out of 7
Exercise 11 _____ out of 15

Total _____ out of 100

Progress Tests

TEST 1 (UNITS 1–5)

Exercise 1

a What's his surname?
b Where's he from?
c How old is he?
d Where does he live? / What's his address?
e What does he do? / What's his job?
f Where does he work / teach?
g Is he married?
h What does he do in his free time?

Exercise 2

a What do you do at weekends?
b Where does she work?
c There is a photo on the television.
d Is there a chemist's near here?
e Can I have a coke, please?
f How many children do they have?
g Hans teaches skiing in Switzerland.
h Is there any milk in the fridge?
i Rosy does not go to work by car.
j Sue and Dave like going to the opera.

Exercise 3

Who do you meet on Saturday evenings?	My friends, Dave and Paul.
How much is a ham sandwich?	£1.30.
What do you do on Sundays?	I play tennis.
Where do you go on Friday evenings?	To the theatre.
How do you travel to work?	By bus.

Exercise 4

a some
b an
c any
d any
e a
f some
g any
h an
i any
j some

Exercise 5

a have
b live
c is
d works
e likes
f doesn't like
g go
h stay
i go
j walk

Exercise 6

a am
b do
c is not, is
d do not
e Does
f does not
g are
h Do, don't

Exercise 7

a (nothing)
b the
c (nothing)
d a
e the
f (nothing)
g an
h the
i (nothing)
j a

Exercise 8

a in
b next to
c behind
d on
e near
f in front of
g on

Exercise 9

Correct sentences

a Kate and Ann are students at Cambridge University.
b Let's go out to the pub!
c On Thursdays I get home at six o'clock.
d Richard live in London.
e At weekends I go swimming.

Exercise 10

a pen (You can read the others.)
b milk (You can drink milk.)
c street (The others are buildings.)
d teach (The others are professions.)
e like (The others are adjectives.)
f man (The others are names of family members.)
g house (The others are rooms.)
h often (The others describe position.)
i American (American is an adjective.)
j we (The others are possessive adjectives.)

Exercise 11

difficult – easy
expensive – cheap
hot – cold
lovely – horrible
wrong – right
old – new
new – old
right – left

Exercise 12

drive a car
play football
go windsurfing
speak French
drink tea
travel by bus
catch a train
listen to music
watch television

TEST 2 (UNITS 6–10)

Exercise 1

a were weren't
b was wasn't
c were weren't
d were weren't

Exercise 2

a can't play tennis
b can speak German / can speak Italian
c can't speak German
d can speak Italian
e can play tennis
f can swim

Exercise 3

a worked
b lived
c earned
d moved
e stayed
f had
g came
h gave
i went
j bought

Exercise 4

a left
b went
c worked
d moved
e met
f got
g live
h teaches
i does
j sells

Exercise 5

a We didn't enjoy the film.
b I didn't take a photograph of my sister
c Angela didn't write a letter to her friend.
d Charles Dickens didn't become a journalist when he was 18.
e Germany didn't win the World Cup in 1986.
f Her father didn't die when she was 14.
g I didn't lose £10 last night.
h People didn't fly by plane 100 years ago.
i That book wasn't very interesting.
j We didn't arrive at school at eight o'clock.

Exercise 6

a Would you like …
b Do you like …
c What would you like …
d Do you like …
e Yes. I'd like a bottle …

Exercise 7

a C b U c U d C e C f U g U

Exercise 8

a some
b a
c any
d any
e some
f some / some
g any

Exercise 9

a How much
b How many
c How many
d How much
e How much

Exercise 10

a No, it isn't. It's more expensive.
b No, it isn't. It's smaller.
c No, it isn't. It's the smallest.
d No, it isn't. It's cheaper.
e No, it isn't. It's the most expensive.
f No, it isn't. It's more modern.
g No, it isn't. It's the oldest.

Exercise 11

Adjective	Comparative	Superlative
dangerous	more dangerous	*most dangerous*
good	*better*	best
bad	*worse*	*worst*
interesting	*more interesting*	*most interesting*

Exercise 12

a first
b second
c third
d twelfth
e twentieth

Exercise 13

a interesting
b start
c day
d buy
e same
f quiet
g new
h old
i east
j before

TEST 3 (UNITS 11–15)

Exercise 1

a driving
b stopping
c working
d using
e looking
f getting
g buying
h thinking
i swimming
j crying

Exercise 2

a am not going
b are … smiling
c is standing
d isn't sitting
e is … eating
f are … doing
am cleaning
g isn't working

Exercise 3

a take, are going
b do … go
c are … working
have
d do … live
Do … like
e do … have
am having
f is ringing

Exercise 4

a It's yours.
b They're his.
c It's hers.
d They're ours.
e It's theirs.

Exercise 5

a They're going to be architects.
b He isn't going to be a ballet dancer.
c Are you going to be a pilot?
d I'm not going to be a policeman.
e We're going to be athletes.
f She isn't going to be a chef.
g Is he going to be a vet?
h I'm going to be an actress.
i He isn't going to be a travel agent.
j Are you going to be an English teacher?

Exercise 6

a I'm going to Moscow to see the Kremlin.
b Paul is going to London to buy some clothes.
c Roger went to India to visit the Taj Mahal.
d Tracey often goes to the disco to dance.
e Tim is going to America to see the Niagara Falls.
f Frank is learning French to get a better job.
g Peter is saving money to buy a car.
h Henry went to Japan to visit Kyoto.
i Chris went to the newsagent's to buy a newspaper.
j Brian and Jane are going to Paris to climb the Eiffel Tower.

Exercise 7

a slowly
b early
c carefully
d well
e hard
f suddenly
g fast
h badly

Exercise 8

a How
b What
c Why
d What
e Who
f Which
g Where
h When
i Which

Exercise 9

a ate eaten
b won won
c lived lived
d had had
e did done
f cooked cooked
g went gone
h drove driven

Exercise 10

Correct sentences

a I went to London last week.
b Have you ever been to France?
c Kate finished her homework two hours ago.
d Did he go to the dentist last week or the week before?
e I haven't seen that film yet.
f I've just bought my plane ticket to Paris – here it is!
g Jim and Cathy won £1,000 last month.

Exercise 11

Colours	Clothes	Weather
blue	jumper	cloudy
yellow	skirt	snowing
pink	T-shirt	foggy
green	tie	sunny
brown	suit	windy

Discussing Terrorism

Series Editor: Cara Acred

Volume 283

First published by Independence Educational Publishers
The Studio, High Green
Great Shelford
Cambridge CB22 5EG
England

British Library Cataloguing in Publication Data

Discussing terrorism. -- (Issues ; 283)
1. Terrorism. 2. Terrorism--Prevention.
I. Series II. Acred, Cara editor.
363.3'25-dc23

ISBN-13: 9781861687111

Printed in Great Britain

Zenith Print Group